PREFACE

THIS book is an amplified version of Ford's Lectures given in Oxford in Hilary Term, 1953. The delay in its reaching the press has been due partly to the need to complete other tasks to which I was committed, and partly to circumstances that have prevented my making more than rare visits to libraries and record offices.

The core of the book is statistical, and the treatment chronological. Thomas Fuller, according to his editor, used to speak of chronology as 'a little surly animal, apt to bite the fingers of those who handled it with greater familiarity than was absolutely necessary'. His description of dates as 'slippery ware' is applicable also to other figures. One of the difficulties of uniting the verbal with the numerical evidence is that, whereas the annalists of the eighteenth century arranged their material by calendar years, the statisticians took as their units of time annual periods that ran, variously, from Lady Day, Midsummer, Michaelmas, or Christmas. Lest the reader should lose sight of this ambiguity, when the reference is to the civil or legal year the date is printed in roman type; when it is to some other annual period it appears in italic. An italicized date indicates a period earlier by some months than the calendar year. In the Statistical Appendix attention is drawn, at the foot of most of the tables, to the day and month at which the relevant accounting periods begin.

It would have been easy to double or treble the number of statistical series in the Appendix. But many sets of figures have been presented in other books of mine, and several more, referred to in footnotes, are accessible in treatises or journals published in recent years. A monograph is not the place for a compendium of statistics.

My debts are many and great. First of all, I must record my gratitude to the University of Oxford for having honoured me with the invitation to give Ford's Lectures. Secondly, I have to pay tribute to the late Mrs. E. B. Schumpeter, who, with characteristic generosity, pressed me to make full use of the fruits of her unpublished work on the statistics of English commerce. If, in the event, I have drawn only on her summary tables, and on her figures of imports of timber and exports of woollen goods, the reason for this restraint was the assurance I had that the detailed tables would, before long, appear in print. Thirdly, I must mention the kindness of the Earl of Harrowby, who not only called my attention to papers relating to the Excise in the archives of the Harrowby Trust, but gave me exceptional facilities for work on these.

I have learnt much about the origins and phases of economic fluctuations in conversations (which they will have forgotten) with J. R. Hicks and Lionel Robbins, and about the operations of currency and finance in the eighteenth century from talks (only too rare) with Jacob Viner. As a teacher for more than eleven years at the London School of Economics, I had the good fortune to be in almost daily contact with R. H. Tawney and F. J. Fisher: I have drawn on the learning of both. Other colleagues in London, members of my seminar at the Institute of Historical Research, and economic historians in other universities, have most liberally provided me with illustrative details, unearthed in the course of their own investigations. I am grateful, in particular, to David Joslin, Peter Mathias, W. H. Chaloner, D. C. Coleman, Lucy S. Sutherland, Julia de L. Mann, Jim Potter, and, by no means least, L. S. Pressnell. The heaviest debt of all, however, is to A. H. John, who has provided me with much information of exceptional value, read the chapters in script, checked the footnotes, and saved me from serious errors. From start to finish, his companionship has lightened my task.

Finally, I must offer warm thanks to Mrs. Gladys Cornwell, who, out of goodness of heart, typed and retyped successive drafts of the book, long after I had ceased to have any claim on her time and skill.

T. S. A.

December 1958

ECONOMIC
FLUCTUATIONS
IN ENGLAND
1700–1800

ECONOMIC FLUCTUATIONS IN ENGLAND

1700–1800

BY

T. S. ASHTON

PROFESSOR EMERITUS OF ECONOMIC HISTORY
IN THE UNIVERSITY OF LONDON

OXFORD
AT THE CLARENDON PRESS
1959

Oxford University Press, Amen House, London E.C.4

GLASGOW NEW YORK TORONTO MELBOURNE WELLINGTON
BOMBAY CALCUTTA MADRAS KARACHI KUALA LUMPUR
CAPE TOWN IBADAN NAIROBI ACCRA

CONTENTS

LIST OF STATISTICAL TABLES

1

THE ELEMENTS

THE title of this book is forbidding: if the attention of the reader is to be held there must be good will from the start. It would be unwise to begin with a disquisition on economic theory—for the fruit of that tree too often turns out to be an apple of discord. And it would hardly be safe to embark on a discussion of the principles and methods of the art of chronology, if only because to do so would be to invite the reader to sleep. It may be best to make use of the most common of all conversational gambits. Even in an age when men torture and kill each other because of differences of opinion on all manner of things, one topic of universal interest lies outside the field of contention: the weather has given rise to no ideologies and no class wars. There is general agreement that it is rarely any better than it should be.

The eighteenth century was an age of diarists and letter-writers, many of whom set down, day by day, observations on what were usually referred to as the elements. If we could accept these at their face value we should be forced to abandon the widely held belief that things are worse ordered for us than for our predecessors. For few in the twentieth century have seen blood streaming down from the heavens, or birds, frozen in flight, dropping like stones to the ground. Few of us have been battered by hailstones as big as quart bottles. And if many have attended a fun fair on the banks of the Thames, no one in our day has roasted an ox, driven a carriage, or set up a row of shops, on the frozen surface of the river itself. Not very long ago[1] heavy rains undermined the earthwork defences of the east coast, and the sea occupied wide tracts of several counties; but there was no such devastation as followed a similar inroad in November 1703, when many thousands lost their lives, a bishop and his wife were killed in their bed, the Eddystone lighthouse was swept away, and the Royal Navy came near to destruction.

[1] On 1 Feb. 1953.

B

The age of the diarists and letter-writers was also an age when men began to record temperatures, atmospheric pressures, the volume of water in the rivers, and the number of hours of sunshine. The first rain-gauge was set up—appropriately in Lancashire—in 1677, and others appeared later at Warminster, Oundle, and Chatsworth. The evidence of thermometers, barometers, and rain-gauges raises doubts as to whether, over the past 200 years, the elements have suffered any real change of heart. On the basis of the recordings, climatologists believe that, whereas the period 1700–50 had somewhat drier weather than what is called 'the standard normal', the succeeding fifty-year period was marked by rather greater humidity. The difference, however, was not pronounced. Though in the eighteenth century there were occasions when flood, drought, or frost wrought havoc greater than any we have known, it would seem that, on the whole, the English of that era enjoyed much the same equable climate as the geography books tell us we enjoy today.[2]

There is, however, an important difference between our lot and that of our forebears. Most of them earned their bread on the soil. Each morning they lifted their eyes to the east for sign of rain to quicken the seed or sun to ripen the crops; each evening they looked to the western sky for promise of better things tomorrow. Concern about the weather is attested not only by the Book of Common Prayer, but also by the saws and proverbs that enriched ordinary speech: a bushel of March dust was worth a king's ransom; April showers brought May flowers. The prodigality or niggardliness of the landlord mattered less than the prodigality or niggardliness of nature; what was happening at Westminster or in the City was of small account compared with what was happening in the heavens. These are things that, somehow or other, seem to have evaded the notice of social historians.

The word 'fluctuation' implies a movement like that of the waves of the sea, an alternate rise and fall, a rhythm of more or less regular duration. But, in the course of time, it has come to be applied to any variation, whether periodic or not; and it is in this imprecise sense that it is used in this work. There is, however, one fluctuation at least that is fairly regular and predictable: the annual rotation of

---

[2] C. E. P. Brooks and J. Glasspoole, *British Floods and Droughts*, pp. 84, 143–4. The figures of the rainfall at Chatsworth from 1761 are given by William Marshall, *Review of the Reports of the Board of Agriculture* (1815), i. 78–79. Other statistics of rainfall are discussed by J. Glasspoole, 'Two Centuries of Rain', *Meteorological Magazine*, vol. lxiii.

the seasons. The effects of this are to be observed in many fields of human affairs, only a few of which, however, can be mentioned here.

The vital statistics of the eighteenth century have yet to be assembled and sifted; but some tentative conclusions about seasonal changes in public health can be drawn from the Bills of Mortality issued, and later printed, by the Company of Parish Clerks of London. Care must be taken in using the monthly figures of baptisms and burials, for the returns for some months cover five weeks and for others only four. If we knew nothing of the ways of eighteenth-century clerks, we might conclude that the incidence of deaths was highest in December; but it is not unlikely that there were stirrings of conscience as Christmas and the New Year drew near, and that the clerks added to the figures for December christenings and burials they had overlooked earlier. When, however, the statistics are presented for quarterly periods the possibility of error is reduced. This book is not concerned specifically with demography, and a single set of figures must suffice:

Average number of christenings and burials in London
for the ten years 1764/5 to 1773/4

			Christenings	Burials
Oct.–Dec.	.	.	4,191	5,803
Jan.–Mar.	.	.	4,160	6,034
Apr.–June	.	.	4,169	5,494
July–Sept.	.	.	3,955	5,031

The seasonal change of christenings is small, but that of burials is significant. Deaths in London seem to have been about 20 per cent. higher in the first three months of the calendar year than in the three months of summer.[3] As one might expect, the Reaper took his main crop in the winter.

Work and play, no less than life and death, were closely attuned to the seasons. One of the major activities of the eighteenth century was war. If it was a matter of prudence to defer the opening of a campaign till the harvest had been reaped, it was of the utmost

---

[3] In spite of the fact that they included only 90 days, as against 92 in the summer quarter. The fall in the number of christenings and burials in July–September may have been the result of the annual migration of the rich to their country seats and of the poor to the harvest fields.

importance to bring it to an end before severe weather set in. A departure from this practice in the cold winter of 1759–60 (when, it was said, cavalrymen froze to death in their saddles) gave rise to biting remarks from Horace Walpole in a letter dated 14 January 1760: 'What milksops the Marlboroughs and Turennes, the Blakes and the Van Trumps appear now, who whipped into winter quarters and into port, the moment their noses looked blue. Sir Cloudesly Shovel said that an admiral would deserve to be broke, who kept great ships out after the end of September, and to be shot if after October.—There's Hawke in the bay weathering *this* winter, after conquering in a storm.' But in the later wars of the century the ancient rule seems to have been observed; and on 15 November 1779 Walpole found comfort in the reflection that 'the devil of a winter is come in that will send armies and navies to bed'.[4]

Most outdoor occupations, including agriculture, seafaring, and fishing, tended to be at their busiest in the summer and early autumn. This was true also of some of the later processes in the manufacture of textiles. Bleaching required dry weather and sunshine. It was usual to expose the yarn or cloth to light and air in the spring and to leave it in the open for several months. But as the days shortened and the sun lost its power, there was little to be gained by continuing the process. On 8 December 1753 J. & N. Philips of Tean wrote: 'At this time of the year we have not the least certainty of goods coming in, 'tis all a chance whether they will whiten or not.'[5] In the early part of the century, at least, the calico printers also were effectively employed for only half the year, since the washing of the fabric could not be carried on in frosty weather.[6] The same was true of several of the heavy industries. It was not easy to produce good bricks in the winter; for the soft, moulded pieces of clay had to be piled in stacks until they were dry enough to go to the kilns to be burnt, and in this state they were highly vulnerable to rain and frost.[7] Building itself tended to decline in the autumn, and the wages of masons, carpenters, and other craftsmen

---

[4] *Letters of Horace Walpole*, edited by Mrs. Paget Toynbee (1903), iv. 340; xi. 53. If men were not to fight in the winter they were not expected, it seems, to train for fighting then. When the Militia was established in 1757 its weekly exercises were confined to the months between May and October.

[5] A. P. Wadsworth and Julia de L. Mann, *The Cotton Trade and Industrial Lancashire, 1600–1780* (1931), p. 295 n.

[6] Ibid., p. 138.

[7] *Eighteenth Report of Com. of Excise, B.P.P.* (1836), xxvi. 17. The development of brick-making in Scotland was held back by the climate.

were reduced after Michaelmas. 'The months following October are not proper to mend the roads in', remarked a writer on the Poor Law in 1787; and hence the highways were neglected at the time when they were most in need of repair.[8] It took about six months to build a merchant vessel: shipbuilding was heavily concentrated in the spring and summer, as is shown by the dates of registration of vessels.[9]

It might be thought that the coal-miners would have been at their busiest in the winter when the demand for domestic fuel was at its peak. In fact, the pits were most active in the summer and autumn: it was considered a misfortune that they drew away horses and carts at a time when these were required by the farmers.[10] When winter rain turned the roads into bogs, and frost or flood put an end to traffic on the rivers, land-sale collieries could supply only customers close at hand, and hence the pit-head price of coal was depressed just when the price in the towns was at its highest. By far the largest coalfield was that of Northumberland and Durham, which found its chief market in the metropolis. In the earlier decades, few collier vessels would face the hazards of the North Sea until the storms of January and February were over, and so the miseries of a London winter were often intensified by a dearth of fuel. In the early months of 1739 coal could be bought in London at 25s. a chaldron: in the following January the price was 70s. No doubt, part of the increase is to be attributed to the outbreak of the war with Spain and the impressment of seamen, but far more of it was the result of the ice that sealed up the Thames to shipping. Before the five weeks of frost that began on Christmas Day, 1762, the price of coal in London was 40s.; in the following January and February it rose to 55s.[11] Needless to say, it was possible for similar increases to take place at other seasons of the year. On 5 May 1782 Horace Walpole wrote of 'an east wind that has half-starved London; as a fleet of colliers cannot get in'. 'Coals were sold yesterday', he added, 'at seven guineas a chaldron.'[12] But such occurrences were far more common in the winter. In the

---

[8] W. Godschall, *A General Plan of Parochial and Provincial Police* (1787), p. 60.

[9] Ralph Davis, 'Seamen's Sixpences: An Index of Commercial Activity, 1697–1828', *Economica*, Nov. 1956, p. 328.

[10] T. S. Ashton and Joseph Sykes, *The Coal Industry in the Eighteenth Century* (1929), p. 122.

[11] Monthly figures were provided by the *Gentleman's Magazine*.

[12] *Letters*, xii. 243.

eighties and nineties the quantity of coal brought to the metropolis was, on the average, 25 per cent. less in the three months December to February than in any other quarterly period. London had warehouses for grain and other produce, but provision for the storage of coal was poor, and the city lived from hand to mouth—as it has done in recent years. In the winter of 1799 there was less than a week's supply in the yards.[13]

Coal had not yet been widely adopted as a source of power, but many industries relied on it for heat; and hence winter shortage of fuel was often a cause of unemployment. Writing of the harsh conditions at the end of 1739, William Stout of Lancaster described how 'many tradesmen were frozen out of their trades and employ, and starved for want of fire, turf and coals being at double prices';[14] and according to the *Annual Register*, the frost of 1762 'put a stop to several handicraft trades'. The records of the iron industry, also, give evidence of frequent anxieties in the winter about the supplies of fuel: in December 1796, for example, Thomas Butler noted in his diary that, unless the frost that had persisted for several weeks broke up, there would be much inconvenience at Kirkstall Forge for want of coals.[15]

There were, however, some industries that tended to be slack in the summer and relatively active in the autumn. The busiest period for malting and brewing was after Michaelmas, when the new crops of barley and hops had been gathered and the weather was neither too warm nor too cold for the brewing of the best kinds of ale. (Customers often expressed a preference for 'nappy October'.) In earlier times most of the annual supply had been consumed by the spring; for, according to Fuller, 'ale went out when swallows came in, seldom appearing after Easter'.[16] And though by the eighteenth century both production and consumption were carried on the year round, most brewers seem to have suspended operations in June and resumed them only in October.[17] Similarly, millers, distillers, tanners, soap-boilers, and candle-makers were at their busiest

[13] *Report on the State of the Coal Trade* (1800), App. 45, pp. 627–8.
[14] *Autobiography of William Stout of Lancaster, 1665–1752*, edited by J. Harland (1851), p. 134.
[15] *The Diary of Thomas Butler of Kirkstall Forge, Yorkshire, 1796–1799* (1906), pp. 98, 102.
[16] Thomas Fuller, *The Worthies of England* (ed. 1840), i. 367.
[17] Peter Mathias, 'Agriculture and the Brewing and Distilling Industries in the Eighteenth Century', *Ec. Hist. Rev.*, vol. v, no. 2 (1952), p. 249.

not in the summer, but after the crops had been got in and the herds had been thinned, in the autumn.

Other occupations less closely dependent on English agriculture were also slack in the summer. There was little or no work for the journeymen tailors between Midsummer and Michaelmas.[18] For some obscure reason the makers of ropes disliked the light of day. (Perhaps the hangman—an important functionary at this time—preferred that the making of his gear should be kept dark.) Some ropeworks were set up in caverns, as in the Peak District at Castleton; but those in the open air operated only at night, and, in the summer, nights were short. According to a nineteenth-century report of the Royal Mint, the Irish and others who made a living by uttering false coin laid aside their crucibles and dies in the summer —less, it would appear, because, their deeds being evil, they shunned the glare of the sun, than because of the opportunity of turning an honest penny in the cornfields.[19] At this time, indeed, large numbers of craftsmen and labourers left their ordinary vocations to take up the scythe or the rake. On 19 June 1762 Henry Hindley of Mere countermanded an order for linen yarn from Hamburg, because it was then too late for this to be turned into cloth before the weavers would leave their masters to work on the land. Generally the linen-weavers were back at their looms by the middle of September; but if the summer were backward, or the crop abnormally heavy, the return might be delayed. On 18 August 1770 Hindley reported that 'our hay harvest is but just ended, and the corn begun, so that all the workmen are in the field'. Towards the end of September they were still there, and as late as 26 October Hindley was unable to execute an order for cloth because, though the harvest had at last been reaped, 'a plenty of apples now imploys many workmen making syder'.[20]

Even the business of teaching and learning was seasonal. William Stout of Lancaster tells how, from the age of ten or twelve, he and his brother 'were very much taken off the school, especially in the

[18] Paul Mantoux, *The Industrial Revolution in the Eighteenth Century* (1928), p. 72 n.

[19] *Report of the Royal Mint* (1849), p. 185.

[20] Hindley MSS. Wiltshire County Record Office. It was a desire to overcome the seasonal fall in the supply of yarn, resulting from the employment of women in the harvest fields, that led the Society of Arts, in 1760, to offer a reward for the invention of a machine that would spin six threads at a time. Mantoux, op. cit., p. 220.

spring and summer season, plough-time, turf-time, hay-time and harvest . . . so that we made small progress in Latin, for what we got in winter we forgot in summer'.[21] There is a deplorable tendency for the same thing to happen to undergraduates today.

More important even than this drain of labour from manufacture in the summer was the seasonal decline in the rainfall. If the economy of the nineteenth century rested on coal, that of the eighteenth was closely dependent on water. Large amounts were needed to cleanse the wool, ret the flax, wash the yarn, and full, dye, and finish the fabrics that were the staples of English manufacture. Maltsters, brewers, and distillers needed great quantities, and so vital was water to the tanners and paper-makers that some correlation can be established between their output and the rainfall. In many summers when the springs dried up operations were brought to a standstill.

Water was not only a raw material of industry: it was also the chief source of power. 'If I have water I will drink wine; but if I have no water, I must drink water.'[22] Though this was said of the miller, it was equally true of the fuller, ironmaster, steel-tilter, scythe-maker, and others whose industry required the use of heavy hammers, large bellows, or grindstones. Since, at any one place, there was rarely enough water for all, disputes were frequent and fierce: in a literal sense local politics centred on the village pump. There was perpetual conflict between the bargemen on the river, who wanted a clear passage, and the millers who built weirs and deflected water to their ponds. And there was conflict between the millers and other manufacturers who made use of water-power. In parts of Yorkshire the fullers were able to work only when water could be spared by the corn mills,[23] and it was customary for them to suspend operations between Whitsuntide and Michaelmas.[24] The Coalbrookdale Iron Company had often to blow out its furnaces for eight or more weeks in the summer, for when the flow of water was small and the blast feeble, both the quantity and the quality of the metal were such as to make working unprofitable.[25] In the summer drought of 1767 all four furnaces of the Carron Works were idle for three months, and it was because of this that James Watt was called

[21] Stout, op. cit., p. 5.   [22] Fuller, op. cit. i. 120.
[23] J.H.C., vol. xxviii (1757–61), p. 138.
[24] W. B. Crump and G. Ghorbal, *History of the Huddersfield Woollen Industry*, p. 16.
[25] A. Raistrick, *Dynasty of Ironfounders*, p. 108.

in to install a fire-engine to return the spent water to the reservoir.[26] The correspondence between Peter Stubs, a file-maker of Warrington, and the Sheffield tilters who supplied him with steel abounds with references to the state of the streams. On 10 August 1800, for example, Walker & Booth wrote, 'There has been 10 cwt. of cast [steel] for you waiting 6 weeks, and not yet done: the water is so very scarce.' It was an exceptionally dry season, with a drought unbroken for seventy-four days, but similar hold-ups were reported in years when the total rainfall was not abnormally low.[27]

John Bright, who was interested in water (not only as a teetotaller, but also as a salmon fisher), observed in one of his less solemn moments that there was almost always either too much or too little of it.[28] Manufacturers of an earlier generation than his had reason to fear floods hardly less than droughts; for when heavy rains raised the level below the mill, the pressure of 'back-water' might put a stop to the wheel.[29] They paid close attention to the rate of flow. Joseph Rogerson, who owned a scribbling mill at Bramley in the West Riding, used a scale of measurement as fine as that sometimes employed in dispensing whisky. On 2 April 1808 he wrote in his diary, 'Our dam runs over a stream as thick as my thumb.' This meant that the level in his pond was dangerously low; the wheels of some of his competitors had already ceased to turn. A month later, on 2 May, things were better: 'Our dam runs over a stream as thick as my wrist.' But heavy rain followed; and on 1 June Rogerson records, 'Dam runs over a stream as thick as my arm'—a state of things that might, if unchecked, have had consequences no less serious than if the stream had dried up.[30] Floods might hamper production by bringing transport to a stop—not only by road but also by river. In the autumn of 1764 inundations in the Thames Valley brought distress to the bargemen, who were put out of work for two months.[31]

Trade, no less than industry, was subject to seasonal change.

[26] H. M. Cadell, *The Story of the Forth*, p. 166. I am indebted to Dr. I. F. Gibson for this reference.

[27] Stubs MSS. The University of Manchester.

[28] In an inaugural address on *The Love of Books*, on the opening of the Birmingham Reference Library, 1 June 1882.

[29] *J.H.C.* xxviii. 142.

[30] Diary of Joseph Rogerson, *The Leeds Woollen Industry, 1780–1820* (ed. W. B. Crump), Thoresby Society, xxxii. 84–86.

[31] G. J. Symons and G. Chatterton, 'The November Floods of 1894 in the Thames Valley', *Journal of Meteorology* (N.S.), vol. xxi (1895), p. 189.

Impediments to transport and epidemics of influenza and other diseases had adverse effects in the winter. If we may judge by the experience of London factors, wholesale dealing in woollens tended to be slack at this season, to improve in the spring, and reach a peak in the summer.[32] Fairs played an important part in the traffic in live-stock and other produce, and more of these seem to have been held in August and October than in any other month of the year. And retail trade in clothing and other wares was most active—as, indeed, it was even in the later nineteenth century—after Michaelmas, when money earned in the harvest fields was being transferred to shop-keepers and pedlars.[33]

Overseas commerce moved in step with the seasons in other parts of the globe, and the arrival and departure of vessels varied with the winds that blew in distant latitudes. England drew material for her houses and ships from the forests of Norway and the areas fring-ing the Baltic. The logs were most easily moved to the rivers when the ground was thick with frozen snow; and if the winter were mild there might be a hold-up of supplies. On the other hand, severe frost in the spring might keep the saw-mills sealed up and cause delay at the ports: the sawn timber could be shipped only when the ice had cleared from the Baltic and the Sound and the Belt were open. Masters of vessels trading with the Far East preferred to leave the Thames between December and June, so that they could reach the Indian Ocean during the south-west monsoons; they sought to set sail for home before the end of January—again so as to catch favouring winds and avoid storms in the Atlantic.[34] In the trade with the American mainland the shipping calendar was similarly determined. The vessels set out in March or April, and were back in time for a second voyage in August or September; during the months of winter they were laid up in British ports.[35] Yet again, in the triangular commerce with Africa and the West Indies it was necessary to adhere closely to sailing time-tables, and, in particular, to get away from the islands on the homeward journey before the

---

[32] Conrad Gill, 'Blackwell Hall Factors, 1795–1799', *Ec. Hist. Rev.*, vol. vi, no. 3 (1954), p. 268.

[33] In R. D. Blackmore's *Lorna Doone* (1869), ch. xxxi, there is mention of 'that time of the year, when the clothing business was most active on account of harvest wages'.

[34] C. N. Parkinson, *Trade in the Eastern Seas 1793–1813*, p. 106; *The Trade Winds* (ed. C. N. Parkinson), pp. 152–3.

[35] Herbert Heaton in *The Trade Winds*, p. 199.

beginning of August, when the hurricanes set in. Naturally, rates of
marine insurance varied from season to season with the risks of the
sea: they were generally at their peak in the winter, but, for the
voyage between the West Indies and England, they doubled on
1 August.[36]

The movement of shipping affected the state of employment in
British ports. Activity in the riverside trades of London fluctuated
with the comings and goings of the East Indiamen; it was fortunate
for the dockers that many of the homeward-bound vessels reached
London River in the summer when departures were relatively few
and there was little loading to be done. The pressure to make up
cargoes before the busy season for sailing opened in December led
to great activity in the export trades in general. And when, each
September, the 'first of August ships' from the West Indies docked
at Bristol the landing of their cargoes of muscovado was followed
by high employment at the refineries.

Little study has yet been made of seasonal movements of prices.
Naturally, grain was relatively cheap in the months immediately
following the harvest. But, from the day the first shoots from the
winter or spring sowing appeared, the eyes of farmers and dealers
were on the soil. At least as early as April forecasts could be made
of the coming crops, and, as time went on, the prospective yield had
an increasing effect on prices. Nevertheless, the major influence was
exerted by visible stocks in the granaries, and, generally, as these
dwindled, prices increased. For the decade 1792–1801 the average
quarterly price of wheat varied as follows:[37]

Oct.–Dec.	Jan.–Mar.	Apr.–June	June–Sept.
67s. 10d.	69s. 3d.	70s. 4d.	71s. 6d.

The prices of cattle and meat were generally at their lowest about
Michaelmas (29 Sept.) and reached their highest point in the winter
about Candlemas (2 Feb.).[38] Those of coal in London and a large
part of the east and south of the country, were regulated by the
associated colliery proprietors of the Tyne and Wear; but, as has
already been mentioned, severe weather meant both increased
demand and curtailed supply; and, on the average, prices were

[36] Richard Pares, in Parkinson, op. cit., p. 183.
[37] The figures are averages for the ten-year period of the average quarterly
prices given in the *Report on the Corn Trade between Great Britain and Ireland*
(1802), App. table G, pp. 171–91.
[38] Daniel Defoe, *A Tour through England and Wales* (Everyman ed.), i. 9.

highest in December and January.[39] For obvious reasons, the prices of imported materials varied with harvests abroad, and with seasonal changes in shipping and trade. Produce from the Orient tended to be relatively cheap after the half-yearly sales of the East India Company in March and September; and the prices of tropical commodities followed the shipping calendar from the West Indies. As Mr. Stern has observed, 'Sugar prices clearly reflected the annual cycle by rising from the beginning of the year to a virtual famine level in June, relieved by the arrival of the first West Indiaman, and dropping to a low level in December, when all supplies had been unloaded and made available.'[40]

Movements of imports and exports had effects on the foreign exchanges. The existence of dealers who were ready to buy, sell, or hold foreign money at any time tended to reduce, but did not eliminate, the seasonal variations in rates. In the early part of the century Britain was, on balance, an exporter of agricultural produce; in the sixties she was, as often as not, a net importer; and before the end of the century the growth of population and manufacture had produced a situation in which she normally depended on foreigners for a large part of her food and raw material. The change in the role of Britain from exporter to importer of grain is reflected in the seasonal movements of rates of exchange. In the early part of the century sterling rose in value from October to December; towards the end of it, what is now called the autumnal drain is clearly marked.

Average London rates on Hamburg

	Jan.	Feb.	Mar.	Apr.	May	June
1701–20	33–10	33–9	33–10	33–10	33–9	33–9
1781–1800	34–7	34–9	34–10	35–0	34–10	34–7

	July	Aug.	Sept.	Oct.	Nov.	Dec.
1701–20	33–7	33–7	33–7	33–9	33–11	34–0
1781–1800	34–8	34–7	34–7	34–5	34–5	34–7

[39] *Report on the State of the Coal Trade* (1800), App. 10, pp. 578–87.
[40] Walter Stern, 'The London Sugar Refiners around 1800', *Guildhall Miscellany*, Feb. 1954. 'Nothing can be more fluctuating than the Market for sugar,' wrote George Maxwell in 1743, 'the continuance of an easterly wind for a few weeks shall raise it, and a westerly wind with the bare expectation of the arrival of Ships shall lower it again.' Richard Pares, 'The London Sugar Market 1740–1769', *Ec. Hist. Rev.*, vol. ix, no. 2 (1956), p. 262.

Another set of figures that show pronounced seasonal change is that of the numbers of bankruptcies. In the period 1742–79 about 12,000 bankruptcies were recorded, and these were distributed by quarterly periods as follows:

Nov.–Jan.	Feb.–Apr.	May–July	Aug.–Oct.
3,424	3,318	2,931	2,343

Perhaps those versed in eighteenth-century legal or administrative practice may be able to offer a simple explanation of the concentration in the period between November and April. But it is at least possible that seasonal changes in the availability of currency played a part. There were two points of time at which what economists call the transactions demand for money was especially high: in the early autumn, when the crops were being moved and wages paid out on a large scale, and about Christmas, when merchants and manufacturers made up their accounts and called for payments. When allowance is made for the weeks that had to elapse before legal proceedings could be taken, it is not surprising to find that the monthly figures of bankruptcies registered a peak in November.[41] (It was not only because of its fogs that this came to be known as the month of suicides.) In the same way, pressure on monetary supplies may explain why the second highest figure for bankruptcies was in February—in spite of the fact that this is the shortest month of the year.[42]

It was observed by Jude the Obscure that there was a flaw in the terrestrial scheme by which what was good for God's birds was bad for God's gardeners. The turn of the season that was welcome to some might be dreaded by others. The dry summer weather that favoured the grain-growers was disliked by the graziers; and the frost that made transport by road easier might halt traffic on the rivers and canals. If the wages of builders and tailors fell as the weather grew worse and the days shortened, those of the seamen

[41] Several commercial crises occurred in November. Macpherson calls attention to the high figures of bankruptcies in Nov. 1778 and Nov. 1792. *Annals of Commerce* (1805), iii. 629; iv. 254.

[42] The monthly averages of bankruptcies in this period ran as follows: Jan. 27·0; Feb. 29·6; Mar. 27·7; Apr. 29·0; May 28·0; June 23·2; July 22·6; Aug. 21·5; Sept. 19·4; Oct. 19·3; Nov. 31·0; Dec. 26·8. The figures are taken from the *Gentleman's Magazine*, 1742–79. Those of Silberling for 1779–1830 show a somewhat different distribution, but there is the same rise in the winter and fall in the summer. Norman J. Silberling, 'British Prices and Business Cycles, 1779–1850', *Rev. of Economic Statistics*, Prel. vol. v. (1923), Suppl. 2.

were raised. How far it was possible to meet such disharmonies by a dovetailing of activities it is difficult to say. The merchant, who had usually more than a single market overseas, could adjust his dealings to the conditions that prevailed on each sea lane or at each port. Industrialists, too, had usually more than one iron in the fire. Some combined manufacture with farming; and a producer of textiles, like Joseph Rogerson, could console himself for weather that put his wheel out of action by reflecting that it was good for his crops. So also with many of the workers. Spinning and weaving alternated with work on the land, and since industrial regulation was weak, all but the highly specialized could turn fairly easily from one job to another. Each season brought its own dangers; but, on the whole, there was less likelihood of widespread interruption of activities in the summer and autumn than in the seasons of austerity. And the fact that at harvest time there was work for large numbers of men and women who normally had little to do suggests that, on balance, employment reached an annual peak between July and September. As with the lower creation, man's activity tended to ebb in the winter.

II

Many of the annual, like the seasonal, variations of output arose from the weather. There are no valid statistics of the output of agriculture, but changes in the yields can be inferred from the ups and downs of prices of grain and animal products. These are by no means a perfect guide, for there was an international market for foodstuffs, and dearth or glut on the Continent or in Ireland might affect prices here: hence it is important to pay attention to verbal as well as statistical evidence. It should be added that, since the weather varied from place to place within the country, good crops in one region might synchronize with poor crops in another; and, in the first half of the century, before the improvement of transport had gone far, there might be wide differences in prices. Moreover, there were local differences in the times of sowing and reaping. ('I am of opinion with the old folk in the West of England', wrote Cobbett, 'that God is almost always on the side of *early* farmers.'[43] But what was early in the West Country might be too early in the north.) Thus it happens that reports on the state of the crops at

[43] William Cobbett, *A Year's Residence in the United States of America* (1813), p. 110. I am indebted to Mr. J. Potter for this reference.

particular times from different areas often conflict. It is only of
the widespread aberrations of the weather that account will be
taken here.

Cereal farming in England rarely suffers from drought. For, as
Fuller observed, the clay lands are far more extensive than the
sands, and the clay may remain moist through months of dry
weather.[44] The producers of wheat feared most of all a cold winter
followed by prolonged frost in the spring and heavy rain in the
summer. Barley was a spring, or Lent, crop. It was hardly affected
by the state of the weather in the winter; but a cold spring was
generally harmful, and, though it stood up to rain better than wheat,
a wet summer usually meant a poor crop. Oats, also, were sown in
the spring. A late frost might do much damage to the crops, but the
chief fear was of drought: in 1719 the oats were so badly scorched
that, in the south of England, the price was nearly as high as that
of wheat.[45] Sometimes sudden changes in demand might affect
the price of a particular grain. In the early months of 1736 it was
reported that, because of a Bill to restrain the consumption of
spirituous liquors, 'distiller's barley bore no price' at all at Bear
Quay, the chief London market.[46] And in 1745–6, when other grains
were relatively cheap, the price of oats rose sharply—no doubt
because of a great consumption by the horses of the military during
the Rebellion. Generally, however, the short-term movements of
prices were similar for each of the grains—partly because wheat,
barley, rye, and oats were, in some degree, substitutes, but mainly
because any extreme of temperature or rainfall, in the spring,
affected the yield of all.

For the graziers the worst enemy was drought. The chief visita-
tions of cattle plague seem to have come through infected livestock
or hides, brought from the Continent. But runs of hot summers were
conducive to the spread of the disease. Moreover, late frost or prolonged drought, which led to a dearth of hay and roots, often made
it necessary to kill off healthy cattle in the autumn. Although there
was an immediate increase in the supply of meat, hides, and tallow,
there inevitably followed a shortage of these, as well as of dairy
produce, in the next two or three years.

The flockmasters, on the other hand, suffered most in years of
excessive rain, which brought outbreaks of sheep-rot; but for them,

[44] Fuller, op. cit. i. 116.   [45] Stout, op. cit., p. 95.
[46] *Gentleman's Magazine* (1736), p. 163.

as for the cattle farmers, severe frost in the winter and spring might spell ruin. There were times when the output of pastoral farming moved in a direction opposite to that of arable farming, but (as will be seen from the following chronological survey) in years of excessive cold all branches of agriculture suffered together.

During the greater part of the last decade of the seventeenth century the prices of wheat and other grains had been extraordinarily high. But in 1700 the weather took a favourable turn, and the 'eight barren years' were followed by three in which the crops were abundant. Foodstuffs were so cheap that many farmers were in arrears with their rents; and when in March 1702/3 Lord Stanhope tried to enforce payment, his attorney reported that the tenants had been unable to dispose of their crops: 'all their corn lyes dead upon their hands'.[47] Heavy rains in the spring and early summer, however, were followed by poor harvests, and the great gales and floods of the autumn, which impeded the movement of grain, brought a further increase of prices. At Lady Day wheat at Windsor had sold for as little as 3s. 9d. a bushel; by Michaelmas the price was 5s. 3d., and by Lady Day, 1704, 7s. 3d.

The dearth was not prolonged; and four warm, dry summers in succession again brought abundant supplies of food of all kinds. In 1708, however, the weather took an adverse turn, and by Michaelmas the price of wheat had risen to 6s. 6d. Far worse was to follow. In October there came a great frost which continued to the middle of March; the Thames was frozen up and the whole country was in the grip of ice. It was not until late in May that the hawthorns began to blow and the elms showed the first signs of green, and not until the middle of June that the wheat began to form in the ear.[48] Like its predecessor, the summer was cold and wet, and the harvest wretched.[49] At Lady Day wheat was already as high as 8s. 1d.; by Michaelmas it had reached 11s. 6d., and the same famine price was recorded at Lady Day, 1710. There were reasons for this conformity: on 24 October the government had put in force the old statutes

[47] T. H. Baker, *Records of the Seasons* (1883), p. 173, citing Evelyn; J. H. Plumb, *Sir Robert Walpole*, p. 16.

[48] Thomas Short, *A General Chronological History of the Air, Weather, Seasons, Meteors . . .*, cited by Theophilus Thompson, *Annals of Influenza* (1852).

[49] For the whole year 1709 the recorded rainfall was 26½ inches, against a supposed average for this period of 19½ inches (T. Tooke, *History of Prices*, i. 36). The same figure for the average rainfall is given by William Coxe, *Travels into Poland* (1792), i. 36.

against forestalling, regrating, and engrossing,[50] and, for fear of being accused of these offences, dealers would not sell—or admit to having sold—at prices higher than those prevailing just before the proclamation. Fears of the spread of riots, such as had broken out in Essex, may also have exerted an influence. High as it was, the price of wheat probably fails to reflect the degree of shortage. At Briton Ferry in South Wales, bread was so short that the people had to subsist on cockles, and some, it was said, looked more like skeletons than men.[51]

Large numbers of cattle and sheep perished in the long frost, and there was little grass in the spring of 1709. In May of the following year fat lambs sold for as much as 10s. 6d. each.[52] The shortage of meat and milk was hardly less serious than that of bread. Even before the rise in price had gone far, in 1708, there was an outbreak of fever, and as hunger increased the number of burials mounted.[53] A decade that had begun in plenty ended in almost universal distress.

Fortunately, the harvest of 1710 was favourable. And though the yields of wheat were light in 1711, 1713, and 1715, and those of barley and oats extremely poor as the result of drought in 1714, the existence of substantial exports of grain suggests that England was free from hunger.[54] Pastoral farming, on the other hand, fared poorly. There was an epidemic of cattle disease, which, beginning at the time of the famine, continued for four years. Lack of rain in the summer of 1714 and severe frost in the winter of 1715–16 led to shortages of hay, oats, and turnips.[55] In 1719 the summer was so dry that farmers in the south had to buy water for their herds, and large numbers of cattle were slaughtered: cows that would normally have fetched £4 were sold for 30s.[56] There was an immediate rise in the prices of butter and cheese, and in the following year beef was at the uncommonly high price of 5d. a pound.

During the early twenties the weather was generally kind, though

[50] Proceedings in Council respecting the Scarcity of Corn in 1709. B.M. Add. MS. 38353, ff. 195–207. I have to thank Dr. A. H. John for a copy of this.

[51] A. H. John, *The Industrial Development of South Wales, 1750–1850*, p. 18.

[52] Baker, op. cit., p. 177.

[53] According to the Bills of Mortality, burials in London (for years beginning in Sept.) rose from 16,100 in 1707 to 22,100 in 1709, and to 24,700 in 1710.

[54] See Table 3.

[55] The rainfall of 1714 was only two-fifths of that of 1709.

[56] Stout, op. cit., p. 97; Baker, op. cit., p. 180.

drought in the summer of 1723 bore heavily on the pastures and enforced the killing of good cattle.[57] But in 1725 the summer was cold and wet; the growing wheat was affected by blight and there were fears of a failure of the harvest.[58] In September, however, the weather improved, and though the price of wheat was relatively high (6s. 10½d.) there was sufficient grain to allow of fairly large exports to France and other countries, where the yields had been abnormally low. As Tooke pointed out, there is no evidence of popular unrest, as there is for nearly every other period when the statistics suggest shortage.[59] The dearth of 1725 cannot have been acute.

In the following season the harvest was satisfactory; but in 1727 harsh weather led to a partial failure of the crops, and in 1728 conditions were equally bad. 'We had a very wet spring and late seeding, and cold summer', wrote Stout, 'so that the corn did not get its feeding, and a great blast in summer, which scorched [the] corn.'[60] A hard frost that began in January 1729 also tended to force up prices; and for the first time in the century, England was, on balance, an importer of wheat (though not of barley). Again, there was an epidemic of fever. Perhaps because London was able to draw on foreign supplies of grain more readily than other places, the number of deaths here rose only slightly. But in 1729 the figures of burials at Norwich were double those of the year 1726; and similar increases were registered at Leeds and other places.[61]

Throughout the thirties the weather was generally good. Year after year, Stout wrote of great harvests (and of the poverty of the growers resulting from low prices). Exports of wheat were especially high in 1733, and again in 1734, when war in Europe put a temporary stop to the flow of grain from Poland. The hot summers that ripened the wheat meant the slaughter in the autumn of many cattle: between 1732 and 1735 beef and pork sold at 1d. to 2d. a pound, and butter at 2½d. or 3d.[62] Gales and floods in the early months of 1735 were followed by summer rains which, 'in many

[57] William Stout observes that 'the summer was exceedingly droughty, so that the people were straitened to keep their cattle alive, and especially for water; and the corn was burnt up, little hay got, and no sale of cattle, nor fodder to subsist them in winter' (loc. cit., p. 102).

[58] According to Jethro Tull, cited by Sir Joseph Banks, *The Causes of Disease in Corn, called by Farmers the Blight*, p. 74.

[59] Tooke, op. cit. i. 38.   [60] Stout, op. cit., p. 113.

[61] For details see Tooke, i. 40; *Thoresby Miscellany*, vol. i, pt. 2, p. 160; and the *Gentleman's Magazine*, passim.   [62] Stout, op. cit., pp. 121–7.

places laid the corn flat'.[63] There was an outbreak of disease among the flocks; thousands of sheep, it was said, were not worth offering for sale, and one lot of a hundred went at Leighton for 6d. apiece.[64] Conditions improved, however, in the following year; and, though food riots were reported in some parts of the country in 1737, the shortage was local and arose from exports to the Continent, where conditions of dearth prevailed.[65] In the two following years the weather was kind to both corn and livestock, and the decade ended in plenty.

In December 1739 the elements once more showed ferocity. The story, as told by the author of a work entitled *Contentment in God*,[66] is similar to that of 1709.

An unheard of frost seized with extraordinary severity on the world and the elements, so that it is scarcely possible to number or relate the many strange occurrences that took place through its violence. Men felt so oppressed that days passed by unheeded. One would and could hardly speak; one sat and thought, yet could not think; if anyone spoke a word it was with a hard, set face. Many hens and ducks, even the cattle in the stalls, died of cold; the trees split asunder. Not only beer but wine in cellars froze. Deeply sunken wells were covered with impenetrable ice. Crows and other birds fell to the ground frozen in their flight. No bread was eatable, for it was as cold and hard as a stone. In May no sign of verdure was yet to be seen; it was still cold in July, and vegetation was then still further hindered by drought. The harvest was not over till late in the autumn, and by the middle of October the frost returned before the fruit in the gardens had had time to ripen.

Between Michaelmas 1739 and Michaelmas 1740 the price of wheat rose from 4s. 11d. to 7s. 10½d., and in the following winter the scarcity was intensified by a freezing up of the corn mills 'so that meal advanced a third part'.[67] In December 1739 the Assize price of the peck loaf in London was 23d.: a year later it was 39d. According to one observer two barren winters in succession swept away half of the sheep; the starving cattle were unable to produce calves; and the oxen were so weak that it was only with difficulty that the seed was got into the ground.[68] The scarcity of hay and roots, as usual, meant that large numbers of cattle were driven to the slaughter houses; and though, for a time, beef could be had at 1d. a pound

[63] *Gentleman's Magazine* (1735), p. 386. [64] Baker, op. cit., p. 185.
[65] *Gentleman's Magazine* (1737), p. 315.
[66] Cited by Baker, op. cit., pp. 189–90.
[67] Stout, op. cit., p. 135. [68] Baker, op. cit., p. 190.

there was a steep rise in the prices of dairy produce. Only a few years earlier butter had sold at $2\frac{1}{2}d$.: now it cost $7d$. Cheese which had been at $15s$. was now $35s$. a cwt. Even more serious for the poor in the north was the increase in the cost of potatoes—from $2s$. $6d$. to $10s$. a load.[69] Cold and hunger between them raised the number of burials in London by 20 per cent.; and at Tiverton, where, it was said, nearly a twelfth of the inhabitants perished, grass grew up in the streets.[70]

The three summers that followed brought excellent crops: by 1743 the price of wheat was down to $2s$. $11d$.—the lowest recorded at Michaelmas in any year of the century—and the peck loaf in London sold at $17d$. 'They have had a very fine harvest here and bread never cheaper than at present, and great plenty of everything else', wrote the sugar factors, Lascelles and Maxwell, to a correspondent in the West Indies, on 16 September 1743.[71] In the autumn of 1745, however, misfortune came to the graziers. 'There rages a murrain among the cows,' wrote Horace Walpole on 29 November 1745, 'we dare not eat milk, butter, beef, nor anything from that species.'[72] The shortage of animal foods was intensified by losses of sheep as a consequence of heavy rain and snow in the following three years.[73] But the run of good harvests continued, and in spite of the fact that the cattle plague persisted until well into the next decade, it would be as misleading to apply the word 'Hungry' to the forties of the eighteenth, as it is to those of the nineteenth, century.

The winters of 1749 and 1750 were mild and the summers hot. According to Horace Walpole, the temperature in London in July of the second of these years was 'some degrees beyond the hottest in the West Indies', and the Thames was warmer than the hot well at Bristol.[74] The crops were abundant and exports of grain reached new peaks. Heavy rain, however, from March to May 1751 interfered with the spring sowing, and the following harvest was light. The rise in the price of bread was sufficient to lead to food riots in various parts of the country in 1752–3; but better weather brought plentiful harvests in the two following seasons.[75]

[69] Stout, op. cit., pp. 123, 136–8.
[70] M. Dunsford, *Historical Memoirs of Tiverton* (1790), p. 228.
[71] I am indebted to Dr. R. B. Sheridan for this extract.
[72] *Letters*, ii. 155.
[73] There was excessive rain in 1745 and 1747, and heavy snow in the winter of 1747–8. Baker, op. cit., pp. 192–3.   [74] *Letters*, iii. 4.
[75] In the summer of 1755 came 'the greatest fall of rain ever witnessed in the

According to one observer, the summer of 1756 was the wettest in the memory of man.[76] 'Great quantities of grain perished by the wind and rains, and most of what remained proved defective, both in quantity and substance.'[77] At Lady Day, 1757, the price of wheat was 8s. 6d. and in June the peck loaf, which a year earlier had cost 23d., was at 36d. There were extensive food riots in the provinces and an increase of burials in London. The government prohibited the export of corn and the use of grain for distilling, and these restrictions were enforced in the two following sessions also.[78]

The weather of 1757 was excellent. 'For how many years we shall have to talk of the summer of fifty-seven!', exclaimed Walpole: he called it a 'jubilee summer, which appears only once in fifty years'.[79] In fact, it was only the first of a long series. Year after year there are reports of hot dry weather. In August 1759 Walpole wrote of 'this most gorgeous of all summers', and in October he asked, 'Can one easily leave the remains of such a year as this? It is all gold.'[80] Others speak of heat and drought in the two following years, and on 5 August 1762 there is again the evidence of Horace Walpole from Twickenham: 'We have not had a tea cupful of rain till today for these six weeks. Corn has been reaped that never wet its lips; not a blade of grass; the leaves yellow and falling as in the end of October.'[81] It is true that there was heavy rain in the following summer, but plentiful harvests continued until 1764. Exports of grain were at high figures; and the low price of bread was reflected in a rise of baptisms in London.

During these years, however, there was some distress among the raisers of cattle. The low rainfall of 1761 and 1762 caused a shortage of fodder, with the usual effect of first reducing and then raising the prices of meat and other animal products. When in 1764 a Parliamentary inquiry was held into the high cost of provisions, attention was focused on the dearness of beef and pork. It was common form to attribute high prices to combination among middlemen; but, after pointing to the misconduct of the butchers and salesmen,

North' (Baker, op. cit., p. 199), but though there was a sharp local rise in the price of oats, there is no indication of general dearth.

[76] Baker, op. cit., p. 199.   [77] Tooke, op. cit. i. 48.

[78] 30 Geo. II, c. 1; 31 Geo. II, c. 1; 32 Geo. II, c. 2.

[79] Letters, iv. 73, 80.

[80] Ibid. iv. 282, 311.

[81] Ibid. v. 228–9. The rain-gauge at Chatsworth registered only 23·399 inches as against 36·399 in the following year.

the Committee went on to discuss the part played by the weather. It seems that the hot summer of 1762 had produced an 'uncommon plenty of acorns', and this had 'induced the raisers of hogs to fatten [and kill] their whole stock of hogs in that year', with the result that there was a shortage of pork and bacon in the following seasons.[82] The conditions that made the oaks yield so bountifully were responsible for a failure of the crops of hay and turnips, and thus both lessened the weight and enforced the slaughter of many cattle. Hence the high price of beef. Nevertheless, the years from 1758 to 1764 must rank with those of the thirties as a time when the standard of life of the poor was rising. The only exception was in the areas where oatmeal was the staple diet: in 1762, in particular, when the oatfields were scorched, there was hunger in Lancashire.[83]

Severe frost in the winter, and heavy rain in the spring and summer, led to a partial failure of the crops in 1766. The price of wheat rose sharply and in September an embargo was laid on the export of grain—a thing, as Walpole noted, that 'was never done before in time of peace'.[84] The following year saw further deterioration. 'This has been everywhere an *annus mirabilis* for bad weather', wrote Lord Chesterfield to his son on 1 June. 'Everybody has fires, and their winter clothes as at Christmas.'[85] A second bad harvest brought the price of wheat at Michaelmas to 8s. 3d., and a severe frost in the winter added to the distress. Again, in 1768 there were heavy downpours—the rain-gauge at Chatsworth registered a record[86]—and, though the harvest was better than the two that preceded it, the price of wheat was relatively high. The period from the summer of 1765 to that of 1768 was marked also by a shortage of animal foodstuffs. In the autumn of 1765 the price of milk in London had been raised from $1\frac{1}{2}d$. to $2d$. a quart; in 1766 an outbreak of sheep-rot forced up the price of mutton; and in this and the two following years there were complaints of the high cost of dairy produce and vegetables.[87] It was a time of general, if not acute, dearth. In 1766–7, when conditions were at their worst, food riots were widespread.

[82] *Annual Register* (1764), p. 136.
[83] See the chart in Wadsworth and Mann, op. cit., p. 358.
[84] *Letters*, vii. 67.
[85] *The Letters of Lord Chesterfield* (ed. J. Bradshaw, 1892), iii. 1361.
[86] 39·919 inches. Marshall, *Review of the Reports of the Board of Agriculture* (1815), i. 78–79.
[87] *Annual Register*, Sept. 1765, Feb. 1766, Aug. 1766, and 1767 *passim*; Baker, op. cit., p. 208.

In spite of a continuance of heavy rain, the harvest of 1769 was better, and though the prices of grain rose in 1770, those of animal products were relatively low. But the respite was brief. At the end of March 1771 'the face of the earth was naked to a surprising degree. Wheat hardly to be seen, and no sign of any grass; turnips all gone, and sheep in a starving way. All provisions rising in price.' The authority is Gilbert White,[88] who also remarks that, in the following year, butter cost 8*d*. to 10*d*. a pound. In 1772 the crops were again thin, and at Michaelmas wheat sold at 8*s*. 6*d*. It was the run of bad weather that led to the new Corn Law of 1773—just as in 1846 the weather was to rain another Corn Law away. Frost alternated with heavy rain in the winter of 1773–4, and at the following Michaelmas the price of wheat was still as high as 8*s*. There were further deluges in the autumn: 'The Thames is as broad as your Danube and all my meadows are under water', wrote Horace Walpole on 27 September 1774.[89] It was 'a Lancashire year'.[90]

At this time war and devastation checked exports from Poland to western Europe, and contributed to the rise of the prices of grains in England. But deeper forces were beginning to exert a similar and enduring influence. Population was pressing more heavily than before on natural resources and a growing preference for white bread concentrated the demand on wheat. A price of 5*s*. 6*d*. a bushel would have been thought excessive at any time before the middle sixties: a peck loaf would have been considered dear at 25*d*. In the last thirty years of the century it was only when harvests were exceptionally good that prices were as low as these.

From 1775 to 1781 the summers were warm and the wheatfields yielded abundantly. In August 1778 Walpole spoke of the harvest as prodigious (adding that 'in such a season we might have wine and oil had we made preparations for them').[91] In the following year the crop was said to be 'one fourth above a medium'. The peck loaf sold at 23*d*., and once more complaints arose of ruined farmers and distressed landlords.[92] In 1780 and 1781 the wheat was mildewed and in the second of these years the cattle suffered from distemper.[93] For a few months the price of bread was as high as 30*d*., but no evidence has been found of hunger.

[88] Cited by Baker, op. cit., p. 211.   [89] *Letters*, ix. 56.
[90] According to a writer cited by Tooke, op. cit. i. 70.
[91] *Letters*, x. 305.
[92] Baker, op. cit., p. 217.
[93] Ibid., p. 218. In 1780 the rain-gauge at Chatsworth recorded only 19·443

In 1782, however, the spring was unseasonable. From February to May there was either frost, snow, or rain.[94] The harvests this year were bad all over Europe, and efforts were made to bring in grain from the New World.[95] At Windsor the price of wheat was 8s. 1d. at Michaelmas and 10s. 6d. in the following winter, when the price of bread rose to 33d. and 34d. According to the Lord Mayor of London the cost of barley was exorbitant;[96] hence there was an extremely sharp fall in the output of malt, beer, and spirits. The summer and autumn of 1783 were sultry, but though the harvest was better, at Lady Day, 1784, the price of wheat was still as high as 8s. The two seasons of dearth saw food riots in the Midlands and attacks on distilleries in Scotland.[97]

Each of the winters of the following five years was severe. Frost continued in the London area for 89 days in 1784–5 and for 112 days in 1785–6.[98] But the summers were warm and dry and the grain harvests good. In 1788, however, the crops were deficient, and over 5,000 horned cattle perished in the drought.[99] In the following November there was again a great frost, which lasted till January. The Thames was frozen over as far down as the Custom House and a fair was held on the ice at Putney.[1] But though these extremes had the effect of pushing up the price of wheat there was no such dearth as in France, where hunger, as Professor Labrousse has shown, was a precursor of Revolution.[2] A mild spring and warm summer brought larger crops in 1790, and in 1791 there was a return of halcyon weather. 'June is not more June at Florence', wrote Horace Walpole, 'My hay is crumbling away; and I have ordered it to be cut, as a sure way of bringing rain.'[3] But if the grass crop was light, the yield of the cornfields was heavy—so heavy that Britain was once more a net exporter of wheat on a considerable scale.

inches—the lowest point since readings began in 1761. In 1781 the figure was only 23·065 inches. Marshall, op. cit., pp. 78–79.

[94] According to the gauge at Chatsworth, 1782 was a remarkably wet year, with 39·115 inches of rain.

[95] Anne Bezanson, *Prices and Inflation during the American Revolution*, p. 96. Importation was allowed on payment of low duties.

[96] *Gentleman's Magazine*, Feb. 1783, p. 88.

[97] Ashton and Sykes, op. cit., p. 127; Macpherson, op. cit. iv. 44.

[98] According to meteorologists the winter of 1785–6 was the coldest of the century.

[99] Only 19·856 inches of rain fell at Chatsworth in 1788.

[1] Baker, op. cit., pp. 222–5.

[2] C. E. Labrousse, *La Crise de l'économie française à la fin de l'ancient régime et au début de la révolution* (Paris, 1944).   [3] *Letters*, xiv. 445.

The summer of 1792 was less favourable. 'We are sorry to announce, from the best authority, that the late long-continued rains have had a terrible effect on the corn in almost every county within a hundred miles of the metropolis', observed the *Gentleman's Magazine* in July. 'It was uniformly wet, windy, cold, and dark, excepting one dry week in August . . . and at the commencement of September all thoughts of summer were annihilated by the severe frosts.'[4] At Michaelmas wheat sold at 7*s.* 6*d.* The flocks suffered from sheep-rot. In the North fruit was scarce, and there was an acute shortage of potatoes—a matter of consequence for the operatives of Lancashire.[5] Better conditions prevailed in the following two years. But the winter of 1794–5 was one of the most severe on record. A frost that began in December and lasted to the end of March destroyed much of the wheat in the ground; and dry easterly winds in the summer prevented the ears from filling. At Michaelmas wheat cost 11*s.* 6*d.* a bushel, and at the following Lady Day 12*s.* During the autumn and winter of 1795–6 the peck loaf sold at 50*d.* or more. Beef, mutton, and cheese seem to have remained relatively cheap, but again, there was great scarcity of potatoes.

The harvests of 1797 and 1798 were good. In the second of these years the price of wheat was down to 6*s.* 9*d.*, and there were ample supplies of beef, mutton, and pork. In the following year, however, there was once more an outbreak of elemental fury. Heavy rains in August rotted the hay and beat down the wheat, and the deluge continued into the autumn. 'Oh, that God Almighty would stop the Bottles of Heaven!', exclaimed Thomas Butler of Kirkstall on 22 September. The reaping had only just begun. 'Never was known to be such late harvest and bad crops', he wrote on 27 November, 'Very many acres will never be reaped at all but for fodder for cattle':[6] Some of the fields, indeed, were not cleared until January. Worse was to follow. The winter of 1799–1800 was severe; the spring was backward; and, again, heavy rains set in in August. The yields of wheat, barley, and oats were wretched. At Michaelmas wheat was at the unprecedented price of 22*s.* 1*d.*, and in December the peck loaf cost 73*d.* By the following spring beef was at 10*d.*–10½*d.*, and mutton at 11*d.*–12*d.*[7] In January 1799 potatoes had sold

[4] Loc. cit. (1792), p. 670.
[5] From the manuscript Diary of Thomas Rowbottom. Manchester Central Library.
[6] Butler, op. cit., pp. 321, 327.
[7] Baker (citing Tooke), op. cit., p. 235.

in Lancashire at 5½d. a score: in January 1801 the price was 1s. 8d. Nettles (which cost 2d. a pound) together with docks and watercress were used as a substitute, and in a Lancashire village 'scores of poor wretches were wandering in a forlorn state eagerly picking up any sort of vegetables'.[8] It would be easy to multiply the instances of distress. The century ended in conditions verging on famine.

This account of the fluctuations in English agriculture may be open to the criticism that it pays more attention to the periods of dearth than to those of abundance. Men are notoriously more vocal about their distresses than their blessings, and it is easier to find evidence of bad seasons than of good ones. But to some extent the stress is deliberate, for the impact of agriculture on other industries is more easily traced in the years of misfortune. The twelve periods[9] in which the prices of grain and other foods were abnormally high form convenient starting-points for a discussion of short-term fluctuations of general activity. The shortages varied in intensity and duration; and, because of the larger part played in the economy by agriculture, the dearths of the first half of the century had more serious effects than those of the second half. It will be observed that there is no regularity in the occurrence of bad seasons, and this surely ought not to surprise us. For when, in all ages, men have sought a symbol for inconstancy they have found it in the weather; and, as modern scholars have told us, 'rainfall, like the motorist, is no respecter of cycles'.[10] It was the unpredictability of the elements that gave them so much power.

---

[8] Rowbottom, op. cit.

[9] *1704, 1709–10, 1714, 1728–9, 1740–1, 1752–3, 1757–8, 1765–8, 1772–5, 1782–5, 1795–6, 1800–1.*

[10] Brooks and Glasspoole, op. cit., p. 183.

2

THE INFLUENCE OF THE HARVESTS

THE men of the eighteenth century were fortunate in that their rulers had not discovered the income-tax. This is a piece of good fortune for the historian also; for it means that a large part of the revenue had to be raised by indirect taxes, and hence that figures are available for the output, or sale, of a number of commodities produced within the country, as well as of others brought in from abroad.

The Excise had its origin in 1643, when duties were laid on ales, beer, cider, and perry. By 1684 British spirits, vinegar, and mead had been added to the list; and it was to these taxes on liquors that the word Excise was officially applied until well into the eighteenth century. Since, however, when duties were imposed on other commodities, the collection was put under the same management, all indirect taxes, except those under the Customs, came to be spoken of as excise duties.

The Excise was hated, especially by the poorer classes. When in 1733 Walpole made the sensible proposal that the duties on tobacco and a few other things should be collected when the goods were taken from the warehouses, instead of at the time and place of import, he was obliged to abandon it for no better reason than that it was known as an excise scheme. But, in spite of the unpopularity of inland duties, there were never wanting members of the public to put forward some new plan to raise money by a levy on a trade or occupation or act which, for personal or social reasons, they considered obnoxious. In the forties and early fifties, in particular, a spate of proposals came to the Treasury for duties on street signs, barbers' poles, perukes, pawnbrokers, attorneys, chandlers (who were accused of stealing business from established traders), and so on. One memorialist of 1747 complained of 'the new habit of working people to keep dogs which destroy game'. Another, who also wanted to see a licence duty of 10s. imposed on the owners of these 'pernicious animals', suggested, however, that persons qualified to keep greyhounds, setters, pointers, and spaniels should pay only 5s., and that 40s. would be the appropriate fee for a whole pack of hounds. Another advocated the laying of a tax on liveried servants, with higher duties on those who had come from abroad, were Roman Catholics, or had a habit of changing their masters. Yet another saw in taxation a remedy for the improper use of coats of arms, and urged that additional revenue might be raised by granting the right to use the words 'Ensigned of Gentility'—a facility, it was said, that would appeal to many merchants.[1] Fortunately, the Treasury took a realistic view: it was interested in getting revenue, not in reforming society. Most of the new duties imposed during the century were productive, and, in the sense that the yield was far greater than the cost of collection, economical.

It was in times of war that the chief extensions of the excise were made. A duty imposed on malt in 1697 was increased when the War of the Spanish Succession began, in 1702, and the mounting costs of the struggle brought several other commodities into the fiscal net a few years later: candles in 1710; hops, hides, and water-borne coal in 1711; soap, paper, starch, printed calicoes, hackney chairs, cards, and dice in 1712. Each of the later wars of the century led to an increase of existing duties and the imposition of new ones. Taxes were laid on glass and coaches in 1746, on household plate in 1757, and on the value of sales at auctions in 1778. Of those imposed in times of peace the most important for the purpose of this book is the duty on bricks levied in 1785.

The collectors of Excise were not all incorruptible. Clerks sometimes made mistakes, and opportunities for evasion (legal or illegal) were open to producers.[2] Since, however, there is no reason to believe that there were short-term fluctuations in clerkly efficiency or public morality, we may accept the variations in the figures as representing changes of output. Some of these were the result of alterations in rates of duty; but when the figures for several commodities move in the same direction it is reasonable to infer an economic, rather than a fiscal, cause.

---

[1] These details are taken from the typescript of a Calendar, prepared by Dr. H. S. Kent, of a large body of manuscripts (mainly from the Townshend Papers) now in the Commonwealth National Library, Canberra. I am much indebted to the Librarian, Mr. H. L. White, for sending me a copy.

[2] A good deal of beer was brewed by the consumers themselves. There were illicit stills for making spirits. And in some parts of the country people illegally made candles and soap for their own use.

It would be unsafe to assume that because the industries subject to excise duties expanded or contracted the same must have been true of the economy in general. The production of excisable goods was widespread, but there was a tendency to geographical concentration. For the year 1741, it so happens, figures are available of the yield of the duties in each of the fifty regions, or collections, into which England and Wales were divided by the Commissioners of Excise. These varied in size: some were counties, others large towns with the surrounding areas. The figures bring out clearly the dominant position, as a revenue-raiser, of the metropolis: slightly more than a third of the receipts of the Excise came from London. Of the forty-nine country collections the most important was Hertford, which not only made by far the largest contribution to the duties on liquors, but also came first in the yield of those on printed calicoes, paper, and hides. (The Lea valley must have been a hive of industry at this time.) Next to Hertford came Surrey, and after this, in order, Bristol, Rochester, Suffolk, and Norwich. The receipts from the north, the Midlands, and Wales were of minor account: only 21 per cent. of the revenue and only 32 per cent. of the country collections[3] came from north and west of a line running from Bristol to the Wash. At first sight it might appear that the figures are unrepresentative of the nation as a whole. It should be remembered, however, that in 1741 the great majority of the people were in the south and east, and that incomes in the rest of the country were almost certainly below the average.

Several of the duties were collected when the goods were withdrawn for sale: the figures are therefore a guide to consumption rather than output. As Joseph Schumpeter[4] and others have pointed out, prosperity (i.e. high activity) is not synonymous with well-being, nor depression (low activity) with poverty. For later periods the distinctions are important: in times of prosperity people may refrain from consuming the whole of their output, and in times of depression they may maintain their standards of living by drawing on stocks. Sometimes in the eighteenth century manufacturers produced more than they could sell: 'Mr. Thrale overbrewed himself last winter, and made an artificial scarcity of money in the Family

---

[3] Of a total excise revenue of £2,667,638, London was responsible for £903,117, and the country collections for £1,764,521. Details are given in the Harrowby Trust MSS., The Employment of Excise, no. 525.

[4] Joseph Schumpeter, *Business Cycles*, i. 140.

which has extremely lowered his spirits', wrote Mrs. Thrale[5] in 1778. The accumulation of stocks in the hands of producers or merchants was then, as now, a feature of depressions. Nevertheless, especially for those excisable goods that were perishable, the discrepancies between production and consumption can hardly have been great. The mass of the people had very small reserves of purchasing power; consumption varied closely with current income, and this depended on the level of wages and the state of employment. There can be little error in using the figures as an index not only of well-being (and poverty) but also of prosperity (and depression).

Apart from the figures of the Excise, there are others of the output of one or two industries which, like the coal trade of the Tyne and Wear, had some organization of producers or system of inspection. For most of the century there are statistics of the production of copper in Cornwall, and of broad and narrow cloth milled, or fulled, in the West Riding of Yorkshire. The degree of error in the figures is, however, probably far higher than in those of the Excise. The searchers appointed by the Justices in Yorkshire were for long notoriously inefficient and negligent; and the sudden rise (almost a doubling) of the figures that followed a reform of the methods of control in 1765–6[6] suggests that those for the earlier years are not to be relied on. From 1769, however, expert and properly paid inspectors provided information not only of the number of pieces of cloth milled, but also of the yardage; and these are a most valuable guide to fluctuations in one branch of an industry of prime importance to the economy.

There are some tiresome problems of chronology. The reform of the Calendar by Pope Gregory XIII in 1582 had long been accepted by most European nations; but for the best part of two centuries England still adhered to the Old Style—'as if', said an eighteenth-century wag, 'it were a matter of heresy to receive a Calendar amended by a Pope'.[7] When, in 1751, at the instance of Lord Chesterfield, the Julian was replaced by the Gregorian calendar, it was decreed that henceforth the civil or legal year should begin on 1 January, instead of, as formerly, on 25 March. The old system had

---

[5] Peter Mathias, 'The Industrial Revolution in Brewing', in *Explorations in Entrepreneurial History*, v. 210.

[6] By 5 Geo. III, c. 51, and 6 Geo. III, c. 23.

[7] E. Ernst, *Memoirs of the Life of the Fourth Earl of Chesterfield*, p. 412. The quip was attributed by Chesterfield to Walpole—presumably Horace.

had several inconveniences: the 25th day of a month was an awkward time to begin a new year. In dating letters, especially to people abroad, at any time between 1 January and 25 March it was usual to include both years: e.g. 1723/4. But the practice was not always observed; and hence annalists and historians have not infrequently been led into error. It is important to bear in mind that when in any document written before 1752 such words as 'this year' or 'the winter of this year' appear, the annual period referred to began at the end of March.

A second change required to bring England into line with the rest of Christendom was to reduce the number of days in the year 1752 by eleven. This was done by enacting that the day after 2 September should be styled 14 September. Care was taken that the nominal loss of these days should not accelerate the time of payment of rents or other contractual obligations. The length of the excise year was not affected: all that happened was that, henceforth, the day on which it ended was called 5 July instead of 24 June. For some reason unknown, however, the year for the figures of overseas commerce continued to run from Christmas to Christmas, and this meant that there were eleven fewer days of trade in 1752. According to Sir George Clark, 'Trade was, in many of its chief branches, seasonal, and with every country it followed so much an annual course that it is safe to leave this small chronological irregularity out of account.'[8] Nevertheless, the student of fluctuations should keep the fact at the back of his mind.

Neither 25 March nor 1 January is a satisfactory starting-point for the economic historian. In a world in which he was king, the year would begin at Michaelmas[9] when the harvest had been got in, when farmers were counting their gains, landlords fixing their rents, servants in husbandry entering on a new annual cycle, and temporary recruits to agriculture settling again to their ordinary occupations. To the student of fluctuations the annual period that opens in March or January is a hybrid: one harvest determines its complexion in the early, and another in the later, months. When there is a large difference between the yields of the two it is hard to say whether the year should be described as one of plenty or dearth.

The only important statistical series based on the year beginning at Michaelmas are those relating to government finance (though

---

[8] G. N. Clark, *Guide to English Commercial Statistics 1696–1782*, p. 37.
[9] 29 Sept.

even in this case the date was changed, in 1787, to 5 January). As already mentioned, the excise year ran from 25 June (New Style, 6 July), and the year for imports and exports from Christmas Day. For broad cloth in the West Riding the statistical year opened on 13 March, and for narrow cloth on 21 January. Of less importance for the present purpose, the returns of production of linen in Scotland began on 1 November.

For the study of long-term trends, lack of uniformity in the accounting periods is of little consequence; but for that of short-term fluctuations it is a serious matter. To ignore it, as some writers have done, is to run the risk of a serious distortion of the picture. When, as is often the case, a new year opens in the middle of an upward or downward movement, the spreading of the figures over two annual periods may give the impression that the movement was smaller, or longer drawn out, than it actually was. As Mr. H. A. Shannon pointed out, almost the whole production of bricks took place in the two quarters ending 5 July and 10 October. 'It follows that the fiscal years cut production in two, with the halves separated by an almost dead period of six months during which the economic forces may have changed direction.'[10] The method of reduction to calendar years by adding half the figure for one fiscal year to half that for the succeeding one may appeal to a statistician, but its use would bring twinges of conscience to an historian. The effect must be to reduce the amplitude of the fluctuations.

For a few series monthly figures are available, and these can be turned into annual averages for periods beginning in whatever month we please. How much the shape of the movement varies with this choice can be seen from the following examples:

Assize price of the peck loaf in London
(in pence)

July–June		Jan.–Dec.	
1793–4	29·7	1794	30·4
1794–5	34·0	1795	43·7
1795–6	50·0	1796	42·1
1796–7	33·4	1797	33·3

Prices rose sharply in June 1795, when it became clear that the harvest would be wretched, and remained high until July 1796,

[10] H. A. Shannon, 'Bricks: a Trade Index, 1785–1849', *Economica*, Aug. 1934, pp. 300–18.

when, with excellent prospects for the following harvest, they suddenly dropped. The figures for the excise year bring out this concentration, whereas those for the calendar year suggest less intensity and longer duration of the dearth.

Number of bankruptcies

July–June		Jan.–Dec.	
1770–1	350	1771	341
1771–2	398	1772	535
1772–3	623	1773	524
1773–4	405	1774	335

If the only figures we had were those in the second column we might assume that the depression extended with equal severity through two years. In fact, it was largely confined to one—the excise year July 1772–June 1773.

The excise year shares some of the advantages claimed above for the harvest year. It is true that it opens before the main crops are gathered in. But, as has already been indicated, fairly accurate estimates of the coming yield could be made by the beginning of July—indeed several weeks before this—and the level of prices in the summer depended quite as much on these as on the stocks of grain left over from the previous harvests. In the few cases in which it is possible to rearrange the figures, the grouping will be into excise years.

It should be clear from this discussion that, even when there is a strong common influence at work, it would be idle to expect any close conformity, in the short run, between sets of figures based on different accounting periods and hence covering different stretches of time. It is largely for this reason[11] that no use will be made of mathematical methods of correlation: if the humdrum methods of the historian are less precise, they are not necessarily less accurate than those of the statistician. As has been mentioned in the Preface, when the reference is to the civil or legal or calendar year the date is printed in roman type. In all other cases, except for imports and exports (for which the opening date of 26 December is close to 1 January), the date is in italics, and is that of the *end* of the annual period.

The chief purpose of this book is to offer to students a general

---

[11] And because of the inaptitude of the author for such exercises.

D

background against which they may set the stage for their own presentations of particular industries or movements. But a subsidiary one is to discover, if possible, how far back into the century the phenomenon later to be called the trade cycle existed. For this it is necessary to introduce a few simple ideas of the kind that pass through the minds of economists. If any theorist should object that no use is made of the organon brought into being in recent years to explain the trade cycle, the reply must be that the data are too slender to allow of it. If, on the other hand, some pure historian should protest against the injection of theory even at a very elementary level, he may be advised to consider the words, written a century ago, by one who was certainly no economist but a careful and persistent collector of facts:

Facts, according to my ideas, are merely the elements of truths, and not the truths themselves; of all matters there are none so utterly useless by themselves as your mere matters of fact. . . . To give the least mental value to facts we must generalise them, that is to say we must contemplate them in connection with other facts, and so discover their agreements and differences, their antecedents, concomitants, and consequences. It is true we may frame erroneous and defective theories in so doing . . . nevertheless, if they may occasionally teach us wrongly, facts without theory or generalisation cannot possibly teach us at all.[12]

After this digression, we may now turn to consider the possible effects of variations in the harvests on industries other than agriculture, and on economic activity in general.

II

The fact that the supply of non-agricultural products often fell in years when the crops were small does not of itself prove the existence of a causal link between the harvests and the output of industry. Most of the dearths (it so happened) occurred in times of war, and it is impossible to disentangle the effects of the two influences. Moreover, as has already been pointed out, some industries were directly affected by changes in the weather. The frost that killed the sprouting corn, or the heavy rain that beat down the straw, might simultaneously put a stop to the water-wheels or interfere with the delivery of materials. Temperature and rainfall varied between regions, and hence a stoppage of production in one area might

[12] Henry Mayhew, *London Labour and the London Poor* (1864). From the Introduction.

sometimes be offset by more intense work in another. In 1740 when the corn mills in many parts of Scotland were frozen up, those in places where the streams were still open were hard at it, not only on the six working days of the week, but also on Sundays—'an unusual thing there', as the *Gentleman's Magazine* pointed out.[13] But in industries that were highly localized, there was little opportunity for such compensation: a fall in the output of copper ore in Cornwall and of broad cloths in the West Riding in this same year was very probably a result of the great frost.[14] Even industries that were carried on in various parts of the country were affected: a marked decline in the production of both leather and paper was recorded in 1740,[15] and since the figures relate to annual periods ending in the early summer, the decline can hardly be attributed to the failure of the harvest.

In most years of dearth there was a sharp rise in the price of coal, not at the pit-head but in London and other urban centres. But, again, it was the severe weather preceding the harvest that was responsible. Difficulty in getting the collier vessels from a frozen Tyne to a frozen Thames was responsible for the famines of fuel in London in 1703, 1709, 1740, and 1799–1800; and there is evidence of similar shortages elsewhere.[16] Since there were limits to the possibility of piling up stocks in the coalfields, production was restricted. When, after each harvest failure, food riots broke out, a leading part was played by the coal-miners, and their abstention from work tended to prolong the periods of shrunken output. This, however, was a minor matter. The chief influence of the weather on the output of coal was exercised directly and not through the crops.

In another group of industries—those that drew their supplies of materials from English fields—the variations in activity were, however, undoubtedly the results of changes in the size of the harvests. There are no reliable statistics of the output of the millers, but this must have varied with the preceding harvest; and the output of the bakers must have followed, with a short lag, that of the millers. In

---

[13] Loc. cit. (1740), p. 34.

[14] The output of copper ore fell from 11,000 tons in 1739 to 5,000 tons in 1740. The decline in that of broad cloth was from 43·1 to 41·4 thousand pieces. As has been said, no great reliance can be placed on these figures.

[15] Between 1739 and 1740 the output of tanned hides fell from 30·7 to 28·1 million lb. and that of goatskins and other tawed material from 39,200 to 35,900 doz. The production of reams of paper fell from 56,900 to 49,700.

[16] Ashton and Sykes, op. cit., App. F.

some parts of the country the Assize of Bread was enforced, and the price fixed for the loaf was determined by that of wheat. In spite of a growing preference for white, wheaten bread, the so-called inferior grains still played a large part in the diet of the poorer classes: until late in the century oatmeal was of more importance than flour in Lancashire and the north-west generally. Nevertheless, the points of time at which the Statute price of wheaten bread in London was raised to a high figure may serve as a rough guide of acute pressure, and those at which it was reduced as marking the end of the emergency, in the country as a whole. According to the monthly figures in the *Gentleman's Magazine,* the following were the chief periods of hunger, or in other words of low output at the corn mills and bakeries, in the last six decades of the century:

May 1740–June 1741	Dec. 1780–Oct. 1784[17]
Mar. 1757–June 1758	Jan. 1789–Sept. 1790
Aug. 1766–early 1768	Dec. 1794–July 1796
Jan. 1772–Aug. 1775	July 1799–Dec. 1800

For other products of cereals there is more precise information.[18] Changes in the rate of duty and in the regulation of sales account for some of the more marked fluctuations in the output of British spirits. But, at least in the early part of the century, production tended to increase rather than to diminish in times of dearth. There was a rise from 1·7 million gallons in 1709 to 2·2 million gallons in the famine of 1710. In 1725 the output was under 4 million gallons; it remained at about the same figure in the following year when the harvest was poor, but rose sharply in 1727–9, as the shortage of grain increased. Even more striking was the increase from 5·8 million in the favourable year 1739 to 7·4 million in the acute dearth of 1741.[19] It looks very much as though people sought to drown their sorrows in gin. In the later part of the century, however, government action cut off this source of consolation: when supplies of grain were short—in 1757, 1767–8, 1773–4, 1782–4, 1788, and 1796–8—restrictions were placed on the distilling of wheat and barley, and sometimes the use of these, and even of molasses, was prohibited.

Fluctuations in the output of starch conformed very closely to the

[17] More precisely Dec. 1780–Sept. 1781; June 1782–July 1783; Feb. 1784–Oct. 1784.

[18] For the output of spirits, starch, malt, and beer, as well as of soap and candles, see the Appendix to T. S. Ashton, *An Economic History of England: the 18th Century.*

[19] In each case the higher level was maintained when the dearth was over.

volume of the harvests. A rise in the cost of corn was generally sufficient to effect a reduction of manufacture, but when there was a
serious threat of famine, as in 1795 and 1800, the government for-
bade the use of wheat in the making of starch, as well as of its
derivatives, hair-powder and blue.[20]

In the same way, changes in the yield of the barley fields are
reflected in the output of malt and beer.[21] There is a tendency for
the figures of beer to move in short waves: an upward trend for two
or three years is followed by a downward trend of about the same
duration. One reason for this is that, in the early part of the century,
both good harvests and dearths tended to cluster. But, apart from
this, the fact that barley and malt could be stored meant that the
effects of a glut or a shortage were spread over a longer period than
a single excise year.

In most industries a rise in costs could be passed on to the con-
sumer: it was the contraction of demand resulting from the rise in
the price of the finished product that led to curtailment of output.
But in many parts of the country (including the metropolitan area)
the price of beer, like that of bread, was subject to control; and the
increases permitted by the authorities were few. Porter, the most
popular drink in London, was sold, unvaryingly, at 3d. a quart from
1722 to 1761, at 3½d. from 1762 to 1799, and at 4d. thereafter.[22] In
the year following each increase of the Assize price output declined.
There were substitutes for beer, and naturally changes in the availability of these had reactions. In the age of cheap gin in the thirties
and forties sales of beer were relatively low; and during the American war, when tea was expensive, they increased. By far the most
important influence, however, was exerted by the harvests. For not
only did a rise in the cost of barley lead the brewers to contract
their output, but the increased cost of food forced the poorer classes
to reduce their consumption of drink. The tendency of wages to
fall and for unemployment to spread in times of dearth (of which
something will be said below) was a further powerful reason for

[20] Major declines in the output of starch appeared in *1726, 1728–9, 1740–1,
1757, 1765–8, 1770–3, 1775, 1777–8, 1781, 1787–8, 1793, 1796–7,* and *1800.*
[21] For the sake of brevity, no account will be given here of the fluctuations
in the production of malt. It may be pointed out, however, that the reason for
a downward trend in the figures was a substitution, in the later part of the
century, of unmalted for malted barley. A good deal of malt, as well as of
barley, was used in the making of spirits.
[22] The increase in the price of beer in 1762 followed the levy of an additional duty on strong beer and ale on 25 Jan. 1761.

the decline of demand. When Members of Parliament wanted to discover whether complaints of distress were well founded they sometimes called for the returns of the excise on beer.[23] If the figures are an index of activity in an industry that gave employment to many thousands, they are also an index of general—or, at least, working-class—welfare.[24]

The influence of the harvests can be seen also in the changes in the numbers of producers and retailers of beer. These were divided into two groups, the common brewers, who sold by wholesale, and the victuallers, who both brewed and retailed their product. In the first six decades, at least, there was a secular upward movement in the number of common brewers: in 1701 there were 764 and in 1761 1,148 of these. The figures of the victuallers exhibit no trend, but there are substantial short-term variations, most of which are closely in line with those of the crops of barley. The good harvests of the opening years of the century led to an increase from 41,841 victuallers in 1701 to 49,838 in 1704. During the following four years there was some decline, but this was slight compared with what happened after the great famine and the succeeding run of poor harvests. From 46,860 in 1709 the number fell to 32,294 in 1712. The good harvest of this year was responsible for an increase of nearly 9,000 victuallers in 1713; and from this time the numbers remained fairly stable for a decade and then rose to a peak of 46,227 in 1724. The dearths of the late twenties saw a decline to 40,971 in 1729; but in the good years of the thirties the figures again ranged about 46,000. The dearth of 1740 had a relatively small effect: the number dropped only by a thousand in 1741. In the years of abundance in the later forties the numbers were extraordinarily high. But from 1754 a downward movement set in, and after the harvest failure of 1756 this steepened, and the figures remained low into the early sixties.[25]

---

[23] See, e.g., *J.H.C.* xxiii (Feb. 1737/8), 49, 84.

[24] The major falls of output of beer were in *1709–13, 1726, 1728–30, 1740–3, 1757, 1765–7, 1783,* and *1799–1800.* All these coincided with, or followed, bad harvests. Minor declines in *1745–6, 1774, 1788, 1794–5,* and *1797–8* were at times when, for other reasons, economic activity faltered. The figures used are those for strong beer. Those for the output of small beer varied in the same way, but the total output was much smaller.

[25] See Table 2. The numbers of common brewers show similar but smaller changes. They are given in a table in Harrowby MSS., vol. 285, f. 27, which supplies details also of the number of barrels charged for duty on both brewers and victuallers.

The excise returns for tanned or tawed hides naturally reflect the variations in the fortunes of animal husbandry. The number of hides and the revenue from the duty declined in 1727–9 and 1740; but perhaps because of an abatement of the cattle plague (which had kept the tanners short of materials for a decade) the figures were relatively high in the dearth of 1756–7. As a result of the slaughter of cattle in the hot summer of 1762 the output of tanned hides rose considerably in the two following seasons,[26] but the depletion of the herds meant that for some years thereafter the tanners were short of material. Matters were made worse by an outbreak of distemper among the horned cattle on the Continent, which led to the prohibition of the import of hides from Scandinavia, the Low Countries, and parts of Germany in July 1768. The shoemakers, saddlers, and others complained that within the past two years the price of tanned hides had risen from 9s. 6d. to 14s. 6d., and that of calf skins from 18s. to 26s. a stone. Petitioners from Norwich declared that the burden on the poor was such as 'they can hardly conceive':[27] it was not until after 1771 that the shortage was overcome. Similar, but less acute, declines of output occurred after heavy frosts in several of the later years of the century,[28] though how far it was the weather and how far the general economic situation that was responsible cannot be determined.

The fluctuations in the production of tallow candles and soap are closely aligned with those of the output of leather. Again, each period of agricultural shortage, except 1756–7, brought a decline of output. Since, however, supplies of tallow could be imported from the Russians and others, the annual variations were relatively small.[29]

Supplies of wool—the raw material of England's premier industry—varied with the number of sheep. This tended to decline in years of severe frost or continued rain, which often led to outbreaks of sheep-rot; but since staplers and farmers normally held fairly large

[26] The number of hides tanned rose from 31·7 million lb. in 1763 to 34·7 million lb. in 1764. It did not again reach a figure as high as this until 1782, following the killing of large numbers of cattle at a time when the distemper was exceptionally acute. The number of goat skins and horse and cow hides rose from 30·9 thousand in 1763 to 39·3 thousand in 1764.

[27] Annual Register, 9 July, 14 Oct. 1768.

[28] Among them, 1784, 1789, 1797–1800.

[29] The output of candles declined in 1728–9, 1740–2, 1755, 1766–7, 1783, 1785, and 1795–6. For soap the chief depressions occurred in 1728–9, 1734, 1740–2, 1778, 1783, 1787–8, and 1800. See tables viii and ix in Ashton, op. cit.

stocks, manufacture can rarely have been held up for want of wool. There were, however, substantial movements of prices. Fleeces varied in quality: wool from the mountainous regions was generally short and fine, that from enclosed farms in the lowlands tended to be long and coarse; and the nature of the clip depended also on the breed of the sheep and the part of the fleece from which it was shorn. No single series of prices can be selected as representative. But a survey of sets of figures from widely scattered areas suggests, as we should expect, that there was some tendency for the price of wool to rise when the flocks were in poor shape. Equally important, however, as a cause of fluctuations, were the changes in the demand for wool. The cost of raw material was a relatively small element in the total outlay of the producer of cloth or stuffs: what really mattered to him was the demand for the finished product. When this was brisk he tended to buy more wool, and hence rising prices of wool were often cited by contemporaries as proof of growing prosperity in manufacture and agriculture alike. During an upward movement of trade in 1751 and the early months of the following year the price of wool mounted. But in the summer of 1752 there was a sudden break, and on 30 September the *Gentleman's Magazine* reported that 'At Sturbridge fair, there was the greatest quantity of wool ever known, which sold for 3*s*. 6*d*. per tod under last year's prices . . . trade being so bad in the clothing counties.'[30] A similar sudden turn from prosperity to depression in 1777–8 led to such low prices that Bakewell declared that 'it wd. be desirable to grow sheep without wool and confine attention to the carcase only'.[31] The fluctuations of activity in the woollen industry were more often the cause and not the effect of the varying fortunes of the flock-masters.[32]

This account of the impact of agriculture on particular industries is brief, partly because the topic has been discussed elsewhere,[33] but mainly because the chief purpose of this chapter is to suggest ways

[30] *Gentleman's Magazine* (1752), p. 448.
[31] R. M. Hartwell, *The Yorkshire Woollen and Worsted Industry, 1800–50*, pp. 20–21. Thesis presented for the Degree of D.Phil., Oxford.
[32] Most of the prices are those paid at Sturbridge Fair on 31 Aug. The chief periods of high prices were 1717–22, 1728–32, 1740–4, 1757–9, 1763–7, 1774, 1784–90, 1792, 1795–6, and 1799. Prices were relatively low in 1723–7, 1734–9, 1745–7, 1754–6, 1761–2, 1768–70, 1772–3, 1778–9, 1791, and 1793. See Tables 14 and 15.
[33] T. S. Ashton, *An Economic History of England: the 18th Century*, pp. 55–62.

in which the fluctuations in the yield of the soil may have affected the economy in general. Those who are able to accept Say's law in its simple form will see no difficulty here: if supply creates its own demand an increase in the product of the agriculturists must have brought an expansion of industrial activity. But most contemporary writers did not think in such terms: their arguments were expressed in terms of money and prices. If the flow of money were swift and wide there would be prosperity; if it were sluggish and constricted there must be depression. The chief matter in dispute was the source of the stream.

Then, as now, men's views were clouded by their interests. Not unnaturally, farmers and landowners argued that the maintenance of fairly high prices for agricultural produce was a condition—if not the sole condition—of a full circulation of money. If anything happened to reduce their incomes, the incomes of all others must also fall. 'The frozen benumbing temperature of the winter does not damp the growth of vegetables more than the poverty of the farmers doth the interest and spirits of tradesmen', wrote William Allen of Pembroke during the period of good harvests in the early thirties.[34] Since the demand for bread was inelastic (only a little more was consumed when the price declined substantially), grain-growers who produced for the market suffered a loss of income when the harvests increased in size. 'Here's a farmer, that hanged himself on the expectation of plenty', said the Porter in *Macbeth*; and though there is no evidence from the eighteenth century of an increase of agrarian suicide in times of good harvests, there is much that tells of distress. According to an anonymous writer of 1767, cited by Dr. Mingay, 'The farmers are always more afraid of a good year than a bad one. . . . They prefer half a crop with a proportionably advanced price to a full harvest.'[35] If the good harvests persisted the land-owners also might suffer. In the years of abundance at the beginning of the century many farmers were unable to pay their rents; and, again, in those of the thirties many landlords were forced to abate their claims, and in some cases to take over from their tenants the burden of the Land Tax. Even in the later part of the century, when

[34] William Allen, *The Landlord's Companion or the Ways and Means of raising the Value of Land* (1736). According to Dr. John (to whom I am indebted for the reference) there is internal evidence that the passage was written in 1734.

[35] G. E. Mingay, 'The Agricultural Depression, 1730–1750', *Ec. Hist. Rev.*, vol. viii, no. 3 (1956), pp. 323–8.

the trend of grain prices was upward, there were years, such as 1779, when good harvests were followed by complaints of ruined farmers and distressed landowners.[36] If the incomes of the agricultural classes were reduced—so the argument ran—the volume of spending would contract. 'Necessity has compelled our farmers to more carefulness and frugality in laying out their money than they were accustomed to do in better times', wrote William Allen in 1734.[37] It was not a long step from this to say that good harvests slowed down the circulation and led to general depression.

The weight of evidence, however, is against the thesis. In the first place, it fails to take account of the fact that large numbers of farmers produced grain only for themselves and their livestock. These, like the industrial workers, suffered in time of shortage. Others who normally had a surplus for the market, and did pretty well in a year of good harvest, might find themselves with nothing left over to sell when the crops were deficient. It was probably this numerous class that William Stout had in mind when he wrote: 'In this year [1730] there was a great crop of corn . . . and yet it is supposed that the farmers will get more by corn this year than the last year, when it sold at about double the price.'[38] It was the large specialist grain-growers who reaped the windfall gains of scarcity; but when the shortage was acute, prohibition of the use of grain for purposes other than the production of bread, and the more drastic measures taken by hungry rioters, must have set limits to the profits even of these. Nor is it necessarily true that the large-scale farmers were plunged into distress when the harvests were rich. Those in areas not too remote from the sea could find compensation by exporting. They received from the state a substantial bounty on every quarter of grain shipped abroad, and when abundance at home coincided with shortage on the Continent (as in 1734 and 1737–8) they were by no means badly off.

Most farmers produced hay and root crops, bred or fattened cattle, raised sheep, and sold dairy produce. If abundance of wheat were accompanied by abundance of fodder, the fall of receipts from grain might be made up by increased receipts from animal products, the demand for which was more elastic than that for bread. The fortunes of many agriculturists were bound up with those of the maltsters, brewers, tanners, soap-makers, clothiers, and other

---

[36] Baker, op. cit., p. 217.
[37] Cited by Baker, op. cit., p. 185.   [38] Stout, op. cit., p. 117.

industrialists who benefited when materials were cheap: a fall in prices was not incompatible with a rise in the incomes of these farmers.

In the second place, even if the receipts of agriculture as a whole varied inversely with the yield of the fields it does not follow that the same was true of the monetary circulation. There was, among contemporaries, much dispute about the effects of plenty and dearth on the attitude of the workers. Some held that dearness of bread and meat was a spur to activity, and that when food was cheap the poor spent more time in drunken idleness. It is unnecessary to enter into this problem of psychology, for it is plain that the opportunities of work declined with bad harvests and increased with good ones. It would, no doubt, be wrong to assert that less labour was always required to gather a small crop than a larger crop: if the corn had been beaten down by heavy rain more hands might be needed for reaping. But generally an abundant harvest demanded additional labour—if not to reap, at least to move, stack, and thresh the grain.[39] These were thirsty operations, and called immediately for large supplies of ale or beer. When the crop had been got in there was a heavy demand for labour at the corn mills, breweries, and distilleries, from each of which flowed tributary streams of money for the payment of wages. Coin did not remain long in the tattered pockets of the casual workers recruited for harvesting, or even of those employed in transporting or working up the crops. It was quickly passed on to a whole army of hucksters and retailers (the victuallers were not the only ones to increase in number at such times) and from these to wholesalers and manufacturers. The demand for clothing, footwear, and the minor luxuries or comforts of working-class life was raised, not only because earnings were higher, but because when food was cheap there was a larger margin for the purchase of other things. Any curtailment of expenditure by distressed farmers and landlords must have been fully offset.

When the harvests were poor those farmers and landlords whose incomes increased were able, if they wished, to engage more labourers to clean and improve the soil, carry out works of enclosure and drainage, and repair old, and put up new, buildings. Some may also have made additions to their household staffs—though, as Adam Smith observed, there were at such times more profitable

[39] There were complaints by farmers that hands were scarce and wages high in 1764, when the crops were described as prodigious. Baker, op. cit., p. 205.

ways of disposing of foodstuffs than in providing sustenance for unnecessary servants. But the propensity of these classes to consume commodities seems to have been relatively low; and a good deal of the money that came in probably remained dormant in the stocking under the farmer's bed or in the chest of the landowner. In any case, the earnings of workers in manufacture were declining, and a larger proportion of these had to go to keeping body and soul together. Professor Pares points out that the demand for sugar declined in each period of dearth,[40] and the same must have been true of the demand for clothes, footwear, and other requirements of the poorer classes.[41] In these circumstances merchants and wholesalers placed fewer orders: they preferred to hold money rather than goods. In December 1740 a clothier of Bolton wrote, 'Trade is bad and no money stirring. People makes no payments.' And six months later it was the same: 'Our trade was never so bad as now and money never scarcer. The warehousemen at London tells us we must wear our own commodities ourselves.'[42] Some of the coin that would normally have been in the hands of traders piled up in the Bank of England. In 1727, 1740, and 1756 the 'Treasure' was exceptionally high; and though there were other reasons for this, a reduced demand for money for use in transactions arising, directly or indirectly, from the harvests, may very well have played a part.[43]

Sometimes the explanations of stagnation were expressed in 'real', as distinct from monetary terms. For food, like raw material, was thought of by manufacturers as circulating capital. In December 1756 the Mayor and Aldermen of Leeds declared that the stocks of corn were not sufficient to supply the woollen industry;[44] and in November 1766 a petition from Norwich mentions the shortage of grain 'as an evil which must not only be prejudicial to the Kingdom in general but absolutely fatal to the woollen trade'.[45]

[40] Pares, loc. cit., p. 259.

[41] This was a matter on which stress was, rightly, laid by the Anti-Corn Law reformers of the nineteenth century. 'The diminution of the home demand arising from the high price of food is of itself sufficient to account for the distressed condition both of capitalists and artisans.' W. R. Greg, *Not Overproduction but Deficient Consumption the Source of our Sufferings* (1842), p. 27.

[42] Wadsworth and Mann, op. cit., p. 270.

[43] Sir John Clapham, *The Bank of England*, i. 230, 233. In each case the rise of the cash ratio had begun earlier: there was no similar accumulation of the precious metals in the dearths of 1766 and 1773. See Table 13.

[44] *Gentleman's Magazine* (1756), p. 448.

[45] P.R.O., H.O. Papers, Dec. 1756.

Further instances will be given later of the effects of the harvests on employment. But one more may be offered here. A letter to the *Gentleman's Magazine* in September 1756, relating to food riots in Sheffield, 'takes notice that oatmeal was eleven pence halfpenny a peck, and wheat fifteen pounds a load, which is more than double the ordinary price [and] that trade was bad and the people starving'. The editorial comment that 'This has been the general complaint for some months past, but a fine harvest has afforded both work and plenty' may have misrepresented conditions in the autumn of this year, but at least it affords further evidence of a contemporary belief in the association of dearth with depression and of abundance with employment.

So far, attention has been confined to forces operating at home. Another, smaller, flow of money had its source in the international market for grain. The export of cereals was stimulated by bounties and the import hampered by duties. Naturally the quantity shipped to foreign ports varied with the state of the crops abroad. Generally, however, in the year following a good harvest in England exports of wheat, flour, barley, and malt increased in volume, and—though prices were low—also in value. In times of dearth the flood dwindled to a trickle (sometimes because the government prohibited exports) and though high prices were obtained, the total receipts from sales abroad diminished.

After the harvest failure of 1709 the quantity of wheat sent abroad fell to one-twelfth of that of the previous year.[46] There was a similar, but less marked, decline after the light crops of 1725; and in 1728–9 the movement of wheat was, on balance, into, and not out of, this country. A sudden change from dearth to plenty caught the merchants unawares. In 1730, according to Stout, 'They continued the import of corn in Liverpool too long, and there was in Liverpool 33,000 windles of foreign corn, wheat, barley, and rye, and no sale for it after the new came off the grounds; which filled their warehouses so as they have no room for their other merchandise, and it is supposed they lost more by that on hand than they got in the dearth of it; the warehouse room of that on hand is computed at £20 a week.'[47] The risks of the trade were increased by uncertainty about the points of time at which the government might see fit to

---

[46] See Table 3. For barley the figures are 196,000 in 1709, and 93,000 in 1710. John Marshall, *Digest of All the Accounts*, p. 88.

[47] Stout, op. cit., p. 117.

suspend, or to end a suspension of, the Corn Laws. Losses resulting from sudden changes in the direction of the flow of grain were not the least of the causes of instability in eighteenth-century commerce.

During the thirties exports of grain soared, and in 1738 no fewer than 581,000 quarters of wheat and flour were shipped abroad. In the dearth of 1740–1 conditions were worse on the Continent than here, and hence exports continued, though on a greatly reduced scale. But in 1742, when heavy crops were reaped in England, there was also 'great plenty in all Europe so that there was no exportation, which is a great discouragement to the farmers'.[48] Thereafter the trade improved, and in 1750 exports of wheat reached a peak at 948,000 quarters. In the dearth of 1757–8 the net movement of wheat and flour was inward, and outward shipments of barley and malt were small. In the early sixties the normal export surplus was restored. But in the spring of 1765 there was again a reversal. 'It is very remarkable', observed the *Annual Register*, 'that we had scarce done exporting wheat to foreign parts, when the Dutch and Flemish began to pour in on us'; and, in the dearth of 1767–8, when the shipment of corn and its products was prohibited, and the duties on imports removed, there was a high inward balance of grain.[49]

From this time the increase of population and a growing insistence on white bread, even by the very poor, meant that only in years of exceptionally good harvests was there a surplus of wheat for export. Net imports rose sharply in the dearths of 1774–5 and 1783. After a bumper crop in 1791 outward shipments were greater than inward shipments. But this was the swan song of the export merchants: since 1792 there has been no year in which Britain has not been dependent on outsiders for part of her bread.

The flow of money from exporters to corn factors and farmers must have helped to spread prosperity in years of net exports; and the flow to importers who had to make remittances overseas must have had reverse effects in times of shortage. The fluctuations of the trade in grain were sufficiently great to affect the balance of payments.[50] Rates of exchange on European centres moved in an

[48] Stout, op. cit., p. 141.

[49] According to the *Annual Register* (23 May 1768) over £1 million had been paid for corn entered in the port of London alone in 1767.

[50] The official value of grain imports was almost £1 million out of total imports valued at £8¼ million in 1767. In 1775 it was £1·2 million out of a

unfavourable direction in 1710 and again in 1727–9. There is a gap in the weekly figures of these in 1740–1, and it is impossible to say whether the small net exports were sufficient to maintain rates on Amsterdam, Hamburg, Lisbon, and so on. But the shortage of food in England was acute enough to make it pay to bring supplies across the Atlantic. Rice was imported from South Carolina in such quantities as to cause the value of the pound sterling to fall from 8 to 7 colonial pounds.[51] At the beginning of 1757 rates on continental centres were highly favourable; but the large imports of grain in this and the following year drove them down and raised the price of exportable gold from £3. 18s. to over £4 an ounce. In each of the years mentioned above Britain was at war, and there is no way of knowing how far the need to make remittances to the forces may have influenced the movement. But in the periods of dearth of the sixties and early seventies, when peace prevailed, there was the same tendency for rates of exchange to fall and for exports of the precious metals to rise.

Shortages of grain had noticeable effects on public as well as on private expenditure. Increased relief to the poor led to a rise in local rates. The decline of output of commodities subject to excise duties reduced government revenue, and the rise in the cost of provisions led to increased expenditure on the navy and army. When the fall of exports of grain caused a weakening of the foreign exchanges the cost of remittances to the forces overseas and of subsidies to allied powers was increased (as has been observed, most of the dearths were in times of war). Government deficits arising from such conditions tended to raise the cost of borrowing and to reduce confidence. It would be wrong to suggest that the major financial crises of the century were solely the result of the influences considered in this chapter, but dearth certainly created an environment in which men were peculiarly sensitive to political and financial disorders. Rising prices of provisions had something to do with the crisis of 1709 in Paris and Amsterdam and with that of 1710 in London; and, as will be seen later, they played a part in the monetary pressures of 1725, 1767, 1773, and 1783. In the last decade of the century the association of imports of grain with financial

total of £12 million. In 1796 and 1801 about one-tenth of the official values of imports was attributable to grain.

[51] I am indebted to Lady Haden Guest for calling my attention to this. It is taken from her (unpublished) study, 'Robert Pringle and the Charleston Trade, 1734–45'.

stringency is plain. In November 1792 Pitt asked the Bank of England to honour £100,000 of Treasury bills for grain purchased abroad as a safeguard against possible shortage in the following season. This was, no doubt, a minor factor in the panic that began in the same month; but it meant that Britain entered the war against France with smaller proportionate reserves of bullion than would otherwise have been held by the Bank.[52] In 1796 more than £2½ million was spent on imports of grain, and the resulting drain of gold, added to the outward flow due to other circumstances, played no small part in the crisis of 1797. Finally, the prospect of harvest failure in 1799 led to enormous purchases of wheat from foreign sources, with a resulting fall of the exchange on Hamburg, and a rise in the price of exportable gold to the unprecedented figure of £4. 5s. an ounce in the summer of 1800.[53]

[52] Sir John Clapham pointed out that the crisis of 1795 was 'neither due to, nor produced, any dangerous crisis of the treasure' (op. cit. i. 258).

[53] H. I. Macleod, *Theory and Practice of Banking* (6th ed.), ii. 2. For annual prices of gold and silver see *B.P.P.* (1810–11), vol. x; and for a lucid exposition of the relation between harvests and effective demand see R. C. D. Matthews, *A Study in Trade Cycle History*, pp. 28–29.

3

WAR, TRADE, AND FINANCE

I

BRITAIN had the good fortune to fight her battles on the seas or on alien soil. Her farmers and peasants could cultivate their fields without fear that the crops would be trodden down by hostile armies; and there was no call, as there was across the Channel, to turn cities into fortresses able to withstand the prolonged sieges that were a feature of eighteenth-century warfare. It is true that threats of invasion were frequent, and that these produced convulsions in the centres of finance. But the reaction of the mass of the people can hardly be described as one of panic or dismay. 'It is quite the fashion to talk of the French coming here' [wrote Walpole in the summer of 1745]. 'Nobody sees it in any other light than as a thing to be talked of, not to be precautioned against. Don't you remember talk of the plague's being in the City, and everybody went to the house where it was to see it. . . . 'Tis our characteristic to take dangers for sights, and evils for curiosities.' A few months earlier, in February 1744, when the Brest squadron had been well out in the Channel, the coasts had been covered with people eager to witness the engagement. (There was disappointment when the wind changed and Admiral Norris was unable to make contact with the enemy.)[1]

The only campaigns on British soil were minor affairs. In neither the Fifteen nor the Forty-five was there much loss of life or destruction of property. The intruding Scots met the costs of their operations not by plunder or levies, but by taking over the existing instruments of taxation; and after the risings had been suppressed, the government honoured the receipts for taxes given by the Jacobites.[2]

War was the business of professional soldiers and sailors, drawn

---

[1] *Letters*, ii. 9, 124.
[2] R. C. Jarvis, 'The Jacobite Risings and the Public Moneys', *Trans. Lancs. & Ches. Antiquarian Society*, lix. 131–54.

mainly from the upper ranks of society, and was regulated by a code
not very different from that of the duel. The object was not to
destroy the enemy, but to force him into a position in which there
was no alternative to surrender. 'Circumspection and defence', it
has been said, 'prevailed over audacity and offence.'[3] The behaviour
of the belligerents in this age of enlightenment must, indeed, appear
quixotic to a generation inured to total war. When Captain Cook
sailed on his third voyage of discovery he was afforded special protection by the French, Spaniards, and Americans, with all of whom
Britain was at war.[4] When, in 1780, British frigates were wrecked
on the French island of St. Lucia, the Marquis de Bouillé restored
the castaways to their commodore, saying that 'he could not treat
as prisoners men whom the fury of the elements had thrown
defenceless upon the shores of his government'.[5] In England funds
were raised for the relief of American and French prisoners, and
subjects of enemy countries were often allowed to practise their
vocations undisturbed.[6] There was respect for the rights of individuals (at least of those who were not without means). The conduct
of privateers was not always marked by humanity, but it was usually
possible for the officers of a vessel taken at sea to purchase their
freedom. And in all but the last war of the century it was legal for
English underwriters to insure the ships of the enemy. If the normal
state of commerce with France and Spain may justly be described
as one of economic warfare, the severity of the Acts of Trade was
mitigated, from the sixties onward, by the existence of free ports in
the West Indies; and some of these were established in times of war.
When, in 1781, Admiral Rodney confiscated all property and stores
on the Dutch island of St. Eustatius (which was, in fact, an international emporium) his action was denounced by British traders as
'a departure from that line of conduct which has hitherto peculiarly
characterised this nation and her sacred regard to the rights of
mankind'.[7]

Britain was able to draw into her armies large numbers of con-

---

[3] Eric Robson in *New Cambridge Modern History*, vol. vii, ch. viii.
[4] Macpherson, op. cit. iii. 665.   [5] Ibid., p. 668.
[6] Clothing for the French prisoners at York was provided by public subscription in 1760 (*Annual Register* (18 Feb. 1760)). A fund was raised to
relieve the distress of the American prisoners in 1777. *Aris's Birmingham
Gazette*, 5 Jan. 1778.
[7] Macpherson, op. cit. iii. 681–5. Several lawsuits were brought against
Rodney.

tinental and colonial fighting men; and the strain on England and
Wales (with which alone this book is concerned) was lessened by
the alacrity with which the Scots and Irish trooped to the colours.[8]
In England the army was so unpopular that special incentives and
pressures were necessary to bring it up to strength. When, in 1757,
Pitt established the militia, all sorts of shifts were employed to avoid
being drawn in the ballot, and the operation of the Act had to be
postponed because so few of the gentry could be persuaded to take
commissions.[9] In 1760 over £7,000 was subscribed at Guildhall to
be used to bribe men (at four guineas a head) to join the regular
army,[10] and in the later wars of the century other funds were established by private enterprise to make payments to the dependents of
men in the forces—partly with the object of overcoming the reluc-
tance to enlist. The navy was able to conscript large numbers of
able-bodied seamen from the mercantile marine, for it was not difficult to find foreigners to replace these. But pay was poor, discipline
harsh, and without the press-gangs the fleets could never have been
fully manned.

It was among the down-and-outs, the semi-employed, and the
criminal classes that the recruiting squads and press-gangs did most
of their business. 'Only too often', says a naval historian,[11] 'the men
thus raised were but poor creatures, the very sweepings of the
streets.' Felons and debtors were often released from gaol on condition that they enlisted: a fall in the cost of relieving vagrants and
prosecuting felons in the West Riding between 1758 and 1762 was
a result not only of industrial prosperity but also of the taking of
such men into the armed forces.[12] In 1795, when a requisition was
made on the shipowners of all ports, instructions were given to
justices and magistrates to send into the navy all able-bodied idle
and disorderly persons, rogues, vagabonds, and smugglers between
the ages of sixteen and sixty.[13] A few years later Patrick Colquhoun
observed that the impress had reduced very considerably the number of malefactors on the Thames. He added, however, that unless
the powers of the river police were extended the evil would become

---

[8] For the disproportionately large contribution made by the Scots see George
Chalmers, op. cit., p. 138 n., and Josiah Wedgwood's *Letters to Bentley*, ii. 324.
[9] See *Annual Register* (Oct. 1758).   [10] Ibid. (22 May 1760).
[11] Admiral Sir Herbert Richmond, *Johnson's England*, i. 49.
[12] For the figures see Arthur Young, *Eastern Tour*, iv. 404–5. The saving was
offset by relief granted to the families of the militiamen.
[13] Macpherson, op. cit. iv. 340–1.

formidable on the return of peace, 'when so many depraved charac-
ters will, of course, be discharged from the Navy and Army'.[14] It
would be wrong to accept without reservation the judgement of
comfortable civilians on the men who were risking their lives in
the service of their country; but the fact that at least a proportion
of these normally contributed little to industry meant that the wars
were fought with less strain on the economy than might have
appeared to a statistician concerned only with the numbers, and
not with the qualities, of the recruits. As George Chalmers, with
characteristic exaggeration and bluntness, put it, 'the sword had
not been put into *useful* hands'.[15]

These remarks must not be taken to imply that the wars of the
eighteenth century had little adverse effect on economic and social
life. If the loss of life in battle was relatively light, that from the
epidemics that raged in the fleets and camps was heavy. One of the
chief costs of war is the interruption it entails of the education of
the young. Many boys went into the forces before they had acquired
knowledge of a trade: they left the navy and army totally unskilled
except in the arts of war and had to subsist—some may have preferred to subsist—on private or public charity. Expenditure on
vagrants in the West Riding rose from £610 in 1762 to £1,624 in
1764; and the cost of maintaining the poor at Tiverton increased
from £1,190 in 1760 to £1,528 in 1765.[16] An investigation into Poor
Law expenditure for England and Wales made at the beginning of
the American War, in 1776, put the amount at £1·5 million; and
another made when it was over gave an average for the years 1783–5
of £2·0 million.[17] Such figures are not conclusive evidence that war
begat poverty: other conditions may have changed. But it was
generally agreed that the navy and army were not schools of
industry. 'The age that makes good soldiers mars good servants',
said Fuller,[18] 'cancelling their obedience and allowing them too
much liberty.' Many of those turned out from the forces took, or
returned, to smuggling and—the line of demarcation was not sharp
—piracy. The accepted remedy for these was the provision of legal,

[14] *Treatise on the River Police* (1800), p. 52.
[15] Chalmers, *The Comparative Strength of Great Britain*, p. 138. 'There is
no reason to suppose', Chalmers adds, 'that anyone left the loom or the anvil to
follow the idle trade of war during the hostilities of 1756.'
[16] Dunsford, op. cit., pp. 460–1.
[17] Arthur Young, op. cit. iv. 404–5; Sir Frederick Eden, *State of the Poor*
(abridged ed. A. G. L. Rogers), pp. 72, 75.   [18] Fuller, op. cit. i. 51.

if less remunerative, occupation on the sea; and hence, in 1750, 1763–4, and 1785, schemes were launched for the development of fisheries.[19] Other warriors became highwaymen and footpads. 'You will hear little news from England but of robberies;' wrote Horace Walpole on 31 January 1750, 'the numbers of disbanded soldiers and sailors have all taken to the road, or rather to the street: people are almost afraid of stirring after dark.'[20] When the American War ended, the increase of crime was marked. In April 1784 the *Gentleman's Magazine* announced that 'Convicts under sentence of death in Newgate and the gaols throughout the Kingdom increase so fast, that, were they all to be executed, England would soon be marked among the nations as the Bloody Country.'[21] The transition from war to peace brought fluctuations of fortune to many who had fought in the wars of a different order from those to be observed in the statistics of industry and trade.

II

Most students are aware of the peculiar nature of the commercial statistics of the eighteenth century. The figures of total imports and exports were reached by multiplying the quantity of each commodity by an official price, and adding together the values so obtained. Since, however, with few exceptions, the official prices remained unchanged, the aggregate figures reflect movements in the quantity, and not in the actual value, of trade. But if the statistics can throw no light on such matters as the balance of payments, they are well devised for the purpose of tracing short-term fluctuations—though the fact that they relate to periods ending at Christmas prevents close comparison with those of the Excise for annual periods ending in the summer.

Part of English overseas trade escaped the eye of the Inspector of Imports and Exports. Smuggling was a spare-time pursuit of many people of rank (including some, like Robert Walpole, who held high office).[22] It was also the profession of large numbers of skilled and resolute men of humble station. But, though it was well organized, it has left few records and no statistics. Quantities of wool and other merchandise produced in this country were carried surreptitiously

---

[19] Macpherson, op. cit. iii. 275, 386; iv. 74.

[20] *Letters*, ii. 423. In 1763 proposals were made to employ 20,000 discharged seamen in the whale fisheries. *Annual Register* (1763), p. 59.

[21] Loc. cit. (1784), p. 379.

[22] J. H. Plumb, *Sir Robert Walpole, The Makings of a Statesman*, pp. 121–2.

overseas; and a much larger volume of tea, tobacco, silks, and other goods of high value and small bulk was similarly brought in. There is reason to believe, however, that in times of war many smugglers were pressed into the navy or took service on privateers. It is probable, therefore, that the decline in legitimate trade that occurred in most wars was matched by at least an equal decline in illicit trade.

Exports are to be thought of as giving rise to employment and incomes in an important section of the economy. It is necessary, however, to distinguish between exports of English produce or manufacture and exports of colonial or foreign goods previously shipped to this country. The official rating of the second of these was sometimes unduly high—far higher than that of the same goods when imported. In the last decade of the century, when Britain was shipping to Europe large quantities of coffee from the plantations, the overvaluation of this single commodity had the effect of making the upward trend of total exports appear much steeper than, in fact, it was. Moreover, since a large part of the real value of re-exports represents incomes earned in the countries of origin, the inclusion of the figures with those of English exports would give a wrong impression of the influence of foreign trade on activity in this country.[23] Generally, the two moved up and down together; but sometimes, as in 1728–9, 1762–3, 1768, 1773, and 1779, when English exports were depressed, some compensation was afforded by a rise of re-exports.[24] A good deal of the intermediary trade was controlled by the East India Company or by individual traders wealthy enough to hold large stocks of merchandise. When, because of war or other adverse circumstances, European purchases of tropical produce declined, goods piled up in the warehouses of London and other ports. When demand recovered it was possible to pour them on to the market immediately; and hence the figures of re-exports sometimes rise in advance of those of English exports (for which the facilities for storage were small). The chief interest of re-exports to the student of fluctuations is that they pointed the way into, as well as out of, depressions.[25]

---

[23] Some important English industries made use of imported raw materials—linen yarn, raw sugar, cotton, dyestuffs, and so on—but the bulk of the costs of production (and the incomes represented by these) arose within this country.

[24] See Table 5.

[25] The 'inventory' nature of re-exports is stressed by A. D. Gayer, W. W. Rostow, and A. J. Schwartz, *The Growth and Fluctuation of the British Economy, 1790–1850*, vol. i.

If all the commodities purchased abroad had been passed directly to consumers in this country the figures of imports might have served as an index of consumption or well-being. In fact, part consisted of raw materials for use in English manufacture and a further part of produce for re-export; since the trade returns take no account of these different ends, it is impossible to say whether any change in the volume of imports is to be attributed to consumption, production, or the entrepôt trade. For obvious reasons there was a tendency for imports to vary with total exports; but the coincidence was by no means exact. Vessels trading with the Far East, or engaged in the triangular (or multiangular) commerce of the Atlantic, were often away from their home ports for long periods; and much more than a year might pass before the cargoes sent out brought their return in imports. Some little time, moreover, must have elapsed before the increased incomes resulting from an expansion of exports gave rise to a larger demand for consumers' goods from abroad. On the other hand, the fact that foreign or colonial produce had to be brought in before it could be shipped out— whether in the same form or as a constituent in manufactured goods —means that the figures of imports sometimes rise earlier than those of exports. The chief divergencies between the two series, however, were the result of war. Shipments by the government of arms and other supplies to the forces overseas tended to raise the volume of exports; and (except in the War of the American Revolution) subsidies and loans to allied powers reinforced this influence.[27] Usually, such grants involved an immediate shipment of military supplies, but, in any case, the provision of finance must, sooner or later, have been followed by a transfer of real resources. Hence, in each of the major wars, the normal excess of exports over imports increased; and when, with the coming of peace, the soldiers and seamen returned to their homes, and the unrequited payments ceased, the gap between outward and inward trade narrowed.

The following brief survey and the further account of overseas trade in Chapter 6 are concerned mainly with exports of English goods. For the years 1705 and 1712 it is impossible to disentangle the figures from those of re-exports; but the statistics of the shipment of woollens, which must have accounted for between a half

---

[26] Peaks of imports were reached a year earlier than those of exports in 1713, 1724, 1745, 1748, 1767, 1788, and 1795.

[27] For loans and subsidies see *B.P.P., Accounts and Papers* (1868–9), xxxv. 2.

and two-thirds of English exports at this time, may serve as a guide here.[28] In view of the special position of the woollen industry in the English economy occasional reference will be made to woollen exports in other years also.[29]

An economist in search of a cycle would find a study of these figures unrewarding. For so capricious were the influences that bore on trade as to rule out any question of regular, recurrent movements. Storms, earthquakes, and plagues interfered with shipping, and the traffic in grainstuffs was sufficiently great to impart to the figures something of the idiosyncrasy of the yield of the soil. But the chief cause of instability was war. Needless to say, it is not the date of the declaration of hostilities or the ratification of a treaty that is significant. A preliminary cold war (like that with the Americans in the early seventies) might be as disturbing as the fighting itself; and the restoration of good relations between traders might precede by many months that between statesmen. Sometimes the seizure of colonial territories from the enemy might bring an expansion of sources of material and markets; but generally the effect of war was to contract the orbit of trade. In each of the four chief wars of the century there were heavy losses of merchantmen: some were taken or sunk by the enemy and others seized for use as transports by the British Navy. The increase of freights and insurance bore heavily on commerce. Often vessels were forced to sail in convoy: it took time to assemble the ships, and the speed of sailing was reduced to that of the slowest member of the flotilla.[30] Frequently material vital to English industry had to be sought in far places: timber and iron might have to be carried, at high cost, across the Atlantic because the Baltic had been made too dangerous for British merchantmen. And sometimes the closing of an entrepôt—Amsterdam, Antwerp, Hamburg, or Cadiz—meant that English goods could reach their destination only after long detours by sea and land. Often, needless to say, they never reached their destinations. Referring to the year 1778 Macpherson pointed out that the decline in the figures of exports failed to reflect fully the loss to the nation, for 'a considerable part of the goods now exported were carried, not into

[28] The fluctuations of the shipments of woollens conform closely to those of total exports (English exports *plus* re-exports). There is the same decline in 1702, and the same upward movement in 1708, 1710, 1712, and 1714.

[29] For these see the tables compiled by Elizabeth Schumpeter.

[30] For delays of convoys in the War of the French Revolution see Arthur Redford, *Manchester Merchants and Foreign Trade, 1794–1858*, ch. iii.

the ports they were consigned to, but into American and French ports, by prize-masters'.[31]

The War of the Spanish Succession differs from most of the succeeding wars in which Britain was engaged in that it was fought largely on land. Exports fluctuated, therefore, not merely with the success of the navy in keeping the seas open but also, more closely than in the later struggles, with the progress of the armies in Europe. Before the war opened trade had been at a remarkably high level—partly because of the removal of export duties on woollens and grainstuffs in 1700.[32] But the outbreak of hostilities, on 4 May 1702, brought the prosperity of the export trades to an abrupt end. Shipments of woollens declined by about 20 per cent., and total exports (including re-exports) by more than 30 per cent. The conclusion of the Methuen Treaty with Portugal, the victory of Blenheim, and the capture of Gibraltar may have contributed to the revival that took place in 1703 and 1704. But, with a worsening of the military situation in the later months of the second of these years, there was a sharp downward movement of exports of woollens; and, as George Chalmers observed, 'the year 1705 marked the lowest stage of the depression of commerce, during Queen Anne's wars'.[33]

Up to this time government expenditure on the war had been relatively small and had been met out of the proceeds of taxation. The maintenance of outward shipments from 1706 to 1710 may be connected with the demands of the forces in Europe, as well as with subsidies to the allies—though a trade agreement made with the Low Countries in the last of these years may also have stimulated exports. In 1710 the shipment of woollens reached a point higher than any previously recorded. The slight decline of trade in 1711 was a consequence of a financial crisis, of which something will be said later, and the revival of the following year may be attributed to the 'desertion' of their allies by the British forces, which gave rise to expectations of a speedy ending of the war. Hopes were, however, frustrated: war in Spain continued, and it was not until the conclusion of general peace in 1714 that trade was fully restored.

In view of the heavy losses of shipping and a substantial rise in

---

[31] Macpherson, op. cit. iii. 629.
[32] By 11 and 12 Wm. III, c. 20.
[33] G. Chalmers, op. cit., p. 90. There is no figure for the export of woollens in 1705.

rates of insurance,[34] the export trades had not done badly during the war: only in 1702, 1705, and 1711 was the decline in the shipments of woollens sufficient to give rise to distress in the manufacturing areas. But that the war exercised a depressing effect in general is suggested by the long stagnation of the import trade—as well as by the rise in both imports and exports that followed the return of peace.

The Jacobite Rebellion of 1715–16 had only slight effects on English commerce. The intervention of George I in the Great Northern War against Sweden was followed by a decline in imports of iron and timber but seems to have had no seriously adverse influence on English exports—which, indeed, reached a peak in 1717. When, however, in the following August, Britain joined in the Quadruple Alliance and engaged in war with Spain, trade with the Mediterranean, as well as with the Baltic (where Russia was now the antagonist) fell seriously: what, with some exaggeration, was spoken of as 'the almost universal decay of commerce' was attributed by a contemporary mainly to the interruption of relations with Muscovy and Spain.[35] The collapse of credit, following the bursting of speculative bubbles in Amsterdam and Paris, as well as in London, contributed to the depression in 1720; and the outbreak of the plague at Marseilles, which led to drastic quarantine restrictions, also tended to keep down the volume of trade.[36] Hence, although a settlement with Spain was reached in 1720, and treaties of general peace were signed in the following year, it was not until 1722 that English exports recovered. It should be observed, however, that re-exports had risen slightly in 1721.

The return of peace was followed by the abolition of the customs duties on exports of British products (with the exception of some raw materials) as well as of import duties on a variety of commodities used in English manufacture. Later in the century George Chalmers declared that the year 1722, when the Act came into force,

---

[34] For the loss of ships see G. N. Clark, *The Later Stuarts 1660–1714*, p. 250. According to William Stout (loc. cit., p. 70) 'at the height of the war no insurance was made, which, if it had, would have exceeded the profit'. The reference appears to be to 1707.

[35] John Smith, *Chronicon Rusticum Commerciale*, ii. 194 n.

[36] It was the last visitation of the plague in Europe. The disease did not spread beyond Provence and Languedoc and was over by Aug. 1721. But the scare was sufficient to bring trade with France to a halt. K. F. Helleiner, 'The Vital Revolution Considered', *Canadian Journal of Economic and Political Science*, xxiii (1957), 3.

'must always form an epoch, as memorable for a great operation in commercial policy as the establishment of the sinking fund had been in finance a few years before'.[37] There is no need to seek further explanation of the expansion of exports in 1722.[38] As usually happened after a sudden surge of this kind, there was some reaction. But in 1724 progress was resumed and in 1725 exports of English products attained a new record. There was also a remarkable expansion of imports, and the fact that these consisted largely of raw materials, such as wool, iron, and timber, suggests rising industrial activity.

A moderate recession of exports in 1726 probably reflects the collapse of a boom. But the lower level of the three following years, though partly due to bad harvests (which turned the normal outward flow of grain into an inward flow), was mainly the result of a new war with Spain that broke out in 1727 and continued, in a desultory fashion, until November 1729. If imports remained high, the reason is to be found in the expansion of the entrepôt trade: the remarkable rise of re-exports in this war was apparently due to the penetration of markets previously served by the Spaniards.

The thirties saw a strong upward movement of trade. A slight recession in 1731 may have been the result of strained relations with Spain. Another in 1734 was undoubtedly connected with the outbreak of the War of the Polish Succession—even though, under the guidance of Walpole, Britain stood aside from the conflict. And a third in 1739, after four years of steadily mounting exports, was due to renewed hostilities with the Spaniards, which, arising out of the seizure of English smuggling vessels in the West Indies, soon spread to European waters. Cruel weather and the failure of the crops reinforced the influence of the Merchants' War, and in 1740 English exports fell to an extremely low point.

In December 1740 when Frederick of Prussia invaded Silesia a new major conflict opened in Europe. This was a further reason for the relatively poor state of English exports in the two following years. Britain's commitments to Austria brought her increasingly into opposition with France at a time when the Spanish war was still dragging on. 'We have the name of war without the thing; and

---

[37] Chalmers, op. cit., p. 107
[38] An increased incentive to make fictitious entries of exports may have had some effect on the figures; but this cannot have been of much significance. Clark, op. cit., p. 16.

war with France without the name', wrote Horace Walpole, in July
1743—a few days after British and French troops had been in colli-
sion at Dettingen.[39] The substantial rise of exports that took place
this year may have owed something to an abundant harvest, but it
was the international situation that was chiefly responsible. For not
only was the British government speeding supplies of stores to
garrisons and naval stations abroad—there was a notable increase
in exports of lead shot and copper—but ordinary traders were
hastening the shipment of manufactured goods and colonial products to markets which, as all knew, would soon be closed. When,
in 1744, Britain became officially at war with France the figures of
English exports fell sharply; and, partly no doubt because of the
Jacobite rising, there was little recovery in 1745. Whether because
of proposals of peace made by France in the following May, or of
the capture of French islands in the West Indies, or—more probably—of greatly increased shipments of warlike stores, English
exports mounted to a peak, higher than any previously recorded, in
1746. A mild recession followed in 1747. But with the end of the
fighting early in 1748, there was a full recovery of trade. Imports
and re-exports soared; but, though English exports also rose substantially, the boom in these came later in 1749 and 1750.

During the first three years of the following decade exports of
English merchandise remained stable at a level somewhat below
that of the immediate post-war years: it was a time of internal,
rather than external, development. Conflict between the British
and French in India, the opening of hostilities between the two in
America, and a general loss of confidence may explain the minor
recession of 1755. The great earthquake at Lisbon in November
brought serious losses to English merchants; and with the outbreak
of the Seven Years War in May 1756 imports and re-exports declined. From its very beginning, however, this new war entailed
lavish expenditure abroad, and in spite of bad harvests and the loss
of some markets, English exports were held at a peace-time level
from 1756 to 1758. In the following year they rose steeply, and the
figures remained extraordinarily high in 1759–61. Something must
be attributed to the capture of French possessions and markets,
especially in the West Indies. But the chief increase was almost
certainly in the shipments made to the British forces overseas and in
those arising from grants to the allies. Pitt was lavish in subsidies.

[39] *Letters*, i. 365.

In 1758 £1·2 million was paid to the Army of Observation in Hanover; and an annual subsidy of £670,000 was granted to Frederick the Great.[40] As the war increased in intensity the payments to the forces and subsidies to the allies rose; and exports responded. A recession in 1762 may be explained partly by a decline of credit following the financial crisis of the autumn of the previous year, and partly by the declaration of war with Spain, in January 1762, which cut off markets in the Mediterranean as well as in Spain and Portugal. But no less important was a decline in government subventions; for in October 1761 Pitt had resigned his office, and his successors withheld the annual grant that had been made to Prussia. The conclusion of peace in November of this year was followed by a striking expansion of imports and re-exports in 1763. But financial crises in Hamburg and Amsterdam and the cessation of government expenditure overseas kept down the volume of outward shipments: it was not until 1764–5 that a sharp rise in English exports registered the beneficial effects of peace.

In the later months of 1765 complaints of dullness of trade came from many quarters, and English exports were relatively low in 1766–70. Among the causes of depression was the tension with the American colonists, who formed non-importation agreements against British merchants. The lifting of the embargo, following the partial repeal of the Townshend duties, brought some relief to the American trade in 1770; but the quarrel with Spain about the Falkland Islands, which led to a sharp rise of freights and insurance, prevented a full recovery.[41] With the settlement of this dispute, however, all the main channels of trade were open, and 1771 saw a surge of English exports to a figure almost as high as that of 1764. Shipments to Spain increased by about a half and those to the American colonies doubled. The boom must have continued into the early months of 1772, for exports for the whole year were only about 6 per cent. below those of 1771, and it is known that a serious recession set in in the summer. The pace of advance had been such as could hardly have been continued. But the Partition of Poland, war between Russia and Turkey, a crisis in the affairs of the East India Company, a deficient harvest, and, above all, financial panic in the City, produced a sudden collapse. English exports fell from £11·2 million in 1771 to £8·9 million in 1773.

---

[40] Eric Robson in *The New Cambridge Modern History*, vol. vii, ch. xx, pp. 472–3. [41] Macpherson, op. cit. iii. 501.

With the restoration of peace in Europe and better conditions in India there was a recovery of trade in 1774. In one important market, however, it was not a feeling of security but the opposite that led to the quickening of activity. Relations with the colonists were rapidly deteriorating, and dealers in America were concerned to build up their stocks of English wares against the time when these would no longer be procurable. When in 1775 the fears were realized, trade declined; and the downward movement steepened when, in 1778, France and, in 1779, Spain joined in the struggle against Britain. Misfortune succeeded misfortune. Following the American example, the Irish raised volunteers and formed non-importation agreements. The northern powers combined in the Armed Neutrality and restricted access to the Baltic; and there was war with the Mahrattas and Haidar Ali in India. In 1779 the official figure of English exports was the lowest recorded since 1745. Possibly because of the capture of Dutch markets after Holland was forced into the war, trade revived in 1780; but in the autumn a great hurricane wrought devastation in the West Indies, and partly because of the loss of markets in Jamaica and Barbados, exports plunged downward again in 1781. This time the war was fought without allies. There were no loans and subsidies to foreign powers such as had helped to sustain the export industries in the earlier wars; and hence, though imports also declined, the difference between these and exports narrowed. Preliminaries of peace were negotiated with the United States in November 1782, and with France and Spain in January 1783. But the definitive treaties with these powers were signed only in the following September, and the final settlement with Holland was delayed until May 1784. It was not until July of this year that, in the words of George Chalmers, 'we offered thanks to the Almighty for restoring to a harassed though not *exhausted* nation, the greatest blessing which the Almighty can bestow'.[42]

The slow pace of the peace-makers may explain why, after this war, there was no sudden boom of exports, but a gradual improvement over the three years 1782–4. And since there was no real boom there was no real depression, but merely a halt in the advance in 1785. The late years of the war and the early years of the peace had seen remarkable developments in the spinning of cotton, the production of iron, and the application of steam-power; and the result-

[42] Chalmers, op. cit., p. 163.

ing fall of costs must have been largely responsible for the continued
upward movement of exports in the later eighties. But policy also
played a part. Pitt's attempt to liberalize trade with Ireland was, it
is true, frustrated. But after the Eden Treaty of 1786, direct trade
with France reached significant figures—for the first time for
several decades. From 1787 the rate of advance quickened, and in
the four years 1789–92, English exports increased by nearly 50 per
cent. Here was a boom greater than any previously recorded—
based mainly on British technology and a rising demand for British
manufactured goods, especially in the United States. It should be
noticed, however, that the upward movement of imports (as well as
re-exports) was less pronounced.

The outbreak of war with France in 1793 brought a drastic contraction of markets, except in the Far East. Exports revived, however, in 1794, and though in the following year, when Prussia made
peace and Holland transferred her allegiance to France, trade with
Europe declined, the settlement of outstanding difficulties by the
Jay Treaty enabled British exporters to find full compensation in
the United States. In 1796, partly because of the large loan to the
Emperor, English exports achieved a new record. But the defeat of
the Austrian army in Italy, the hostile activities of the United Irish-
men, and financial crisis at home, conspired to reduce trade in 1797.
In the following year war in India led to a halving of exports to the
Far East, but—perhaps as a result of the naval victory of Cape St.
Vincent (in February 1797)—there was a phenomenal expansion of
those to the West Indies. The upward movement steepened in 1799,
partly, no doubt, because of shipments arising directly from government expenditure, but largely in response to a mounting demand
for British manufactured goods in the United States. And, though
in the last year of the century there was little or no further advance,
with the approach of peace in 1801 and its realization in 1802, exports reached figures far higher than ever before.[43]

[43] It is not possible to offer figures of total government expenditure abroad
The amounts paid as loans or subsidies to foreign powers were as follows:

(In £ thousand)

1793	833	1798	127
1794	2,552	1799	850
1795	5,731	1800	1,613
1796	33	1801	690
1797	1,685	1802	285

B.P.P. *Accounts and Papers* (1868–9), vol. xxxv, pt. 2, p. 681.

The War of the French Revolution, unlike its predecessors, saw a general rise of imports, as well as of exports—especially in the years from 1798. The reason for this lay in the large quantities of colonial produce brought to Britain for re-export at a time when some of the entrepôts of Europe were doing relatively little trade. Since there are no accurate figures of retained imports, it is impossible to trace the short-term fluctuations of consumption.

Enough has been said to indicate that war was an important cause of instability in eighteenth-century commerce. Fears of a coming interruption of the channels of trade stimulated exports on the eve, or in the first year, of each major struggle—in 1701, 1743, 1756, 1774–5, and 1792. As the scale and intensity of the fighting increased, imports tended to fall (or to rise only slightly); but, mainly as a result of government expenditure abroad, exports expanded. The dictum that trade follows the flag is not entirely false, but the expansion of exports in war-time appears in a somewhat different light when it is realized that a large part of it was paid for by the British people themselves. As each war drew to a close, contracts between merchants were re-established, and ordinary trade increased. The full recovery of imports was usually attained in the first year of peace— in 1713, 1748, 1763, 1783. But, partly because of a fall in outward shipments on government account, and partly because it took time for industry to adjust itself to peace-time requirements, the booms in English exports came later—in 1714, 1749–50, 1764, and 1801–2.

III

The answer to the question whether war increased or decreased economic activity in the nation as a whole is one that admits of no simple answer. Much depends on the methods by which the costs were met. Though it was possible to obtain help from abroad, the bulk of the resources required had to come from the British people themselves. How far they were obtained by curtailing civilian consumption and how far by increasing production is unknown, but among the relevant considerations is the use made respectively of taxation and loans.

The increases of the Land Tax in 1701, 1740, and 1756 must have done something to cut down spending on consumers' goods, capital goods, or both. In most of the wars the rates of duties on imports were raised, and expenditure on imports declined. Many of the Excise duties, the returns of which are a main source of information on fluctuations, were a product of the wars. When rates were increased there was almost always a decline of consumption. A single example must suffice. A raising of the duty on strong beer by 3*s.* a barrel, followed as it was by an increase of the cost to consumers of $\frac{1}{2}d.$ a quart, led to an immediate fall in consumption from 4·06 million barrels in 1761 to 3·80 million barrels in 1762: it was not until fifteen years later that the earlier figure was again attained. Often, when duties were increased, the revenue fell. The inelasticity of the ordinary sources of taxation led to suggestions for all sorts of taxes—from members of the public, who hoped for rewards for their ingenuity, as well as from legislators. But few of the proposals found acceptance.

In these circumstances, much of the revenue needed for the prosecution of war had to be obtained from loans. The proportion was low at first, but mounted as the cost of maintaining the forces increased: in 1709–11, 1748, 1758–63, 1779–85, and 1795–1801 over 40 per cent. of government expenditure was met by borrowing.[44] Some of the money subscribed must have come out of idle balances, but, as will be seen in the following chapter, a good deal of it was deflected from other channels, and in particular from investment in building and construction. The production of capital goods was relatively low in most years of war.

In modern times much of the finance of governments at war is provided by the banks—either directly or through loans to enable members of the public to subscribe to government issues—and hence the floating of loans tends to an expansion in the volume of money. In the eighteenth century when the Bank of England increased its advances to the state it usually curtailed its loans and discounts to other clients. The tables compiled by Sir John Clapham show that the wars had little influence on the Bank's note issue and deposits (the circulation and drawing accounts, as they were termed). The two together were actually lower throughout the war of 1739–48 than in many of the preceding years of peace. If in the Seven Years War the trend was upward it was only in 1757 and 1762 that the increase was marked. In the American War the figures

---

[44] Except in 1799 when it fell to 31·2 per cent. E. B. Schumpeter, 'English Prices and Public Finance, 1660–1822', *Rev. of Econ. Statistics*, vol. xx, no. 1, table 6, p. 36.

declined, except in 1779 and 1783. And even in the war with revolutionary France, when Pitt pressed heavily on the Bank, the note circulation and drawing accounts were held down except in times of financial crisis.[45] Nor does the cautious policy of the Bank seem to have been offset by an expansion of credit elsewhere. There was no marked increase in the number of private banks, and there is evidence that the London banks, at least, reduced their loans to private customers when they lent to the state. Moreover, the restrictions imposed on the issue of notes of small denomination at the beginning of the American War (in 1775 and 1777) must have had some deflationary effect: it was not until the crisis of 1797 that the ban was lifted.

Nevertheless, it is possible that aggregate purchasing power expanded. For a large part of the circulation consisted of bills of exchange created by traders and manufacturers; and those whose dealings were increased by orders arising from war may have extended their credits. Again, the creation of national debt involved an increase in paper claims that could serve some of the functions of money. This was true even of the long-term obligations of the government: according to a writer of 1725, 'the large and regular interest that has been paid on these state-actions have [sic] exhausted all private hoards and made these securities become like a new species of money, current in everybody's hands'.[46] More potent in promoting liquidity, however, was the issue of short-term instruments—navy bills, victualling bills, exchequer bills, and so on —which could be readily discounted or themselves used in settlement of debts between individuals and financial institutions.

When government expenditure financed by loans increased, resources previously unemployed were brought into use. In the eighteenth century there were large numbers of under-employed men and women, especially in the rural areas; but considerable pressures and inducements were necessary to persuade many of these to take regular work in manufacture. In so far as wars increased the demand for labour they should have seen a rise in both wages and prices.

There are no satisfactory price-indices for the whole of the period. Those compiled by Dr. Gilboy relate to commodities supplied under

    [45] Sir John Clapham, The Bank of England, vol. i, App. C.
    [46] Erasmus Philips, The State of the Nation in respect of her Commerce, Debts and Money (1725), p. 44.

contracts, mostly for fairly long periods, and are insensitive to short-term changes in the volume of money. According to Dr. E. B. Schumpeter they can, however, be used to determine trends over periods as short as those of the wars.[47] The series relating to producers' goods, based on the Admiralty Accounts, record the changes in the cost to the state of a variety of materials required by the navy; and those relating to consumers' goods (exclusive of cereals) may serve as a rough guide to changes in the cost of living other than changes resulting from the state of the harvests. The War of the Spanish Succession saw few movements worthy of comment: the index numbers for both producers' goods and consumers' goods are lower at the end than at the beginning of the war. During the wars of 1739–48 and 1756–63 the upward movement was never more than 10 or 12 per cent.; and during the American War never more than 20 per cent. Increases of this order of magnitude cannot be taken as proof of pressure on available supplies of labour: the rise in the cost of necessary food and material brought from abroad is sufficient to explain them. Some classes of workers—notably sailors—obtained increased pay in times of war; but until the last decade of the century there is no clear evidence of a general marked increase of wages. It is impossible, therefore, to assert that deficit finance led to conditions of full employment in any of the earlier wars. In the struggle with revolutionary France, however, signs of real inflation appeared; and the sharp upward movement of prices was accompanied by complaints of a shortage of men not only in the armed forces, but also in agriculture and manufacture. How far government finance was responsible it is impossible to say; for technical changes, involving large capital investment, were well under way before the war began: it may be that even if peace had continued there would have been some rise of prices and wages.

Apart, however, from its influence on prices, government policy tended to increase instability. For the methods by which loans were raised—in particular the use made of lotteries—encouraged speculative tendencies. Wild hopes of capital gains led to booms in the stock market in a number of war years, including 1710, 1761, 1778, and 1796. Deficit finance continued when the wars were over in 1714–16, 1748–9, 1763–5, and 1783–5 at times when other influences, including an expansion of overseas trade, were tending to increased

---

[47] Elizabeth W. Gilboy, 'The Cost of Living and Real Wages in Eighteenth Century England', *Rev. of Econ. Statistics*, vol. xviii, no. 3.

activity.[48] If in periods of war-time crisis and depression—1711,
1762, 1779, 1797, for example—the gap between revenue and expenditure widened, this was not the result of any conscious desire
to relieve unemployment but of a decline in the yield of taxation.
All that can be said is that if, at such times, the government had
sought to balance its budget the unemployment and distress would
have been even greater.

IV

The gains and losses arising from war were distributed unevenly.
Some industries and regions benefited from government orders
while others suffered from a decline of civilian demand. Some pros-
pered because of the protection from foreign competition afforded
by the rise in the cost of transport and prohibition on the entry of
goods from enemy countries: others declined because of a curtailment of imports of raw materials or of a shrinkage of markets
abroad. The rise in rates of interest enabled some men to grow rich
by lending to the state and made others poor by raising the cost of
borrowing for industrial or commercial purposes. It is impossible to
do more than offer a few illustrations of the redistribution of wealth
produced by conditions of war.

In the earlier decades of the century when England was a net
exporter of grainstuffs, the impediments to the shipment of bulk
cargoes must have tended to contract the market and reduce prices
—to the loss of farmers and landowners and the gain of consumers
in this country. Sometimes these effects were heightened by policy.
In 1709–10 restrictions were placed on the export of grain in the
hope that the French, who were suffering from the famine more
severely than the English, might be forced to surrender. And the
fixing of prices by authority may also have tended to reduce the
incomes of farmers. In the second half of the century when Britain
normally relied on foreigners for part of her bread, the influence of
war told in the opposite direction. It seems probable, moreover,
that the prices of animal products, including that of leather, were
increased by the demands of the navy and army for food, boots,
saddlery, and so on. The fact that the number of cattle and sheep
brought to Smithfield tended to rise in time of war may mean merely
that London, as a main centre of naval and military activity, was
drawing in a higher proportion of livestock than in times of peace.

[48] Other years outside the great wars that saw unbalanced budgets were
1718–19, 1722, and 1734–6. See Table 7.

But the need for more horses for cavalry and transport must certainly have benefited the breeders.

It is natural to suppose that the production of minerals and metals would be stimulated by war. By far the greater part of the output of coal at this period, however, was used for domestic consumption: the chief source of supply was Northumberland and Durham, and employment at the collieries varied with the demand for coal in the hinterland of the ports from Flamborough to Topsham, but especially with that in London. But it varied also with the ease or difficulty of transport by sea. In war-time some of the collier vessels were taken by the navy; and, though the crews of those that remained were given protection from the press-gangs, many of the men enlisted or took employment in merchant ships or privateers. Freights and rates of insurance rose, and with them the price of coal. Exports from the Tyne to London declined in each of the wars of the first half of the century. From 1748 there are figures of shipments from the Wear as well as the Tyne, and the two together, as well as the statistics of imports of coal into London, tell of depression in coal-mining in the Seven Years War and the War of American Independence. The outbreak of the War of the French Revolution was marked by a depression of shipments in 1793–4; and from this point the figures fluctuated considerably (no doubt with the fortunes of the war at sea) rising sharply in 1795, 1797, 1799, and 1800, and declining in 1796 and 1798. The last war is the only one of the century in which, on the whole, employment in the coal industry of the north was well maintained.[49]

At the opposite corner of England the tin-miners were equally dependent on an open traffic by sea. They needed sea-borne coal for smelting their ores, as well as for the fire-engines that pumped the water from the mines. And the smelted tin was sent by sea to London, whence a high proportion was shipped to the Mediterranean and the Far East. Following the outbreak of the War of the Spanish Succession, there was a slump in the industry in 1703 but production recovered and a peak of output was reached in 1710. In the early part of the century England met most of her needs for tin-plate by imports from Germany. But when, with the outbreak of the

[49] In one or two years of the earlier wars, e.g. 1728, 1740, 1756, and 1776–7, shipments were high. The explanation lies in hard winters, which raised the demand for coal. But even severe cold had no stimulating effect on the coal trade at the height of any of the great wars. The figures are given in Ashton and Sykes, op. cit., App. E.

War of the Austrian Succession, foreign supplies were cut off, the English and Welsh producers expanded their concerns, and hence called for larger supplies of Cornish tin. In the early part of the Seven Years War output again expanded. But in both the American and the French Wars at the end of the century, the loss of overseas markets brought depression to the tin-miners; and in 1801 output touched the lowest point for fifty years.[50]

When, in the twenties and thirties, the more accessible supplies of tin ore had been exhausted, the Cornish miners turned their attention increasingly to copper. Most of the ore was smelted in Bristol and South Wales, and shipments across the Bristol Channel were less liable to interruption by enemy action than those of tin to London. But the coal required to work the fire-engines at the mines had to be brought to Cornwall at increased freights; and, in spite of the abolition of duties on this in 1741, during the War of the Austrian Succession the output of copper declined.[51] If in the Seven Years War production was at a relatively high level, the fact that the advance continued when the war was over suggests that the rise was not simply a reflection of the needs of the navy and army but was part of a secular movement. In the American War the output of the Cornish mines declined, but perhaps this was due to the opening up of new supplies in Anglesey rather than to any decline in the demand for copper. For by this time the metal had come to be used extensively for the sheathing of naval vessels, and its importance as a strategic material was such that in 1780 exports, and even the shipment from one British port to another, were prohibited.[52] It is probably this use of copper that was responsible for the high level of production during the war with revolutionary France, though technical improvements—in particular the application of steam power for pumping by Boulton & Watt and others—may have been the dominant influence here.[53]

The effects of war on the iron industry are less ambiguous. At the beginning of the century the English iron-working trades drew their

---

[50] John Rowe, *Cornwall in the Age of the Industrial Revolution*, pp. 4, 14, 58, 104, 174. For the stimulus given to the tinplate industry after 1739 see W. E. Minchinton, *The British Tinplate Industry*, pp. 14–15 and App. D.

[51] John Rowe, op. cit., pp. 41–42.

[52] Macpherson, op. cit. iii. 661.

[53] Figures of output of copper for the years 1726–75 are given by Pryce, *Geologia Cornubrensis*, and for later years by Sir Charles Lemon, 'Statistics of the Copper Mines of Cornwall', *Journal of the Statistical Society of London*, vol. i.

supplies of material largely from Sweden. The price of iron rose sharply during the Great Northern War, and this may have had something to do with the striking advances in the technique of smelting and casting at Coalbrookdale in and after 1709. It was certainly the reason for the setting up of new furnaces and forges in Sheffield and the Furness area in 1716–17. The long peace of the age of Walpole, quite as much as a growing shortage of charcoal, was responsible for the stagnation of the output of bar-iron in the twenties and thirties. New life was infused into the decaying industry of the Weald by the demand for cannon, as well as by the cutting off of supplies from the northern powers during the years 1739–48. It was, however, in the later part of the century that the stimulating effect of war on the production of iron was marked: most of the great new works based on the use of coke for smelting and refining were brought into being in 1756–63, 1775–83, and 1793–1802. In the French War, in particular, the increase in output was spectacular. In 1788 the estimated output of pig-iron was 68,000 tons; eight years later it was 125,000; and by 1802 the figure had risen to 170,000 tons.[54]

Whether the trades dependent on supplies of iron benefited or suffered from conditions of war is uncertain. Some craftsmen, like the anchor-smiths, required the high-quality iron that only Sweden (and later Russia) could supply, and others, like the cutlers and blade-smiths, needed steel, either imported or made from imported bar-iron. Anything that interfered with trade from the Baltic spelt depression for these. There is evidence of activity in the making of swords in 1703, and of the decay of the works when war ended in 1713.[55] But, on the other hand, both in this early war and in its successors, there were many complaints of a decline of employment as a result of the loss of markets for ironwares of all kinds, and especially for nails. It is not even certain that the makers of small-arms, other than those employed directly by the government, were better off, for it was usual to prohibit the export of weapons in time of war. In 1775, however, concern for the Liverpool slavers led to the granting of permission for the shipment of guns, pistols, cutlasses, and powder and shot to the African coast.[56] Though exports of lead and

[54] T. S. Ashton, *Iron and Steel in the Industrial Revolution*, ch. vi.
[55] Edward Hughes, *North Country Life in the Eighteenth Century*, pp. 59–62.
[56] Macpherson, op. cit. iii. 580.

lead shot were high in the first war of the century, they were cut down severely in each of its successors.[57]

The royal arsenals and dockyards were naturally busy in periods of war, and the prosperity must have extended to the surrounding districts. In 1709 and 1710 Acts were passed for enlarging and strengthening the fortifications of Portsmouth, Chatham, and Harwich.[58] Naturally, again, the return of peace brought unemployment. In June 1712, when the War of the Spanish Succession was drawing to an end, some 400 men were dismissed from Deptford and Woolwich.[59] There is evidence of great activity at the beginning of the War of the Austrian Succession: in February 1744 it was reported that 'the people at Woolwich-warren work incessantly day and night, Sundays not excepted, to supply the present large and immediate demand for warlike stores'.[60] In the Seven Years War much labour must have been absorbed in and about the dockyards. In 1757–8 measures were taken to improve the harbours at Dover and Milford Haven; and in 1760 further extensions of the fortifications and docks at Portsmouth, Chatham, and Plymouth were authorized.[61] There is some doubt, however, about the effects of war on the private shipyards. Britain was not without trees, but most of those suitable for the building of ships were in the Highlands and other mountainous areas remote from the rivers and the sea. Hence she had to rely on Norway and the Baltic for most of her timber; and in each of the wars supplies declined. Most of what was brought in, other than that used by the building industry, must have been taken by the Admiralty. Some privateers and small naval vessels were built at small dockyards during the War of the Austrian Succession; but it was not until 1765—a year of peace— that the first warship was built on the west coast of England, and not apparently until 1779, when the supplies of ships from the American colonies ceased, that orders were placed for the construction of naval vessels on the Tyne and Wear.[62] If it was sometimes found necessary to ration the East India Company, it is unlikely

[57] Except in 1739–41, 1743, 1756, and 1777.
[58] Macpherson, op. cit. iii. 12.
[59] V.C.H. Kent, ii. 356. Cited by D. C. Coleman, 'The Economic Significance of the Naval Dockyards under the later Stuarts', Ec. Hist. Rev., vol. vi, no. 2 (1953), p. 143.
[60] Gentleman's Magazine, 15 Feb. 1744.
[61] Macpherson, op. cit. iii. 308–9, 311, 321.
[62] Ibid. iii. 521.

that much lumber was available for building ordinary mercantile ships.[63] In the War of the French Revolution, for which alone figures exist, the annual tonnage of these built in Britain and the empire was generally below that of the peace year, 1787.[64]

The impact of war on the textile industries varied with the purpose for which each fabric was required. In the early part of the century the manufacture of ducks and canvas received special encouragement from the state. Evidence of activity in the production of sailcloth in the War of the Austrian Succession is afforded by the statement of a Warrington manufacturer in 1750 that since the coming of peace he had turned off two-thirds of his 5,000 hands.[65] During the American War progress was such that imports from Russia declined almost to zero. A similar prosperity visited the manufacturers of other kinds of linens. The demand for shirts for the men in the forces in the Seven Years War had spectacular effects on the industry in Scotland, where the output of cloth rose from just over $8\frac{1}{2}$ million yards in 1756 to nearly 12 million in 1761, 'the expansion being limited only by the availability of labour'.[66] That there was high activity in the English industry at the same time is attested by letters from Henry Hindley of Mere to the Hamburg house of Dove & Moller, which supplied him with yarn. Writing on 27 November 1762, Hindley says: 'As we have a Peace I apprehend yarn will be cheaper and plentier with you, for we shall not want near the quantity in these parts as in time of war.' And in the following February he informs his agent that trade is dull and 'not half the quantity of yarn in general will be sold as was last year'.[67] It was not

---

[63] Ibid. iii. 548.
[64] The figures are as follows:

	Tons		Tons
1787	103,714	1795	72,241
1788	86,338	1796	94,972
1789	71,090	1797	84,195
1790	68,695	1798	89,318
1791	68,857	1799	98,044
1792	..	1800	134,198
1793	75,085	1801	122,583
1794	66,021		

Reports and Papers on Navigation and Trade (1807), Introduction, pp. xx, xxi. For the tonnage built in England and Wales see Table 19.
[65] Wadsworth and Mann, op. cit., p. 404 n.
[66] Henry Hamilton, 'Scotland's Balance of Payments Problem in 1762', *Ec. Hist. Rev.* v (1953), 344–57.
[67] Manuscripts in Wiltshire County Archives.

only the requirements of the forces that was responsible for war-time prosperity: the import of the finest linens, in the making of which the French excelled, were cut down; and attempts to establish the manufacture of French cambrics in Sussex seem to have met with some success.[68]

Another industry highly sensitive to competition from France was the manufacture of silk. The fact that this was carried on in London (as well as in other places) meant that Parliament was rarely in ignorance of any distress that might fall on it. The silk weavers received high protection, and, from 1722, bounties were paid on the export of their products.[69] The advantages derived from tariffs were, however, modified by the operations of smugglers; but in times of war many of these were serving in the armed forces or as privateers, and hence the decline in imports of finished silk through legal channels was probably matched by a fall in those that came in clandestinely. There are no continuous figures of output, but the statistics of imports of raw and wrought silk, as well as of British exports of manufactured silk, may serve as a guide. During the War of the Spanish Succession, especially between 1706 and 1711, the quantities of foreign silks brought in were low and exports of British silks high. Again, in 1717–18, when Britain was at war with Spain, imports of raw silk rose sharply, those of manufactured silks fell, and exports of English manufactured silks soared. The silk-weavers, like others, seem to have suffered severely in the famine of 1740;[70] but the return of plenty brought a swift recovery. Imports of raw silk reached a record figure in 1741, and in this year and the two that followed exports of silk fabrics were phenomenally high: it looks as though Spanish markets were being captured. After the outbreak of hostilities with France prosperity was less marked, but exports continued at a level somewhat higher than in the preceding peace. In the Seven Years War, again, the quantities of manufactured silks brought in dwindled and exports of English-made cloths mounted steadily from 1756 to 1760 and remained high in the following two years. Once more, however, peace brought depression. Between 1762 and 1764 the number of people employed by a Macclesfield concern fell from 350 to 180;[71] and in January 1765 it was reported

[68] *Annual Register*, Nov. 1761; Ibid., 1763, p. 100; Ibid., 17 Jan. 1765.
[69] By 3 Geo. I, c. 15.
[70] T. S. Ashton, *An Economic History of the 18th Century*, p. 225.
[71] W. H. Chaloner, 'Charles Roe of Macclesfield (1715–81)', *Proc. Lancs. & Ches. Antiquarian Soc.* lxii. 139.

that the weavers of Spitalfields were starving. Conditions were at their worst in 1768–9, when imports of foreign wrought silks suddenly doubled: there was acute unemployment and rioting in Spitalfields and attempts were made by the men to exclude women from the better-paid branches of the trade.[72] It was the persistence of the distress that led to the passing of the Spitalfields Act in 1773. Not until the outbreak of the American War did good times come again. Already in 1776 there are signs of a revival of enterprise in the preliminary processes. A new throwing mill was set up at Sherborne: wages here were increased, and there was a brisk demand for the labour of workhouse children.[73] In the following year the weavers of London felt strong enough to set up a union to enforce the Spitalfields Act; and the decline of foreign imports that followed the outbreak of war with France seems to have maintained the prosperity. After the post-war boom of 1784 the industry lapsed into depression; but there seems to have been a revival in 1787, and the outbreak of the War of the French Revolution brought conditions of high activity.[74]

Of the effects of war on the largest of all English industries, the manufacture of woollens and worsteds, it is impossible to speak with precision. The product was far from homogeneous: there was a secular tendency for lighter and more varied fabrics to replace the old staples and for the output of stuffs (or worsteds) to increase more rapidly than that of cloths (or woollens). The chief centres of production were in East Anglia, the south-west, and the West Riding of Yorkshire; and each of these had its own special products and markets. Norfolk did a large trade in worsteds with Germany, and Essex and the West Country in fine cloths with Spain and Portugal. In the early part of the century Yorkshire made coarser types of cloth mainly for the home market, but as time went on it produced worsteds and finer kinds of woollens for sale in America and elsewhere.[75] It is not possible to estimate the relative importance of the home and the overseas trade. According to one writer, at the beginning of the century about a quarter of the total product of the industry was exported; and as time went on the proportion must almost certainly have increased. But there were wide differences

---

[72] M. D. George, *London Life in the Eighteenth Century*, p. 182.
[73] Frank Warner, *The Silk Industry*, p. 335.
[74] See table in Macpherson, op. cit. iv. 291.
[75] *An Answer to Sir John Dalrymple's Pamphlet upon the Exportation of Wool*, Anon. (1782), p. 16.

between regions, and between localities and groups of producers in the same region. A well-informed observer, in 1772, said that about nine-tenths of the broad cloths, but only one-tenth of the narrow cloths, made in the West Riding found their markets abroad.[76]

The course followed by exports of woollens and worsteds varied greatly between one war and another. The outbreak of the War of the Spanish Succession led to a sharp fall in the quantities of fabrics sent overseas in 1702. During the remainder of the war, however, exports were well maintained; exceptionally high levels were reached in 1710 and 1712, and, after a brief depression, the figures mounted in the post-war boom of 1714. The beginning of war with Spain led to a steep decline of exports in 1739, and the depression continued during the five following years. But overseas trade recovered in 1746, remained good till hostilities ended, and soared in the first full year of peace, 1749. During the Seven Years War, on the other hand, overseas sales advanced greatly from the start and climbed to a peak in 1760. The following two years were marked by severe depression, but again a post-war boom appeared in 1764. In the American War there was an almost unbroken downward movement: only in the last year of the struggle, 1782, were there signs of recovery. Once again, however, the coming of peace brought expanding markets in 1783–4. Finally, in the War of the French Revolution, a slump of exports in 1793–4 was followed by a sharp upward movement, broken only in 1797, and culminating in a boom in 1800–1.

It is probable that the fluctuations in the home trade were less marked than those in overseas commerce. A demand for clothing and blankets for the forces—partly home trade, partly overseas—must have sustained production of the coarser cloths. How far this influence offset the decline of ordinary trade it is difficult to say. Some indications, however, are given by figures of the prices of raw wool.[77] Long-term movements of these were the result of changes in the size of the flocks of sheep, and in the demand of the public for mutton; and some of the short-term variations were

---

[76] Yorkshire, in particular, benefited from the export of clothing for the Russian troops and white kerseys for the Dutch troops. *J.H.C.* xxviii (1757–61), 136.

[77] For wool prices 1696–1781 see *The Propriety of Allowing a Qualified Exportation of Wool*, Anon. (1782), pp. 83–85. Others from 1759 to 1801 are provided by Marshall, op. cit., p. 119. Generally the prices are those paid at the annual sales in August. See Tables 14 and 15.

due to epidemics of sheep-rot, which reduced supplies of wool as well as of meat. But, as has already been mentioned, most of the sudden rises and falls are to be attributed to fluctuations of demand for wool itself. A rise in 1743–4 may have been a result of large government demands at the beginning of the struggle with France; that of 1756–9 must have been due partly to the needs of the forces and partly to the growth of exports. Again, the two influences in conjunction may explain the increase of prices from 1779 to 1783, as well as that from 1795 to 1800. But that commerce rather than war was the dominant influence in prosperity is suggested by the sharpness of the advance in wool prices that followed the conclusion of hostilities—in 1714, 1748–9, 1763, 1784, and 1801.

The only statistical series of output that cover a long period relate to Yorkshire, and only to one of the two main sections of the industry here. Even so, the figures are partial and defective. They begin in 1727 but for the first ten years cover only the output of broad cloths; and when, from 1738, similar information was collected for narrow cloths, it was for different accounting periods.[78] The officials who compiled the statistics were notoriously careless; there is reason to believe that a large part of the output escaped their scrutiny; for when, in 1766, the system of inspection was reformed, the figures of broad cloths rose to an entirely new level. Hitherto it had been only the number of pieces of cloth milled that the returns purported to give; and since cloths varied considerably in length, even if the figures had been accurate, they would have provided only a rough measure of output. By 1769, however, the new inspectors were able to offer information about yardage, and from this time to the end of the century the figures are all that could be desired.[79]

The earlier, dubious, evidence is that the War of the Austrian Succession gave a stimulus to the industry of the West Riding, for the figures for broad cloths rose sharply in 1744 and those for narrow cloths two years later: in both cases the level was maintained into the early years of the peace. With the outbreak of the Seven Years War production of broad cloths seems to have fallen drastically, and, though there was some recovery, throughout the war production was below the level of the preceding peace. The figures of narrow cloth, on the other hand, show a rise of output in 1756–7, followed by a decline to 1760, and a new rise to peace-

[78] *Supra*, p. 32.   [79] See Table 16.

time levels in *1761–4*. Taken together, the statistics do not suggest high prosperity. In the American War production of both kinds of cloth rose to *1778*, but was at a relatively subdued level from this point to *1783*. Finally, in the War of the French Revolution, after a decline in the first two years, the production of broad cloths (dependent as this was on foreign markets) rose to new heights, while that of narrow cloths (for sale at home) was barely maintained to *1798*; in the last two years of the struggle, however, new records were achieved. Clearly the statistics of wool and woollens will not bear any generalization about the effects of war on industry.

The only other textile trade for which statistics of production are available is that of printed goods, made of silk, linen, cotton, and wool, or a mixture of these.[80] Throughout, there is a marked upward trend. But war seems to have brought a fall of activity in *1728* and *1740–6*. During the Seven Years War the fortunes of the printers fluctuated: output declined in *1756–7*, rose spectacularly from this year to *1761*, and declined again in *1762–3*. In the American War the experience was somewhat different. There was an increase in the first two years, *1776–7*, depression to *1780*, and a high output thereafter. Up to this point of the century the fluctuations seem to have been closely bound up with those of the linen industry, not only in England but also in Scotland and Ireland. But cotton, no doubt, had contributed an important part of the fabric; for during the first three-quarters of the century the chief use of cotton yarns was in the weft of materials of which the warp was linen, worsted, or silk. Only after the inventions of the late sixties and seventies, however, is it possible to speak of a cotton *industry*.[81] After the American War, if not before, printed goods seem to have consisted mainly of cotton: the sharp increase of output that followed the cancelling of the patents of Arkwright is evidence of this. During the period of the War of the French Revolution the production of cotton yarns rose at extraordinary speed, and with it the output of printed fabrics. There were slight

---

[80] See Ashton, *An Economic History of England*, Appendix, table x.

[81] Retained imports of cotton declined in each of the first three major wars. High figures were reached in 1775–81, and there was a boom in 1782. Powerful expansionary influences were at work in the War of the French Revolution. The imports of cotton, already at a record figure in 1792, almost doubled in the following decade. Only in 1793 and 1797 was there recession. See figures in Wadsworth and Mann, op. cit., App. G, and McCullough, *Dictionary of Commerce*.

recessions in *1793–4* and *1797*, but, in the main, the story is one of great progress, culminating in boom conditions in *1800*. It is obvious, however, that the causes lay in the realm of technology and that war or peace was a minor consideration to the printers.

Little is known of the varying fortunes of the trades that made up these materials into garments and other consumers' goods. For one article of dress, however, the Office of Excise provides an eloquent table. During the greater part of the century well-to-do people of both sexes made extensive use of gold and silver braid. It is not surprising, therefore, that the output of gold and silver wire should have risen at times when, as in *1714, 1717, 1725*, and *1736–7*, other series indicate conditions of general prosperity. It is incontestable, however, that there is a special connexion between gold braid and the successful prosecution of war. The Lords of the Admiralty were perhaps behindhand in recognizing this; for it was not until 1748 that rules were laid down about the dress of all ranks from admirals to midshipmen.[82] In the army, however, it had always been important to be able to distinguish, at a glance, between those who might give, and those who must obey, orders; and the amount of gold braid on the uniform was the index of the degree of authority of the wearer. Naturally, the demand for gilt wire rose sharply in times of conflict. The outbreak of the War of Jenkin's Ear led to a rise of production in *1740* (it was one of the few instances of industrial activity in this dismal year) and the merging of the war into the struggle with France caused a further increase in *1745–9*. Again, output rose sharply in *1756*, and soared when the number of men in the forces reached a peak in *1760–4*. Possibly because of some change in civilian taste, less use was made of this form of adornment in the later decades of the century; for the long-term trend was downward. But the suddenness of the decline of production in *1783* suggests that the armed forces had helped to sustain demand during the preceding years of the American War. Relatively high figures were recorded when the war with France became intense between *1795* and *1801*, and yet again in *1804* when the Peace of Amiens was broken.[83]

Figures of production of another commodity without which, in modern times, it is impossible to wage war tell a different story. The men of the eighteenth century were ignorant of the strategic

---

[82] C. Lloyd, *The Nation and the Navy*, pp. 145–6; M. Lewis, *The Navy of Britain*, p. 279.   [83] See Table 17.

importance of the duplicate or multiple form, and though they recognized the importance of the pamphlet and the broadsheet, relatively few of them seem to have found war-time occupation in the field of information and exhortation. Perhaps for this reason, perhaps because of impediments to the import of rags, there is no sign of any marked increase of the output of paper in times of war. Apart from that of wall-paper (about which something will be said later) production seems to have declined sharply in the War of the Austrian Succession; and though relatively high figures are recorded for 1756–60, the later stage of the Seven Years War brought recession. The rise to a new level of output in the years following each of these wars is evidence of release. There are clear indications of a fall in the quantities of paper manufactured between 1776 and 1780;[84] but an alteration in the system of assessment makes it impossible to pronounce on the state of the industry in the remaining years of the American War. Production declined sharply in 1794, and though it seems to have recovered, there is no indication that it shared in the expansion of industry in general that marked the closing years of the century. With the approach of peace in 1801, however, there was a considerable advance.[85]

The output of glass, another commodity which had little or no place in the operations of war, will receive attention in Chapter 4. One branch of the industry, however, the manufacture of bottles, was clearly affected by the fall of imports of wine that took place in the later wars of the century. The production of glass bottles declined from 260,000 cwt. in 1755 to 166,000 cwt. in 1759, and though it moved upward from this point to 1763, it failed to attain the former peace-time level. In the American and the Revolutionary Wars the experience was repeated. A rise of consumption of beer (little of which was bottled) suggests that war-time austerity brought a change in the drinking habits of the public: in 1780 and 1798, in both of which the consumption of beer was exceptionally high (and that of wine probably low), the output of bottles touched its lowest points.[86]

---

[84] It should be mentioned, however, that the number of copies of newspapers printed in England increased steadily during the war—from 12,600,000 in 1775 to 15,273,000 in 1782. Adam Anderson, *Origin of Commerce*, iv. 522.

[85] This brief account is based on figures kindly provided by the Office of Excise. For a scholarly account of the development of the industry in the eighteenth century see D. C. Coleman, *The British Paper Industry, 1495–1860*, ch. iv. See also *Report of Inland Revenue 1870*, ii. 22–25.   [86] See Table 18.

Wars led to changes of other social habits. The inevitable separation of families and friends seems to have brought an increase of correspondence. According to a return of the gross and net revenue of the Post Office made in 1716, the ending of the War of the Spanish Succession was followed by a decline in the number of letters. In particular, the coming of peace 'lessen'd very much the Foreign correspondence, and made a Conveyance for the Portugall Letters (that in time of War came thro' England to Holland) to go there by way of France, by which His Majesty is deprived of that Postage which amounted to about Five Thousand Pounds a Year'. It is added that, 'The Ship's Letters that produced a Considerable Post are also much lessen'd since the Peace'.[87] No information can be offered about the number of letters carried during the later wars of the century. But between 1790 and 1800 the net revenue of the Post Office doubled; and though, as has been said, this was a period when nearly all economic series show a rise, the fact that receipts from postage continued to grow in the years of crisis and depression no less than in those of rising prosperity, suggests that the influence of war was dominant.[88]

Enough has been said to indicate that wars led to a redistribution of activities among industries. It is equally clear that they led to a similar redistribution of prosperity regionally. In war-time there was a tendency for money to flow from the provinces to the capital; and the remittance of the proceeds of taxes and subscriptions to loans was matched by a flow of commodities. The concentration of the military in the neighbourhood of London, and the provisioning of warships in the Thames estuary, increased the normal movement of foodstuffs from the country areas. In the war of George II cattle disease reduced the sale of beasts at Smithfield, and, for this reason, from 1745 the number of sheep brought to this central market increased greatly. High figures of sales at Smithfield are recorded for cattle between 1756 and 1762, and for sheep between 1759 and 1762. An even greater expansion took place in the American War; and the same upward trend was resumed on the outbreak of the war with France in 1793.

The transport of other provisions and manufactured goods to London in times of war was on such a scale that freights for return carriage were sometimes extremely low. Most of the increase of traffic was by road, for the transfer of coasting vessels to the navy,

---

[87] Harrowby MSS., vol. 285.   [88] Macpherson, op. cit. iv. 548.

and the danger of capture by enemy privateers, tended to reduce carriage by sea.[89] It seems safe to include the road hauliers in any list of those who benefited from war.

On the other hand, fears of rebellion or riot sometimes led to the posting of troops in the provinces, and this produced some reversal of the flow of money. Industry and trade in Scotland profited from the presence of English regiments after the 'fifteen and 'forty-five. Since there were few garrison towns in England troops sent to the provinces had to be quartered in ale-houses, and this meant that regiments were often split into detachments and scattered among many small towns. It is hardly to be believed that the news that the soldiers were coming was greeted very differently by the village maidens than by the heroines of Miss Austen; but among local magistrates, clergy, and others in positions of authority it created dismay. Nor was it welcome to the innkeepers, who seem to have been meanly reimbursed. Billeting of troops was especially disliked in times of general shortage. In 1729 complaints were made that the presence of soldiers in Lancaster was forcing up the cost of living: 'there being 100 horses, they eat much corn, which sharpens the market for meal'. The publicans were offering 2s. a week above 'the King's pay' to anyone who would maintain a dragoon with meat and hay. In 1741 it was estimated that the troop quartered in the same town was costing the innkeepers £20 a week for hay, and nearly as much for meat and drink.[90] But benefits were reaped by others. As a Quaker, William Stout could not do other than deplore the presence of soldiers in the town, but as an honest shopkeeper he was bound to admit to compensations. According to his estimate, the dragoons and the Jacobite prisoners together brought at least £3,000 into Lancaster in 1716.[91] In the last war of the century Pitt's policy of erecting barracks in widely scattered parts of the country was probably welcomed by the publicans, as it certainly was by those responsible for law and order. It must have given a stimulus to the

[89] Writing in 1702 William Stout remarked that, 'This war put a stop . . . again to communications by sea betwixt this country [Lancashire] and London.' During the Seven Years War, it was said, ten times more goods were carried from Yorkshire to London by land than in time of peace; and the charges for bringing back wool were lower. *J.H.C.* xxviii (1757–61), 143.

[90] Stout, op. cit., pp. 115, 137–8.

[91] Ibid., p. 93. For the hostility to quartering see Sir John Fortesque in *Johnson's England*, pp. 68–69.

building trades at a time when, because of the calling-up of men, and the high cost of mortgages, there was little demand for new houses. And, again, the local shopkeepers must have benefited.

To sum up: the wars of the eighteenth century led to the acquisition of new territories and new markets. They may have created employment for men who would otherwise have been idle or engaged in anti-social activities. They stimulated some branches of production, and drew remote communities into the main currents of national life. It is possible to point to a few—very few—technical inventions to which they gave rise. On the other hand, they involved many losses in men and ships, and in intangible human qualities. If there had been no wars the English people would have been better fed, better clad, certainly better housed, than they were. War deflected energies from the course along which—so it seems in retrospect—the permanent interests of England lay. At this stage of development the chief need of the country was an efficient network of main roads and inland waterways; and, as will be seen, war tended to retard the creation of this. If England had enjoyed unbroken peace the Industrial Revolution might have come earlier.

These assertions and conjectures will not today find universal acceptance, for several young scholars have recently laid stress on the long-term benefits that may accrue from the extension of the sphere of the state which is an acknowledged outcome of war. But whatever differences of opinion may exist on these large issues, there will be few to dispute that, whether for good or ill, the wars of this period tended to accentuate the short-term oscillations of activity.

4

BUILDING AND CONSTRUCTION

I

FLUCTUATIONS arising from the weather and from wars have occurred in all parts of the earth at all periods of time. In simple societies, in which nearly the whole annual output consists of things intended for consumption in the near future, they must be the principal, if not the only, kinds of fluctuation. But as wealth increases, a growing part of the nation's output comes to consist of things that yield their return not once and for all, but over a long period of time. Before the days of factories and elaborate machinery the chief durable capital goods were dwelling-houses and means of transport (including ships and harbours, roads, improved rivers, and canals). No doubt the long-term trends in the production of these were determined by the growth of population and income; but the short-term fluctuations, with which this book is concerned, are to be explained (like the short-term fluctuations in the output of consumers' goods) by changes in expectations of profit and in the volume of resources made available to those who directed production.

Harvest failures and epidemics which led to more deaths and fewer marriages may have tended to damp the hopes of the builders; and the prospects of gain from improvements of highways and waterways may have been smaller in times of war than in times of peace. If so, two main causes of fluctuations in industries concerned with consumers' goods must also have influenced investment in building and public works. But we cannot see far into the minds of the entrepreneurs of the eighteenth century, and nothing more can usefully be said about changes in expectations of profit.

More information is available about the volume of resources put at the disposal of builders and constructors. Most houses were built of materials—stone, brick, clay, wood—obtained locally, and there is no reason to think that the physical conditions of supply of these was subject to much variation. But now and then excise duties were laid on some of the components of houses, and the resulting rise in cost may have had some effect on the building industry. Far more important, however, were the variations that took place in the supply of timber, a commodity the price of which played a very large part in the cost of dwellings, ships, and public works. Wisely or unwisely, Englishmen had chosen to use their land to produce grain and livestock rather than trees, and to meet their need for timber largely by import from Norway and the coastal areas of the Baltic. As has already been pointed out, the volume shipped was closely affected by the conditions of the weather in these parts. But since fairly large quantities of timber were held by English merchants (partly because it was desirable to allow time for the wood to season) it was usually possible to meet a temporary shortage by drawing on stocks. When, however, as a consequence of war, there was prolonged interruption of shipping on the sea lanes from northern Europe, the supply of wood fell and building and construction declined.

More influential than variations in the provision of any single material, however, were those in the supply of loanable funds. For in building and construction, more than in most other industries, the entrepreneur was dependent on others for his working capital. In London (and, no doubt, elsewhere) men known as land-jobbers obtained leases of fairly large pieces of ground and sub-let plots to the builders—for the first year or two at a mere peppercorn rent. Most of the master builders were working bricklayers, masons, or carpenters, who engaged fellow craftsmen to help them to complete a cottage or a row of small houses. They were usually able to obtain materials on credit and get money to pay wages and meet other charges by mortgaging the building in process of construction. In the same way, the production of ships, other than naval vessels, was carried out by men of small means, or by groups of artisans, who got their materials on credit from timber-merchants and mortgaged the unfinished vessel. Public works were the responsibility of companies, trusts, improvement commissioners, and local authorities, all of which raised part, at least, of the funds they needed by borrowing—though river and canal companies usually started operations with an issue of shares.[1] Sometimes these bodies raised money on the personal bonds of the trustees, commissioners, or

---

[1] For the financing of builders see George, op. cit., ch. ii, and for that of public utilities, L. S. Pressnell, *Country Banking in the Industrial Revolution*, pp. 367–8.

shareholders, and in times of stress they might be forced to have recourse to the sale of annuities.

In the eighteenth century mortgages were rarely, apparently, for a fixed period of time: either borrower or lender might at any half-year end give six months' notice to terminate the contract or vary the rate of interest. Often, it is true, in rural areas, mortgages might be left undisturbed for a generation or more. John Parsons, for example, who borrowed £160 from James Harding of Mere in 1751, still owed the same amount on the same mortgage in 1778, and perhaps later.[2] But in many parts of the provinces, as in London, the rate on both mortgages and bonds moved freely (though only by steps of a half of 1 per cent.).

In industries concerned with consumers' goods a rise of a half or of 1 per cent. in the rate on loans makes little difference to the cost of the product. But in those concerned with buildings and means of communication (where a long time must elapse between the beginning of an enterprise and the return of profits) it is of the greatest consequence. A rise in the rate of interest might not merely check new enterprise but bring projects already begun to a halt. Nor was it only the quantity of production that suffered: when rates of interest rose, builders would be tempted to economize in land, reduce the depths of foundations, and make use of inferior bricks and timber. Jerry-building was partly, at least, a consequence of dear money.

One function of the rate of interest is to distribute loanable funds among would-be borrowers according to the relative strengths of their demands. As the rate rises, step by step, more of these would-be borrowers have to go away unsatisfied, and production declines gradually. But in the eighteenth century the range of possible rates on mortgages and bonds was limited. No instance has been found of a rate below 3 per cent.; and the Usury Laws prohibited borrowers from offering, or lenders from receiving, more than 6 per cent. until 1714 and more than 5 per cent. during the rest of the century. The existence of this upper limit is of the utmost importance to an understanding of the fluctuations of the period. Once the critical point had been reached further borrowing might become impossible. This, it may be said, in passing, is one reason why so many manufacturing concerns sought to finance themselves, internally, by the ploughing back of profits. But the structure of

[2] Hindley MSS. Wiltshire Archaeological Society.

the building industry did not lend itself readily to the practice; and, though large public utilities might sometimes evade the Usury Laws by the sale of annuities, this method was not open to the small concern.[3] Hence the abruptness that characterized the depressions in building, and the peculiarly high rate of bankruptcy among builders.

It was not, then, simply through a rise in the cost of borrowing, but through interruptions to the flow of funds, that depression came to the industries that are the subject of this chapter. When the rate of 5 per cent. had been reached builders and contractors might be getting all the loans they wanted or, on the other hand, many of them might be in acute need of more. If we want to know the degree of scarcity we must look to other sources of information.

A man of means who wished to build a country mansion or a town house for his own use might perhaps ignore conditions in the capital market: even in years of acute shortage of funds some building took place. But if such a man contemplated putting up a house as an investment he would surely consider the yield he could obtain by buying other assets and, in particular, government stock. If he already held such stock, his decision whether to sell and use the proceeds for building would depend on the market price of the stock. And if he decided to leave his holding undisturbed and raise the funds he needed by borrowing, he would find that the value of any securities he might lodge against the loan was closely bound up with the price of the Funds. Moreover, he would find that, within the range of 3 to 5 per cent., the rate of interest he would have to pay on his loan would vary inversely with this price. Recent investigations by Dr. A. H. John and Mr. David Joslin show that the movement of rates on mortgages given by London insurance companies and banks followed closely, with a short lag, that of the yield on the Funds (though, to compensate for the greater trouble, risk, and illiquidity of mortgages, the rate on these was usually about 1 per cent. higher than this yield). There

---

[3] The impossibility of raising money on mortgages in 1799 led to the sale of annuities by landowners (Pressnell, op. cit., p. 346). Examples of the issue of annuities by canal companies can be found in the early nineteenth century. In June 1814, when again it was impossible to obtain mortgages, the Stratford on Avon Canal Company resolved to raise £30,000 in annuities at 10 per cent.; and in Oct. 1815 it was decided to raise a further £10,000 by the same means. For these details drawn from the Minute Books of the Company (British Transport Commission's Historical Records) I am indebted to Mr. Charles Hadfield.

is evidence that the same was true of some, at least, of the mortgages given by private lenders in the provinces. Thus, for example, between January and April 1778, the quotation for the 3 per cent. consolidated stock fell from 72 to 61. In April the rate on a mortgage for £10,000 (granted by a Wiltshire landowner, James Harding, to one Albinius Martin of Silton in 1772) was raised from $3\frac{1}{2}$ to 4 per cent.; and in May the trustees of the Droitwich roads increased the rate they paid to mortgagees from 4 to $4\frac{1}{2}$ per cent.[4]

Evidence exists that rates of interest in some parts of the country were normally higher than in London. This seems to have been so in the outports and, to a higher degree, in the rising industrial areas of Lancashire, Yorkshire and, towards the end of the century, Northumberland and Durham. Opportunities for investment were considerable in these regions, and the demand for money, or capital, correspondingly high. Unfortunately no local series of rates on mortgages, bonds, or bills are available, but it is reasonable to assume that, since the provinces were closely linked by trade with London, rates would move up and down freely with those at the centre. The fact that the general level was a little higher may have made the Usury Laws more effective: the ceiling would be reached earlier.

The yield on government stock is, then, the chief representative of a whole family of long-term rates, and the price of the Funds may be taken as an index to the supply of loans available to builders and contractors. There was no upward or downward limit to the movement of this price: it reflects the degree of scarcity of money, not merely within the bounds set to other indices by the Usury Laws, but at all levels.[5] Long ago, Mr. A. H. Shannon showed how, after 1785, the output of bricks (which may be taken as an index of building) moved up and down, subject to a lag of about a year, with the price of the 3 per cent. Consols. In the discussion that follows it will be assumed that, for earlier periods also, the price of government stock was one of the determinants of the volume of building.

It remains to mention a minor matter. Students of cyclical movements in the nineteenth century have observed that Consols often

---

[4] Hindley MSS. Wiltshire Archaeological Society; Pressnell, op. cit., p. 555. In view of the financial situation at this time both these increased rates were remarkably low.

[5] See Table 9.

behaved like debentures, rising in price in the period of recovery from a depression but tending to fall in the boom. As Professor Rostow has pointed out,[6] this second tendency was the result of the fact that, in the boom, other securities giving promise of higher yields were put on the market, and drew investors away from Consols. In the eighteenth century, however, there were few other competing securities—the Bubble Act of 1720 saw to that—and hence the price of Consols remained high, and reached its peak, in the boom. (Consols, in fact, behaved in the same way as equities in the nineteenth century.) The fact that the 3 per cent. annuities were sometimes falling at a time when the output of bricks was still rising is no disproof of this statement. For conditions of boom and decline usually showed themselves earlier in the capital market than in output, and the lag was greater in building than in most industries.

Little need be said of the other statistical material available for a study of fluctuations in building and construction. When the Seven Years War broke out in 1756 a proposal was made to raise revenue by an Excise on bricks. This was rejected on the grounds that such a tax would discriminate unfairly between those parts of the kingdom that used bricks and those that used stone or other material. The economic historian cannot but regret the decision. For if the Excise had been levied, the returns would have provided an index of activity in building for a substantial part of the century: it was not until 1785, following the action of Pitt in subjecting bricks and tiles to taxation, that figures of the output of these materials became available.[7] Fortunately, however, another set of statistics can be used as a guide to fluctuations at an earlier period: in 1746 (again in time of war) a duty was imposed on glass, and annual figures of production exist from the following year.[8] Glass used for bottles is listed separately and can be ignored for the present purpose. Some of the remainder must have taken the form of crystal, mirrors, beads, and other ornaments; but by far the greater part was, without doubt, used for windows. Glass offers a less satisfactory index of building than bricks, for some (though not a large part) of the output was exported. But the fact that from 1785 onward the two series move in much the same way suggests

---

[6] A. D. Gayer, W. W. Rostow, and A. J. Schwartz, *The Growth and Fluctuation of the British Economy 1790–1850*, i. 258.

[7] See Table 21.

[8] See Table 12.

that the statistics of glass may serve to reveal fluctuations before, as well as after, this date. As with the brick index, the figures move up and down with the price of the Funds, though, again, with a lag of about a year.[9]

For the period before 1747 the only excise returns that have any bearing on houses are those of the output of stained paper, or, as we call it, wall-paper. At this time wall-paper was a luxury: only the well-to-do could afford to adorn their homes with it. Unlike bricks or windows, wall coverings need to be replaced fairly frequently and hence the volume produced has only a tenuous connexion with new building. All that can be said is that it may have tended to increase more rapidly than usual in, or following, years of high activity in putting up houses. At least it is unlikely to have done so when building was depressed.[10]

Other statistical series that may help to identify fluctuations include the returns of imports of deals and those of fir timber. The first have relevance to building, and the second to both building and construction. For the early decades they are almost the only guide.[11] At the other end of the century figures of the number of insurance policies taken out against risk of fire may be used to supplement other information about the output of houses.[12] For shipbuilding, the evidence is meagre: it is not until 1787 that figures of the number and tonnage of ships built in British yards were assembled.[13] For public works, the only statistical material is the number of Acts relating to roads, rivers, and canals passed in each year. These, as Dr. Pressnell has pointed out, are neither an index of the inception of schemes—a matter of importance in the study of fluctuations—nor an index of performance. The Act came some time after the project had been put on foot but some time before operations began. Mere numbers of Acts, moreover, tell us little,

[9] Since glazing takes place at a late stage of building, the effect on the output of glass might well follow, rather than coincide with, that on the output of bricks. But monthly or quarterly figures would be necessary to demonstrate the existence of such a lag, and these do not exist.

[10] See Table 11.

[11] The fluctuations in the two are generally, but not invariably, in the same direction. The figures used here are those obtained by adding the official values of the two for each year. See Table 10.

[12] The Fire Insurance Duty was introduced on 24 June 1782 at the rate of 1s. 6d. per £100. On 5 July 1797 the rate was increased to 2s. I am indebted to Mr. H. A. L. Cockerell for the figures in Table 20.

[13] The figures for Britain and the Empire are given *supra*, p. 73 n.; those for England and Wales in Table 19.

for projects varied greatly in size, and not all of them came to fruition. But for the last years of the century there are also details of the amount of capital and loans authorized by Parliament, and these are of value in helping us to detect the points of boom and slump.

II

Information about the state of building and construction in the first half of the century is meagre, and there must be an element of conjecture in the story that follows. The boom in the erection of houses and the improvement of waterways that had marked the closing years of the seventeenth century seems to have come to an end in 1701, for there was a sharp decline in imports of timber in this year of crisis. In spite of the outbreak of war in the following year, there was a quick recovery, and until 1709 imports were at a relatively high level. Among other large buildings put up at this time were Blenheim Palace, several Oxford and Cambridge colleges, the first Pump Room and Assembly House at Bath, and the cloth hall at Halifax. Many civic improvements, such as the paving and lighting of streets, were initiated, and work was begun on the construction of a dock at Liverpool. Straws in the wind support the belief that 1707, in particular, was a year of considerable activity— among them the passing of the first Turnpike Act of the century, and a measure to regulate building in the metropolis. (This last bit of evidence is significant, for rarely did the City fathers trouble themselves with such matters, except when building was brisk.)[14]

Between 1709 and 1711 or 1712[15] there was a drastic decline in imports of timber. No doubt the scarcity of food at this time led to a fall in the demand for housing, and the calls of the navy and army may have curtailed the supply of labour available for building. But of at least equal importance was the deflexion of capital to the state at a time when the war reached its most intense stage. Although it was legal for ordinary borrowers to offer as much as 6 per cent., so long as it was possible to obtain something like this by buying government annuities there was little incentive to put one's money into bricks and mortar.[16]

[14] John Summerson, *Architecture in Britain, 1530–1830*, pp. 192–4; Walter Ison, *The Georgian Buildings of Bath*, p. 49; Mark Searle, *Turnpikes and Toll-bars*, i. 362.

[15] There is no figure for 1712.

[16] In 1711 the Tory government passed an Act for the erection of fifty new

With the coming of peace in 1713 these pressures were removed, and Englishmen were able to turn again to the improvement of their physical estate. The fall in market rates of interest was sufficiently great to make it safe for the government to lower the legal maximum to 5 per cent. in 1714, and three years later it was able to convert a substantial part of the public debt to a basis of 5 per cent. or less. Other bodies followed suit. In June 1716 the harbour trustees at Whitehaven lowered their rate of borrowing from 6 to 5 per cent., and in June 1718 they made a further reduction to 4 per cent.[17] Demobilization had provided the builders with the necessary labour; and conditions of peace on this side of the North Sea allowed of an adequate import of timber (though in 1716–17 shipments were somewhat depressed by England's participation in the Northern War). It was at this time that part of the area between what is now Regent Street and Hyde Park was developed;[18] and, according to a contemporary, the number of new buildings put up in the metropolis in 1716–18 was 'a full fifth of the whole in 1695'.[19] There was similar activity in public works. In 1717 the turnpike principle was applied to the area south-east of London,[20] and in the next three years many schemes were put on foot for the improvement of rivers—in the north of England especially. The boom in building and construction was borne on the wave of optimism that culminated in the Bubble of 1720. Stock-piling may account for some of the large imports of timber this year, but most of these probably went immediately to the builders; and when the speculative wave receded it left behind something more solid than the worthless stock and irrecoverable debt that are usually thought of as its only product.

The government normally followed the practice of raising temporary loans in anticipation of the year's revenue, at 5 per cent. In 1721, as a result of the crisis, it had to offer 6 per cent.[21] Perhaps a difficulty in obtaining money for building may explain the fall of

churches; but only twelve were actually built and most of these at a later period.

[17] P.R.O., C. 137/117. I am indebted to Dr. L. S. Pressnell for this reference.
[18] John Summerson, *Georgian London*, p. 81.
[19] *A Computation of the Increase of London and the Parts Adjacent* (1719), p. 9.
[20] By the Act authorizing the Bermondsey, Rotherhithe, and Deptford Turnpike.
[21] See J. J. Grellier, *The Terms of all the Loans which have been raised for the Public Service* (3rd ed., 1805).

imports of timber, but the depression was short. The year 1721
itself saw the passing of Acts for the improvement of the Weaver
and the Mersey and Irwell (projects for which, however, had been
laid down before the crisis); and in the following year, when plans
were made for a bridge to join Westminster and Lambeth, it was
reported[22] that 'upon the presumption of this edifice all the proprietors about town are at work to contrive the building of Squares,
Streets, Public inns etc. etc. in Tuttle Fields and upon the Prince's
Waste on Lambeth side'. The increase of houses called for a
development of public utilities; and in 1722 the Chelsea Water
Company was authorized to develop basins in Chelsea from which
the water was to be pumped to a new reservoir in Hyde Park.[23]
The upward movement continued, and especially high imports of
timber suggest conditions of boom again in 1724. When Defoe
wrote the Preface to the third volume of his *Tour* in 1726 he called
attention to important changes in the face of London since the
publication of the second volume a year before. They include a
new East India House, a new South Sea House, 'Mr. Guy's Hospital
in Southwark', a new 'little city of buildings, streets and squares at
the west end of Hanover and Cavendish Squares', and the foundations of a new stone bridge over the Thames between Fulham and
Putney.[24] At the same time the area around Burlington House was
being developed.[25] The growth of what were then the western
suburbs was so great that in 1726 permission was given to increase
the number of hackney carriages by a hundred.[26]

From 1725 to 1727 imports of timber, though absolutely large,
were declining, and it is possible that in the last of these years
activity in building abated. But in the autumn a further conversion
of debt (planned ten years before) was effected, and in 1728 imports
of fir and deals registered another peak. In the metropolitan area
building went on apace: in 1730 two new parishes were created,
and at Deptford the increase of the dock and dockyard population
was so great that the old church no longer sufficed and a new
parish of St. Paul's was established.[27] In the provinces also activity
was high: work on Queen Square—the first stage in the development of Upper Town—at Bath began in 1728, and Sir Oswald

[22] In a pamphlet cited by Searle, op. cit., p. 13.
[23] Macpherson, op. cit. iii. 121.
[24] George, op. cit., p. 331.   [25] Summerson, op. cit., p. 84.
[26] Macpherson, op. cit. iii. 134.   [27] Ibid., p. 157.

Moseley's Exchange at Manchester was erected in the following year.[28]

The period from 1721 to 1729 saw considerable investment in means of communication also: in various parts of the country waterways were improved; proposals were made to link rivers by canals; and in 1724–5, in particular, large numbers of plans were put forward for turnpiking main roads.[29] Writing of 1729, Adam Anderson remarks on the rise in the value of land—a reflex of the fall in the rate of interest—from 20 or 21, to 25, 26, or 27 years' purchase; and adds that large sums were being laid out for enclosing and improving lands and opening mines.[30] As has been seen, after 1725 there was some decline in overseas trade: the development of building and construction was part of a great wave of investment in the resources of England herself rather than in those overseas.

There are signs that the boom in building came to an end in 1730. Writing of London, Mr. Summerson observes that 'in the thirties expansion slowed down almost to a standstill', and it seems likely that it was the early years of the decade he had chiefly in mind.[31] From 1729 to 1733 imports of timber were at a subdued level, and in December 1733 it was reported that 'the rage for building is much abated'.[32] There is, moreover, little evidence of activity in public works at this time. Since the nation was at peace, food plentiful, and rates of interest low, it is not easy to point to any simple cause for recession. We have here, it would seem, an instance of a process, familiar to students of business cycles, by which the deflexion of an unduly high proportion of income to the creation of capital goods creates tensions that must lead to recession. It should be noticed that, just as the high activity of the late twenties was associated with a depression of English exports, so the relative depression of building in the early thirties was associated with a revival of overseas trade: it must not be assumed that activity in general languished.

[28] W. Ison, op. cit., p. 32.

[29] W. B. Crump and G. Ghorbal, op. cit., p. 62; T. S. Willan, 'The River Navigation and Trade of the Severn Valley', *Ec. Hist. Rev.* viii, no. 1 (1937), p. 72. Eighteen Turnpike Bills reached the Statute Book in 1725, and ten in 1726.   [30] Macpherson, op. cit. iii. 147.

[31] John Summerson, *Georgian London*, p. 93.

[32] James Sharp, *Survey of the Canal from Waltham Abbey* (Dec. 1773), cited by Robert Whitworth, *The Advantages of Inland Navigation* (1766), pp. 5–6.

From 1734 to 1738 imports of timber were at a higher level, and though the expansion of London was less marked than in the twenties a good part of the City was rebuilt and many dwellings converted into warehouses.[33] Year after year Acts were passed relating to the projected bridge across the Thames from Westminster to Lambeth, though it was not until January 1739 that the first stone was laid. Among other Acts relating to public works in the provinces was that passed in 1737 authorizing the first Duke of Bridgewater to make the Worsley Brook navigable to Manchester.[34] Many years were to pass before either Westminster Bridge or the canal was completed, but the fact that plans were laid down and money raised is indicative of the direction of enterprise at this time.

The outbreak of war with Spain was not marked by any financial crisis, but all the principal stocks fell in price, and it may have been a tightening of credit that led to a sudden decline of imports of timber in 1739. At no point from this time to 1750 did the quantity of fir timber and deals brought in approach the average for the two previous decades. The dearth of 1740–1 may have deflected demand from housing to food, and though at no point except during the Rebellion of 1745–6 were the prices of stock inordinately low the economic circumstances of the forties were clearly unfavourable to long-term investment. According to Mr. Summerson, 'the war period of 1743–8 seems to have witnessed building activity at its lowest ebb'.[35]

Even before the war came to an end, however, there were indications of activity, if not in building itself, at least in the supply of building materials. From 1747 figures of the output of glass are available, and these show a steady rise from 43,000 cwt. in 1748 to 82,000 cwt. in 1754.[36] Even more spectacular was the increase in the output of stained paper from 442,000 yards in 1747 to 1,067,000 yards in 1753. A growth in the import of timber began only in 1750 and it was not until 1752 and 1753 that it was strongly marked. It seems possible that what would in any case have been

[33] Macpherson, op. cit. iii. 217; John Summerson, op. cit., p. 93.
[34] Searle, op. cit. i. 16.
[35] Summerson, op. cit., p. 94.
[36] The greatest annual increase was between 1747 and 1748 but a sharp rise was usual in the year after the institution of a new duty, either because the first figure was for something less than twelve months or because it took time for the newly appointed officials to extend their surveillance to the whole industry.

a period of prosperity for builders was turned into a boom by the fall in rates of interest that were associated with Pelham's conversion of debt from 4 to $3\frac{1}{2}$ per cent. (in 1749–52). This was the time that saw the erection of several important structures (including the Horse Guards) in London,[37] and large developments in building and means of communications in the provinces. In the industrial north, in particular, there were many schemes for the improvement of highways: whereas only eight Turnpike Acts relating to Lancashire had been passed in the first half of the century, no fewer than thirteen were authorized between 1750 and 1754.[38] For the country as a whole the number of such Acts passed in these years was ninety-three.

The calendar year 1754 seems to have seen a recession in building. There was a sharp fall in the imports of deals and fir timber. Already in the excise year 1754 there had been a marked decline in the output of stained paper, and in 1755 there occurred, for the first time since the series began, a reduction in the figure for the output of glass. In November 1754 the Court of Governors of St. Bartholomew's Hospital recommended certain economies on the grounds that 'it is impossible that the present revenues of this hospital, which are greatly lessened by the fall of rents and by empty houses in London, can maintain the present number of patients which are so greatly increased by the enlargement of this hospital'.[39] The recession may have been the result of a temporary decline of demand or some restriction of credit that was not registered in the price of long-term securities. It came too soon to have been a consequence of the semi-crisis of 1755: the causal relations must surely have run the other way (over-investment in building may have been a major influence in the collapse of the boom). Once again, however, the lull in activity was short; and during the early part of the Seven Years War the trend of output of glass was upward. It is true that there was a decline in 1759 but this was no more than a reaction following a spectacular increase in the preceding year. It is true, also, that there was a small decline in the imports of timber in 1760. But if the building of houses fell off a little at this time it is difficult to believe that the same can have been true

[37] Summerson, op. cit., p. 99.

[38] Wadsworth and Mann, op. cit., p. 305. The Manchester Infirmary was put up in 1753.

[39] Minute Book of St. Bartholomew's Hospital, 1754. I have to thank Dr. Arthur John for a copy of this minute.

of works of construction. The years 1759–60, which saw the inception of the Duke's canal from Worsley to Manchester, the completion of Smeaton's Eddystone Lighthouse, the erection of Roebuck's Carron Ironworks, and the beginning of what contemporaries called Pitt's bridge across the Thames at Blackfriars, can hardly have been marked by depression.

It is not easy to set an initial date to any social or economic movement. But what was known as 'improvement' seems to have arisen in the early fifties and to have got under way in the middle of the Seven Years War. Sometimes the initiative came from existing corporations, but generally new bodies of commissioners were set up by Acts of Parliament for paving, lighting, and in other ways ameliorating, the physical conditions of the larger towns; and these in time took on new functions. 'This growth of local authorities', writes Dr. Plumb, 'is the most important social development of the second half of the eighteenth century and the least stressed.'[40] The pioneers were London and Westminster. In 1753 and 1754 proposals had been made for filling in the open sewer of the Fleet Ditch and building a new bridge across the Thames at Blackfriars. In 1760 an Act was obtained for widening and improving the streets of the City, and in 1761 another allowed of improvements to the approaches to London Bridge. In the same year a body of public-spirited men in Westminster obtained the first of a number of Acts that allowed them to defray the costs of improvement by levying a rate on householders; and it was not long before other towns followed suit. At Manchester the Court Leet had shown more initiative than similar bodies elsewhere, but it was a move in the right direction when in 1765 Commissioners were appointed to effect civic betterment. Four years later similar action was taken at Birmingham.[41]

There are several signs of improvement in London in 1760: one (which must be deplored) was the removal of the old City gates.[42] But in the following three years rising rates of interest, and two financial crises, brought the movement to a halt. From 1761 to

<hr/>

[40] J. H. Plumb, *England in the Eighteenth Century*, p. 86.
[41] Arthur Redford, *The History of Local Government in Manchester*, i. 100–1, 107–8; Conrad Gill and Asa Briggs, *History of Birmingham*, i. 157. For civic improvement in London and Westminster see Summerson, op. cit., ch. viii.
[42] They were sold to a carpenter, who paid £177. 10s. for Aldgate, £91 for Cripplegate, and £148 for Ludgate. *Annual Register*, July 1760.

1763, indeed, all the indices point to a decline of building and construction in the country as a whole; and it was not until the war and demobilization were over that constructive activities were resumed.[43]

Once the floating debt created by war-time finance had been funded, however, private credit expanded and rates of interest declined. Writing of this period, Sir John Sinclair remarked that 'the value of the stocks was increasing every day; and mortgages were obtained for immense sums, on private security, at three and a half *per cent*.'[44] It was in these conditions of easy money that there occurred what was probably the biggest building boom of the century, fed, as the figures show, by a rapid expansion in the import and output of materials. As early as 1764 a newspaper referred to 'the many piles of new buildings that are daily arising in the metropolis' (and deplored the use of defective bricks which resulted in the tumbling down of houses before they were completed).[45] In the following year it was observed that 'the rage, or at least hurry, of building is so great at present, that the bricks are often brought to the bricklayers before they are cold enough to be handled; so that some days ago the floor of a cart, loaded with bricks, took fire in Golden Lane, Old Street, and was consumed before the bricks could be unloaded'.[46] A pamphlet of 1767 reports that 'London now extends to Marylebone, to Tyburn, to Chelsea, to Brumpton, and some thousands of houses have been built within these last 3 or 4 years which has drained the country of all sorts of labourers and mechanics and raised wages'.[47] There were big developments in town planning. In 1766 John Gwynn produced his scheme for the reconstruction of London, and three separate Acts were passed for improving the streets and regulating buildings.[48] In the same year a temporary bridge across the river was opened at Blackfriars, and authorization was given for another from Chelsea to Battersea. Early in 1767 a plan was submitted to the Common Council to raise more than a quarter of a million

[43] Imports of timber were low from 1760 to 1762; the output of stained paper declined in *1762–3*, and that of glass in *1763*. The imposition of the window tax in 1762 may have played a part here.

[44] Sir John Sinclair, *History of the Public Revenue* (3rd ed., 1803), i. 519.

[45] *The Morning Chronicle*, cited by M. D. George, op. cit., p. 74.

[46] *Annual Register*, 17 July 1765.

[47] *Considerations on the Scarcity of Corn and Provisions* (1767).

[48] Summerson, op. cit., pp. 103–4, and *Architecture in Britain, 1530–1830*, pp. 235, 311; Macpherson, op. cit. iii. 444.

pounds to pay the artificers of London Bridge, embank the Thames, repair the Royal Exchange, and rebuild Newgate Jail;[49] and in the following year the Adam brothers began their work on Adelphi.

Nor was activity confined to the metropolis. It was in 1767 that John Wood began to build the Royal Crescent at Bath, and in this same year the foundation stone of the first house was laid for James Craig's New Town at Edinburgh. In 1765 no fewer than forty-three Bills for the improvement of highways came before Parliament and a General Turnpike Act was passed. Large numbers of men were at work digging navigations in the North and the Midlands; in May 1767 £100,000 was raised in London for the Forth and Clyde Canal.[50] There was, moreover, great activity in the construction or improvement of harbours as well as in the bridging of rivers and the drainage of land in various parts of the kingdom.[51]

The following figures may give some indication of the scale of 'improvement' in the country as a whole. Between 1763 and 1768 the output of glass increased from 99,000 cwt. to 138,000 cwt. and that of stained paper from 1,387,000 yds. to 2,257,000 yds. The value of timber imported in 1762 was £56,000,000; by 1769 it had risen to £110,000,000.

There seems to have been a pause in the upward movement in 1769–70;[52] but a sharp increase in imports of timber in 1771 and in the output of glass in 1772 suggest a return of conditions of boom. The effects of the crisis of the summer and autumn of 1772 were, however, especially serious for the builders and contractors. In Scotland the Monkland and the Forth and Clyde companies were in difficulty, and work on the building of New Edinburgh was suspended.[53] Bankruptcy was the fate of large numbers of builders: it was only by offering part of their properties in a lottery that the Adam brothers were able to escape it.

The indices of output and import of building materials suggest muted activity from 1773 to 1775—though it was at this time that the great Building Act for London was passed, and several plans were presented to Parliament for the improvement of harbours

[49] *Annual Register*, 19 Oct. 1765; 14 July, 19 Nov. 1766; 23 Jan. 1767.

[50] Henry Hamilton, 'The Failure of the Ayr Bank, 1772', *Ec. Hist. Rev.*, vol. viii, no. 3 (1956), p. 406.

[51] For improvements to harbours see Macpherson, op. cit. iii. 391, 447, 467.

[52] The output of glass declined in 1769–71 and that of stained paper in 1770. Imports of timber fell in 1770.

[53] Hamilton, op. cit., pp. 414–15.

in various parts of the country.[54] By 1776, however, conditions were favourable for expansion. Perhaps because of the decline in overseas commerce, it was easy to obtain funds for investment at home: in Scotland, it was said, over half a million was lent at 3 per cent.[55] In the excise year from July 1776 to July 1777 the output of glass reached a peak. In London, wrote Horace Walpole: 'Rows of houses shoot out every way like a polypus, and so great is the rage of building every where, that if I stay here a fortnight without going to town, I look about to see if no new house is built since I last went. America and France must tell us how long this embarrassment of opulence is to last.'[56] The passing of an Act to regulate the sizes of bricks and tiles, and to prohibit combinations to raise the price of these, would seem to indicate pressure on supplies of building materials.

Again, the boom came to a sudden end. The cost of the war led to substantial increases in the duties on glass and stained paper,[57] which are sufficient in themselves to explain the drastic fall in the production of the first in 1778 and of the second in 1779. But the war had wider effects. High rates of freight and insurance made it expensive to ship timber across the North Sea, and imports of this fell by about a third in the years 1778–82. Even more important was the influence of war on the cost of money: early in 1778 the yield on the 3 per cents. was above the critical point, and the impossibility of further borrowing led to a suspension of work on buildings, roads, and canals. In 1779 the Forth and Clyde Company appealed to the government itself to complete the navigation.[58] In the general depression of this year the demand for housing declined: it was said that there were more than 1,100 houses in the City unoccupied.[59]

The depression was severe and prolonged. In 1781 the government borrowed £12 million on terms that gave a yield of 5½ per cent.[60] (There were protests in Parliament against such extravagant

---

[54] Macpherson, op. cit. iii. 535, 554, 577, 587.

[55] Ibid., p. 593. The reason given for the low rate was that large sums formerly employed in the American trade 'were thrown into the hands of the banks and bankers at three per cent, which they used to allow for money payable on demand'.

[56] Cited by M. D. George in *Johnson's England*, i. 167.

[57] The increased duties on glass came into force on 5 July 1777.

[58] Macpherson, op. cit. iii. 641.   [59] Ibid., p. 647.

[60] For every £100 advanced the government gave £150 of 3 per cent. stock, plus £25 of 4 per cent. stock, and a chance of drawing a prize in a lottery.

finance.) The consequences for private enterprise were pointed out by Macpherson in the following words: 'Such high interest with government security evidently makes it extremely difficult, if not quite impossible, for individuals to borrow any money, *upon legal interest*, either for the extension of commerce and manufacture, or the improvement of agriculture.'[61] Even when the war was over the existence of a mass of floating debt kept short-term rates high: 'Every one must remember how impossible it was for individuals to borrow money on any security for any premium towards the end of 1784', wrote George Chalmers.[62] Hence it was not until 1785 that any noticeable rise in the output of glass was recorded, and not until 1788 that a figure as high as that of 1777 was attained. The delay in the recovery of building had serious social effects, for since population was growing rapidly congestion became acute. It was not only industrialization that was responsible for overcrowding in slums at this time.

From 1785 statistics of the output of bricks are available. As with other series, the initial rise in the figures may represent no more than a widening fling of the net by the excise officials. But the brickyards were certainly busy in 1787 and 1788; and though there was recession in the following year, an increase of production of over 120 million bricks in 1790 reflects the beginning of a spectacular building boom. In 1793 duty was paid on no fewer than 909 million bricks—a number far greater than any previously recorded and not to be surpassed until 1806. The growth in the output of glass was less pronounced, but the high level maintained from 1789 to 1794 also bears witness to conditions of intense activity. Imports of timber fell sharply in 1789 (perhaps for the same reason as led to the decline of output of bricks in 1789) but mounted to an entirely new level in the following four years. The extraordinarily high figure for 1792 may reflect the anxiety of merchants to build up stocks before the war clouds broke; but it is probable that most of the timber brought in, both in this year and in 1793, went to meet current needs. So great, indeed, was the demand for wood that serious inroads were made on home-grown supplies. In a letter from Strawberry Hill on 8 June 1791, Horace Walpole

[61] Macpherson, op. cit. iii. 686.
[62] Chalmers, op. cit., p. 186. A high 'transactions' demand for cash also tended to keep rates of interest high. The reasons for high rates after each of the major wars are made clear by J. R. Hicks, 'The Future of the Rate of Interest', *Trans. Manchester Statistical Society*, Mar. 1958.

tells of the devastation wrought in the neighbourhood of Richmond, and also gives a graphic account of the boom:[63]

The Duke of St. Albans has cut down all the brave old trees at
Hanworth, and consequently reduced his park to what it issued from—
Hounslow Heath; nay, he has hired a meadow next to mine for his
embarkation; and there lie all the good old copses of oaks, ashes, and
chestnuts directly before *your* windows, and blocking up one of my
views of the river! but so impetuous is the rage for building, that his
Grace's timber will, I trust not annoy us long. There will soon be one
street from London to Brentford; ay, and from London to every village
ten miles round! Lord Camden has just let ground at Kentish Town
for building fourteen hundred houses—nor do I wonder; London is, I
am certain, much fuller than ever I saw it. . . . Nor is there any complaint of depopulation from the country: Bath shoots out into new
crescents, circuses, squares, every year: Birmingham, Manchester, Hull
and Liverpool would serve any king in Europe for a capital, and would
make the Empress of Russia's mouth water. . . .

At the same time the number of Turnpike Acts increased and
the canal mania developed. The following figures of Bills for
river navigations, canals, and railways (wagon-ways largely to
feed the canals) speak for themselves.[64]

	Number of Bills	Authorized capital
		£
1788	3	115,000
1789	3	133,500
1790	8	377,400
1791	10	803,700
1792	9	1,063,600
1793	26	3,159,700
1794	18	2,588,500
1795	11	384,732
1796	14	1,306,000
1797	8	157,000
1798	5	192,000
1799	1	35,000
1800	10	539,000
1801	11	932,000
1802	8	277,000

Many of the companies authorized in 1793 and 1794 must have
been initiated before the outbreak of the war. The financing of

---

[63] To Miss Mary Berry. *Letters*, xiv. 447.
[64] *Select Committee on Cash Payments* (1819), vol. iii, App. G. 6, p. 291.

these was, without doubt, one of the chief reasons for the spate of country banks of the years 1790–4. Projects on such a large scale could hardly have been carried through without inflation, and pressure on limited resources must have led, sooner or later, to a collapse of the boom and to financial crisis. As it was, international politics brought panic in 1792–3: the output of bricks fell sharply in 1794 and that of both bricks and glass in 1795. The boom in building and construction was over.[65]

It is true that in 1796 there was a revival of interest in canals,[66] and that in the excise year 1796 the output of both bricks and glass moved upward a little. It was remarked in a pamphlet that the erection of buildings 'in the present war, for the first time, has received no material interruption'.[67] The man who wrote this was evidently unaware of the activity that had persisted throughout most of the Seven Years War, and he was wrong in his view of the contemporary situation. For in 1796 and 1797 the output of building materials was far behind that reached in the years immediately before the war. The crisis of 1797 (accompanied as it was by an additional tax on bricks) led to a deepening of the depression in building, and not until 1800 are there signs of recovery. Some other works of 'domestic melioration' seem, however, to have suffered less than building: stimulated, no doubt, by rising prices of foodstuffs, agriculturists were active with schemes of enclosure and drainage. But the number of Acts for making roads, bridges, canals, and harbours, and for paving and other improvements remained far below that of 1793. Possibly the restriction of cash payments, which opened the door wide to inflation, may explain a modest revival that took place at the end of the decade.[68] Some of the schemes may have been financed (at 5 per cent.) by the banks and insurance houses; but these institutions did not generally provide funds for the ordinary builder.[69] Towards the

[65] The imposition of additional duties on bricks and materials used for making glass on 17 Apr. 1794 may have been partly responsible for the decline. If the legislature had sought to deflect resources from building to the purposes of war, it could hardly have found a better instrument. Probably, however, it thought only of revenue.

[66] The number of Bills was 14 and the capital authorized £1,306,000.

[67] *Reflections on the Present State of the Resources of the Country*, p. 15.

[68] The figures for 1800 and 1801 do not fully reflect the revival of interest in works of construction. Very large sums were authorized and raised for the building of docks.

[69] Support for this view is provided by the following passage from H. A.

end of the century work on houses at Bath was almost at a stand-still, and contemporaries wrote of the desolate appearance of parts of the town where ranges of buildings had been abandoned at all stages of construction.[70]

In an expanding economy the growth of income and output leads to acceleration of the rate of investment. This is sufficient to explain why the course of building and construction should have been generally upward in eighteenth-century England. It is a commonplace among economists that fluctuations in the capital-goods industries are always greater than those in the consumption-goods industries, and the figures in the Appendix afford illustrations of this. Again, it is agreed by economists that, sooner or later, up-ward movements in these industries must exhaust themselves or die down because of a tendency for investment to outrun saving; and perhaps this is what happened in 1727, 1733, 1754, 1767, 1770, and 1789—though in most of these instances it is possible to think of extraneous forces that may have been responsible for the temporary decline.

Generally, however, in the eighteenth century, the chief cause of the halts in the upward movement was war. This led to the im-position of taxes on building materials, to a shortage of shipping, and a cutting off of supplies of timber. It was largely shortage of timber that was responsible for the depressions of building in 1709–12, 1716–17, and 1739–48; and this may have played some part in the later periods of slumps as well. More seriously, war led to the deflexion of resources from building and construction to the armed forces and the industries that ministered to these. It is un-likely that enlistment had much effect on building—as it had on shipping. But generally wars led to a rise in rates of interest. This may be explained simply by saying that there was an increase in

Wyndham, *A Family History, 1688–1737*, p. 133. The writer, in 1815, was opposing the revival of a scheme, authorized in 1767, for a navigation on the Ouse and Swale. 'The Acts have been in force during many years of the peace succeeding the Seven Years' War when the rate of interest was lowest; and during the last fourteen years, when the circulation of paper money arising from the restriction of bank cash payments has given such facility to specula-tions of internal development, that the attention of Parliament has lately been almost as much employed in watching and checking useless and improvident projects as in forwarding those that are useful and good.' I am indebted to Dr. A. H. John for this reference.

[70] Ison, op. cit., p. 43.

borrowing by the state and that the demand of the public for government obligations did not keep pace with the supply at the previously existing rate of interest. (An economist would say that in time of war the demand for money increased. From precautionary motives people sought to hold larger cash balances at a time when the demand of the state for money balances to finance current translations was especially high. In order to induce people to release part of their liquid reserves the state had to offer a larger incentive in the form of a higher return on government stocks.)[71]

High rates of interest must surely have contributed to the decline of building and construction in the later years of the War of the Spanish Succession. They can, however, have had little to do with the depressions that occurred between 1713 and 1760. For during this long period the yield on the Funds never rose to the critical point at which the supply of loans to builders fell off. The halts in the development of the capital goods industries in 1721, 1733, and 1755 were no doubt the result of temporary stringencies of which something more will be said in the following chapter; and the long period of stagnation between 1739 and 1748 must be explained in terms either of shortage of timber or of low expectations of profit. Thereafter, however, the major depressions—those of 1761–2, 1778–84, and 1794–9—seem to have been a direct result of upward movements of interest that cut off builders and contractors (their powers of borrowing limited by the Usury Laws) from the market for funds.

It is another commonplace of economic theory that investment in capital goods has multiple effects on incomes and employment elsewhere. When large numbers of men were engaged on buildings and public works their demand for consumers' goods spread prosperity widely; and when few were so employed depression tended to become general. The fluctuations considered in this chapter had repercussions throughout the economy.

[71] J. R. Hicks, *A Contribution to the Theory of the Trade Cycle*, pp. 140–2.

5

FINANCIAL CRISES

I

I⊤ is impossible to understand the course of industrial fluctuations without reference to the media of exchange. In the early part of the century the chief forms of money were silver and gold coin, notes issued by the Bank of England or by the London private banks, and promissory notes and inland bills, created by individual borrowers or lenders. Other instruments—Exchequer bills (first issued in 1697), Navy bills, Army and Transport debentures, and East India bonds—could be passed from one person to another in payment of debts; but, since these bore interest, their velocity of circulation was small, and they are to be thought of as securities that might serve some of the purposes of money, rather than as money itself.[1] In the second half of the century the supply of means of payment was augmented by the notes of the new country banks and by the drafts of these banks on their correspondents in London.

Each of the chief forms of money had its special use: coin for retail trade and the payment of wages; notes for dealings in real estate; and bills for commercial transactions. But each could be exchanged for the others and use was made of whichever happened to be most accessible or least costly. Bank of England notes and the notes of the London private bankers circulated mainly in the metropolitan area; and country bank notes exchanged freely only within the regions in which they were issued. But commercial paper passed from hand to hand among traders and manufacturers in all parts of the country.

A promissory note was an undertaking to pay a stated sum of money to a certain person at a certain point of time. It could be passed on, with or without endorsement, but it seems to have circulated only within fairly narrow limits. The bill, on the other

[1] The existence of such securities reduced the tendency to hoard money. Of the national debt as a whole, George Chalmers observed that 'besides yielding an annual profit, it was equally commodious for all the uses of life; since it could be easily pledged or transferred' (op. cit., p. 99).

hand, had wide currency. It was an instrument by which a man demanded payment of another, usually at a date some months ahead. When a bill had been 'accepted' by the drawer or his agent, it became a promise to pay, and, like a bank note, could be used as a substitute for coin: all that was necessary was for the person who passed it on to give his guarantee by putting his signature on the back. Each person who took it did so because of his confidence in the drawer, the drawee, and the endorsers. A bill drawn by one obscure man on another was hardly likely to circulate or to be discounted at a low rate. Hence, before entering into business relations, a trader would often stipulate that he should receive a bill drawn on some firm of repute with whom the customer had previously arranged a credit. A bill on a well-known London concern was far more likely to circulate than a promissory note or a bill on a small trader in a remote part of the country. When in 1786 the Derby bankers, Thomas Evans & Son, agreed to supply cash to Samuel Oldknow by discounting paper, they wrote 'Bills at two months on a good House in London, either your own drawings or endorsements will suit us'. They added, 'We do not much like notes, tho' we have the utmost confidence in the drawer, because if we happen to have any particular occasion for money, they are not regularly discounted in London; and indeed our own opinion is against the custom of passing notes'.[2]

In most provincial centres there were men who, having connexions with the metropolis, were willing to supply their neighbours with bills in return for cash and, equally, to supply cash in return for bills. Some of them went farther: in addition to discounting bills, they were willing to take deposits and make loans against bonds and other securities, paying out coin or their own notes, and supplying drafts on their correspondents in London. They became country bankers.

The bill drawn on the reputable London house, and, later, the draft of a country bank on a London bank, were the means by which transactions were settled not only between the provinces and the metropolis, but between one provincial area and another. It was through them that conditions of plenty or shortage at the centre were transmitted to the periphery—that changes in short-term rates of interest in London were followed, very quickly, by corresponding changes throughout the country.

[2] George Unwin *et al.*, *Samuel Oldknow and the Arkwrights*, p. 177.

Since a commercial bill usually grew out of a particular transaction, it was commonly supposed that it owed its worth to the commodities transferred by this. In law, however, a bill conveyed a title not to any specific set of goods but simply to a payment out of the assets of the parties to the bill. Many bills had no connexion with any transfer of commodities. They were drawn by one man on another in return for a promise to repay a larger sum, or to render a similar service, at the same or some future time. Such accommodation bills were often regarded with suspicion, but, as Henry Thornton pointed out, there was nothing essentially disreputable in making use of them. 'The fictitious bill', he remarks, 'may, in many cases, be a bill given by a person having a large and known capital, a part of which the fictitious bill may be said, in that case to represent.'[3] The 'real bill' had no firmer basis than this. The chief objections to accommodation bills were not that they did not represent commodities (for once in circulation they could be used in ordinary trade) but that they were often drawn for speculative purposes, and that, whereas the existing volume of trade set limits to the number of commercial bills, there was no restraint on the number of accommodation bills that might be put into circulation. Several of the inquests into the crises of the eighteenth century attribute the trouble to an excessive creation of bills of this kind.

In a system such as that outlined here the supply of means of exchange was highly elastic. And so also was the demand. All but the very poor held some coin or notes to meet day-to-day obligations and contingencies, and most business men kept by them a supply of bills, or held a deposit with a bank which enabled them to obtain bills (or drafts) at will. When men were optimistic they tended to hold goods or securities, and cut down their holdings of ready money, relying on their ability to discount bills if they needed more cash. They would allow others to draw on them at dates far ahead, and might be willing to renew bills payable to themselves when these reached maturity. In the same way, the country banker tended to hold low stocks of coin, relative to his notes and deposits, trusting to his ability to replenish his reserve by drawing on his London correspondent. He could lend freely because the needs of most of his clients could be met by notes and bills.

[3] Henry Thornton, *The Paper Credit of Great Britain* (ed. Hayek), pp. 85–86.

Prosperity, however, often engendered speculation. Commodities were bought not to meet current needs but in the expectation of resale at increased prices. Securities were purchased not for the income they yielded, but in the hope of capital gains. Funds could be obtained by the drawing of accommodation bills. Stimulated by easy money, a boom developed. New projects were set on foot— some of them unsound from the start, and others incapable of yielding profits as early as had been promised. Sooner or later disappointment brought a check to enterprise and invention, and the boom gave way to a slump.

Once confidence was shaken men thought less of the opportunities of gain than of the dangers of failure. The merchant or trader, conscious that there were bills in circulation for which he was responsible, became uneasy lest those payable to him should not be honoured at maturity. He became circumspect in drawing, accepting, or endorsing bills, especially bills of long date, and sought to exchange any he still held for notes of the bank. Instead of buying commodities and securities he tended to throw those he had on the market and hold cash instead. Some who had bought with borrowed money found that the amount they could get for their goods and securities (which had now fallen in price) was insufficient to cover their debts; and each failure increased the probability of others. 'In the midst of this terror', wrote George Chalmers of the crisis of 1793, 'the whole city of London was frightened by the *rule of three*. It was an easy calculation, by which it was demonstrated, that, if one house failed for a million, ten houses might fail for *ten millions*.'[4]

At the first hint of danger, the banker, no less than the merchant or manufacturer, sought to limit his commitments and strengthen his reserves. But his position was difficult. On the one hand, his customers were bringing in bills for discount on an abnormally large scale; on the other, his London correspondent was pressing him to reduce his drawings. If he refused further loans men might doubt his soundness as a banker; yet the Usury Laws prevented his charging more than 5 per cent. and so of employing dear money as an instrument for reducing the volume of discounts and loans. If a rumour arose that his reserves were inadequate the public would return his notes and demand coin. It would take time to obtain more gold and silver from London, and, in the meantime, the fact

[4] Chalmers, op. cit., p. 295.

that the banker's assets might equal his liabilities would avail him
nothing. If he were forced to close his doors there would almost
certainly be a run on other bankers, and these, in turn, might go
down. The whole region might find itself with notes that no one
would accept, and trade and manufacture might be brought to a
halt.

The pressure of the country banks on their London correspondent
banks would cause these, in turn, to seek to strengthen their reserves, which normally consisted of Bank notes and coin; and the
Bank of England would find itself called on to increase its issues at
the very moment when its reserves of gold and silver were falling.

The men of the eighteenth century usually attributed their em-
barrassments to a shortage of money. But, as Adam Smith pointed
out, it was the rise in demand for legal tender rather than any
curtailment of supply that was at the root of the trouble.[5]

Even such general complaints of the scarcity of money do not always
prove that the usual number of gold and silver pieces are not circulating
in the country, but that many people want these pieces who have
nothing to give for them. When the profits of trade happen to be greater
than ordinary, over-trading becomes a general error both among great
and small traders. They do not always send more money abroad than
usual, but they buy upon credit both at home and abroad, an unusual
quantity of goods, which they send to some distant market in hopes
that the returns will come in before the demand for payment. The
demand comes before the returns, and they have nothing at hand
with which they can either purchase money, or give solid security for
borrowing. It is not any scarcity of gold and silver, but the difficulty
which such people find in borrowing, and which the creditors find in
getting payment, that occasions the general complaint of the shortage
of money.

In this statement it is implied that financial crises spring from
over-trading and undue extension of credit. But a sudden and
intense demand for money—what modern economists call a high
liquidity preference—might equally well arise from fears generated by political forces. Even when trade was at a moderate or
low level and credit reasonably restricted, the threat of war or
invasion might give rise to hoarding. At such times men would
seek to exchange their bills for hard money, and refuse to enter
into new engagements or take payment in forms other than cash

[5] *The Wealth of Nations*, bk. iv, ch. i (Everyman ed.), p. 383.

—or notes that could, beyond doubt, be turned into cash. There would be what George Chalmers and others called 'an impaired circulation'.[6]

Long before rules for the treatment of crises were laid down by economists, it was recognized that the remedy was for the monetary authority (the Bank of England or the government itself) to make an emergency issue of some form of paper which bankers, merchants, and the general public would accept. When this was done the panic was allayed; rates of interest (which, legally or not, had been driven up) were reduced; and men regained trust in each other. But the restoration of industry and trade took time: the duration of the period of recovery was usually proportioned to the intensity of the preceding crisis.

The expansions and contractions of purchasing power were accentuated by forces operating abroad. Most of the fluctuations of credit were international, for since many financial concerns had branches, or agencies, in Amsterdam, London, Hamburg, and Paris, optimism or pessimism in one centre spread rapidly to another. If, however, credit (and therefore money incomes) expanded more rapidly here than elsewhere this might lead to unduly large purchases of goods and securities abroad and hence to an abnormally high demand for foreign moneys which must force down rates of exchange and give rise to an export of treasure. The fall of the reserves of the Bank would force it to contract its discounts, and, in due course, other banks and mercantile houses would follow suit. In fact, as will be seen, an external drain was often the harbinger of an internal drain: the knowledge that gold and silver were leaving the country intensified the desire to hoard it.

No adequate study has yet been made of the crises of the eighteenth century. Brief accounts of some appear in books on particular institutions, such as the Bank of England and the East India Company, but the treatment is incidental to the main theme. Even in the massive volumes of W. R. Scott[7] the story is coloured by its relation to joint-stock enterprise, and little is said of the effects on ordinary manufacturers and traders. No attempt will be made here to treat of the crises in detail. The object is simply to identify the

---

[6] The phrase used by Chalmers, op. cit., p. 289.

[7] W. R. Scott, *The Constitution and Finance of English, Scottish and Irish Joint-Stock Companies to 1720* (1911).

points of time at which optimism gave way to anxiety and this to
panic, and to trace the connexion between the crises and the fluctuations of output already considered.

It is possible to obtain relevant information from newspapers
and the records of business concerns. But the essential facts can be
read, and the timing of the crises most clearly detected, in a few
statistical series relating to finance. In the great work of Thorold
Rogers quotations are given for Bank stock, East India stock, and
the Consolidated 3 per cents., the yields on which may be taken as
representing rates on long-term investment.[8] For short-term rates
the best index is the price of the bonds of the East India Company.
These bore a fixed rate of interest; they were issued in various
denominations, could be turned into cash on demand at the end of
six months, and were readily transferable. 'India bonds', wrote
Mortimer,[9] 'are the most convenient and profitable security any
person can be possessed of, who has a quantity of cash unemployed, but which he knows not how soon he may have occasion
for. . . . There is as little trouble with an India Bond, as with a
Bank Note: it is not indeed current in the common course of business, but may always be sold in office-hours, at any of the public
offices, as well as at Jonathan's Coffee House.' The bond was less
bulky than cash and less likely to be stolen, since the holder might
have to give proof of his title. Merchants, banks, and insurance
companies bought India bonds as a means of reconciling their
desire for a steady income with their need for liquidity. Normally
the bonds passed at a premium: a fall to a discount was a symptom
of monetary stringency and a low state of confidence.[10]

In the eighteenth century the Bank of England was already the
lender of last resort: in each crisis hard-pressed debtors came to
it for aid, and timorous creditors unwilling to hold bills and promissory notes brought these to be turned into Bank notes or coins
for hoarding. The demand for cash is reflected in the Bank's income from discounts, which rose sharply in the years ending in
August 1734, 1748, 1754, 1758–9, 1762, 1764, 1767, 1773, 1778, 1782,

[8] J. E. Thorold Rogers, A History of Agriculture and Prices in England,
vol. vii, pt. ii.
[9] Mortimer, Every Man his own Broker (5th ed., 1762), p. 181.
[10] Some account of these bonds is given in L. S. Sutherland, The East India
Company in 18th Century Politics, pp. 23–24. See also Dr. Sutherland's
'Sampson Gideon and the Reduction of Interest, 1749–50', Ec. Hist. Rev.,
vol. xvi, no. 1 (1946), pp. 15 seq.

1785, 1793, and 1797. Very often—and in all the serious crises—a high level of discounting at the Bank is found in two consecutive years.[11]

Equally valuable as a means of detecting crises are the figures of the bullion held by the Bank against its liabilities for notes and drawing accounts (deposits). The ratio between the two declined when the demand for bullion for export increased or (since 'bullion' included coin) when more gold and silver pieces were withdrawn by the public for use in transactions or for hoarding; and, naturally, it fell also at times when the demand for Bank notes rose. Among years in which the ratio was especially low were 1720, 1725, 1745, 1763, 1767–9, 1772–3, 1778, 1783–4, 1793, and 1796–7.[12]

Another statistical guide to the crises is the course of rates of exchange. Generally this was upward when confidence was growing, and downward when credit was over-expanded or fears arose of the stability of the polity or the economy. As has already been said, one of the earliest signs of impending crisis was often (though not invariably) an adverse movement of the foreign exchanges. Paradoxical as it may appear at first sight, however, when crisis came there was usually a sudden and more or less violent upward, or 'favourable' movement of rates. For at such a time men held money in high esteem; and just as those who had goods or securities sought to sell these for cash to hold, so did those who had bills or other claims on foreign centres. As Jacob Viner has pointed out, they sold these to other Englishmen for English money. Anyone willing to give up sterling could get money in Amsterdam, Paris, or Madrid cheaply: anyone who wanted sterling had to pay dearly in foreign money for it. No one who remembers the flight from the dollar—the flight to the pound—in the summer of 1914 will think it strange that the exchanges should have risen sharply at each threat of war or insurrection in eighteenth-century England.

A final set of figures that helps to identify crises is derived from the records of the bankruptcy courts.[13] It is true that the light it throws is uncertain. For the bankruptcy courts were not the only channel of insolvency: large numbers of people who were not engaged specifically in trade were excluded from their jurisdiction,

[11] Clapham, op. cit. i, App. E.
[12] See Table 13.
[13] For statistics of bankruptcies see Chalmers, op. cit., p. 291, and Ashton, *An Economic History of England*, Appendix, table xvi.

and, in any case, creditors often preferred a settlement by agreement.[14] Moreover, the figures relate not to the number of bankrupts but to that of dockets struck and not rescinded, or to commissions issued. Dockets might be taken out and commissions issued against the several partners in a concern as well as against these collectively; and there were other causes of double or multiple counting. But though, for these reasons, a relatively small difference in the figures between one year and the next must be ignored, a substantial increase may be taken as evidence of a change of economic weather. For, as was pointed out by Lord Kaims,[15] when activity increases and people are roused to adventure there must be larger losses as well as larger gains: as trade mounts to a boom the figures of bankruptcies rise, partly because a growing competition for resources and markets squeezes out the weaker producers and traders, and partly because it is at such times that unsound projects, predestined to early death, appear in large numbers. Nevertheless, the highest figures of bankruptcies were always registered in the year following a crisis.

II

It remains to set down in chronological order the dates at which movements in the prices of securities, rates of exchange, and bankruptcies suggest the advent and the disappearance of crises. The opening weeks of the first year of the century saw great pressure. According to Scott, the court of the Old East India Company, eager to strike a blow at the Bank of England (which supported its rival, the New Company), first collected cash, so as to drain the City of specie, and then presented some £300,000 of Bank bills for payment, in the hope that the Bank would be unable to honour them. The plot failed; the Bank retaliated; and William Sheppard, the banker of the Old East India Company, was forced to suspend payment.[16] 'These stories of organised runs', remarks Sir John Clapham, 'are not all certainly authentic. The more trustworthy of them have often a

---

[14] For the anomalies of the law of bankruptcies see E. Welbourne, 'Bankruptcy before the Era of Victorian Reform', *Cambridge Historical Journal*, vol. iv, no. 1 (1932), pp. 51–52; and for defects in the statistics see L. S. Pressnell, *Country Banking in the Industrial Revolution*, pp. 445–8.

[15] Chalmers, op. cit., p. 289.

[16] Scott, op. cit. iii. 217.

political background.'[17] It is beyond question that there was a financial crisis at the beginning of 1701, and it is equally beyond question that international politics played a major part in it. For it was just at this time that Louis XIV was sending his troops to occupy the barrier fortresses in the Spanish Netherlands, and, as all well-informed men knew, this meant that before long England would once more be at war with France. It is unnecessary for the present purpose to determine how far conditions at home, and how far those abroad, were responsible for the anxiety that led merchants to cut down their commitments, call in their loans, and sell their holdings of securities and bills for cash. On 4 January Bank stock was at 122; a month later, on 1 February, it had fallen to 106; and on 6 March it was as low as 97. During the same weeks the rate of exchange on Amsterdam rose from 35–7 on 3 January to 36–1 on 4 February and from that to the extraordinarily high figure of 37–2 on 4 March. The Bank of England seems to have acted correctly: it met the intense demand for cash by an emergency issue of sealed bills. By 9 April Bank stock had risen to 103½ and by 17 April to 110. Correspondingly, the exchange on Amsterdam had fallen to 36–8 on 1 April and to 36–1 on 2 May. The crisis was over.

The actual declaration of war against France, on 15 May 1702, caused scarcely a ripple on either the stock or the exchange market; for business men had been given long warning and had gradually adjusted their holdings of cash, stock, and foreign moneys to the needs of the situation. The general effect of war was to force down the value of securities and sterling alike; but there were at least two occasions between 1702 and 1713 when a marked inverse movement of the two series—indicating a crisis—appeared. The first of these was in the late months of 1704. A sudden fall, at the end of October, in the prices of the stock of the Bank, the Africa Company, the two East India Companies, and the Million Bank was (according to Scott) the result of victories of the French in Spain and Germany and insurrection in Hungary.[18] At the beginning of September Bank stock had been at 129½; three months later it was at 116. The corresponding fall in the stock of the Old East India Company was from 131 to 119; and the rise of exchange on Amsterdam from 34–3 to 34–11. Obviously the crisis was less acute than that of 1701; but the propensity to hoard was strong enough to necessitate an issue of interest-bearing bills by the Bank, as well as of bonds by the East

[17] Clapham, op. cit. i. 226–7.   [18] Scott, op. cit. iii. 220.

India Company, and it was followed by an increase in the number of bankruptcies and a decline of business activity in 1705.[19]

In 1706 the issue of a large annuity loan depressed the prices of existing securities, and the transfer of the proceeds of a loan to Prince Eugene forced down rates of exchange on European centres.[20] In the twelve months ending in June 1707 the number of bankruptcies increased very sharply.[21] All the signs of crisis appeared. But recovery seems to have come quickly, and, though there was much in the political situation to cause anxiety, the following two years saw at least modest prosperity.

In 1710, however, there was an acute financial panic. The poor harvest of 1708 and the failure of that of 1709 had led to a fall, to a very low figure, of exports of grain; and from July of that year to September 1710, rates on Amsterdam were below 34. Official figures of the export of gold and silver are of little value, if only because they take no account of the illegal export of British coin; but it should be noticed that they reached a peak at this time. There is evidence also of an expansion of credit and of the development of a speculative boom in the City. Large numbers of companies were floated for insurances 'on marriages, births, christening services etc.' as well as against fire; and there was a growth of private lotteries.[22] In the summer of 1710 grave fears arose of a Jacobite rising, and when on 8 August Godolphin fell from power the internal drain of coin, which had begun a little before this time, was intensified. In the words of Clapham, the Treasury of the Bank of England in August was 'very empty'. Still greater pressure came with the dismissal of the Whig ministry in October, when rumours of invasion brought a run on the Bank that necessitated an emergency issue of sealed bills. Conditions of crisis are reflected in the following figures which are, in each case, the first available for the month:

1710	Bank stock	East India stock	Rate on Amsterdam
Sept.	113½	124½	33–9
Nov.	95¾	113¼	34–8
Dec.	105½	124	35

[19] Between July 1703 and June 1704, the number of bankruptcies recorded was 61; in the following year it was exactly double—122. Both imports and exports declined.

[20] Scott, op. cit. iii. 292.

[21] From 117 in 1706 to 259 in 1707.

[22] Macpherson, op. cit. iii. 23; Clapham, op. cit. i. 227.

It was at this time that Jonathan Swift transferred his party loyalty to the Tories. The change of allegiance did not, however, prevent his wish to invest in the Whig Bank. 'If the fellow that has your money will pay it, let me beg you to buy *Bank Stock* with it which is fallen nearly thirty *per cent* and pays eight pounds per cent and you have the principal when you please: it will certainly soon rise.' So, Swift wrote Stella on 26 October, when the crisis was at its height. A fortnight later, on 8 November, he announced that he had written Stella's mother about the possibility of such an investment, and added, 'Would to God mine [his money] had been here, I should have gained one hundred pounds, and got as good interest as in Ireland, and much securer. I would fain have borrowed three hundred pounds; but money is so scarce here there is no borrowing, by this fall of stocks. 'Tis rising now, and I knew it would: it fell from one hundred and twenty nine to ninety six.'[23]

Needless to say, the fall in Bank stock and the impossibility of borrowing were results of the same cause. The effects were felt far outside London. 'This is such a time as we never had before', wrote a northern commercial traveller in November, 'I cannot see but other people are as hard sett to get Money for their Masters' notes as I am . . . I cannot take money from people whether they have it or noe.' And in the following year another northern business man, Henry Liddell, remarked, 'Now on the best land security no money can be had; credit is so sunk.'[24] In the course of 1711, however, the financial situation improved, and the remaining two years of war saw no further acute pressure.

The Treaty of Utrecht was signed in March 1713. But, with an ailing monarch and uncertainty about the succession, the atmosphere in the City was one of distrust. At the end of January 1714 a false rumour of the death of the Queen led to a sudden fall in the price of the stocks, a rise in rates of exchange, and a run on the Bank; but the scare was soon over, and when, on 1 August, death came to Queen Anne, the news was received with hardly a tremor in the stock and exchange markets.

A year later, however, when apprehension arose of rebellion in Scotland, stock prices weakened and rates of exchange began to move up. On 24 July there was a run on the Bank which was

[23] *Journal to Stella*, cited by William Cunningham, *Growth of Industry and Trade*, pp. 642, 644.
[24] Edward Hughes, op. cit., p. 158 n.

attributed to a Tory stratagem. Henry Liddell told a friend that the
Bank had been forced by this to make two calls on the subscribers
to the Circulation, 'which puts a great stop to Trade of all sorts'.[25]
Early in September 1715 the Earl of Mar hoisted the standard of
the Pretender: from a price of 131 at the beginning of the month
Bank stock fell to 118 at the beginning of November, while the rate
on Amsterdam rose from 36 to 36–6. After the defeat of the Jacobites at Preston on 11 November there was a reversal of these movements, and early in January Bank stock was as high as 128 and the
Amsterdam rate down to 35–11. Though the rebellion had not yet
run its course, the crisis was over.

During the following two years of cheap money securities rose
substantially in price, and at the beginning of March 1717/18 Bank
stock sold at 162. But before the end of the month the King's speech
indicated a high probability of war with Spain, and the news
brought an immediate fall (to 152), which again was associated with
an upward movement of the exchanges. A year later, in March 1719,
news was received that the Pretender was in Spain, and that a
Spanish fleet was preparing to convoy transports to England. On
2 March Bank stock had stood at 157: within a week it had fallen to
146. During the course of the month East India stock fell from 210
to 194 and the Amsterdam rate rose from 34–11 to 36. But this, like
the other Jacobite crises, had no lasting effect. Neither in 1716 nor
in 1719 was there any significant increase in the numbers of bankruptcies.

For the first eight years the War of the Spanish Succession had
been financed largely by short-term borrowing. But the crisis of
1710 had deranged public finance, and in the following year the
unfunded debt had grown so large that the government was unable
to redeem it, or even, in the prevailing conditions of business, to
raise sums sufficient to meet the interest charge. When faced by
similar difficulties in the past the state had generally overcome its
difficulties by offering its creditors exclusive rights to some region
of finance or trade, in return for a reduction in the rate of interest
and the advance of further moneys. It was in this way that in 1694
the Bank of England, and in 1698 the New East India Company, had
been brought into being. But since in 1711 neither of these bodies
could be induced to make additional loans, Harley decided to create
a new company to take over a large part of the existing debt. In

[25] Edward Hughes, op. cit., p. 413.

return for their annuities the creditors of the state were to be given stock in this company, which, in consideration of a grant of a monopoly of trade with the South Seas, was willing to accept from the government an annual sum considerably less than that previously payable on the debt taken over.

The South Sea Company never engaged seriously in trade, but it carried boldness to the point of sharp practice and downright fraud in its financial dealings. After the end of the war in 1713 the trend of rates of interest was downward, and after Walpole's (or Stanhope's) conversion of public debt in 1717 the prices of stocks rose substantially. It was this rise that set the stage for the greatest speculative boom and crisis of the century. In February 1719 the South Sea Company offered to convert the Lottery Loan of 1710 into its stock (in return for 5 per cent. interest and an additional sum for management) and in November of the same year to do the same for the whole of the national debt, except that held by the Bank and the East India Company. Since the amount of its stock that was to be given for a unit of the public debt was not fixed, it had a vested interest in a rising market: if South Sea stock stood high, less of it would be needed to exchange for the government obligations and the surplus would represent profit to the Company. The directors gave stock as bribes to politicians, accepted their own stock as security for loans, and took other measures to create a bull market. In April 1720 they made a new issue of £2 million at 300, and thereafter the stock soared until, at the beginning of June, it reached 800. On the 15th of this month the directors offered £5 million for subscription at 1,000, 10 per cent. of which was to be on application, and the remainder by instalments to be spread over five years.

By this time all rational calculations of annual dividends had gone by the board. Men bought South Sea stock simply in hope of further capital appreciation. There was much dealing on narrow margins, buying for future delivery, and traffic in options. The inflation of the stock of the South Sea Company infected other securities. Company promoters put forward all kinds of projects and the shares of these unincorporated concerns also mounted. Sooner or later the boom must have come to an end, for it was impossible to meet more than a fraction of the subscriptions out of current savings. In the event, it was the issue of writs against the unauthorized companies, on 18 August, that brought the frail structure to the ground. The stocks of these bodies fell well below the margins on which they were held, and speculators had to sell other securities to meet their liabilities. Bank stock fell sharply, South Sea stock spectacularly. Early in the following month the crisis heightened; and when on 24 September the Sword Blade Company (banker to the South Sea Company) suspended payment there was widespread panic. On 17 September South Sea stock sold at 550; eleven days later it was down to 190. At the beginning of the month 5 per cent. India bonds had been at a premium of £1. 5s.; by the beginning of November they were at a discount of £1. 10s. There was a run on the Bank which brought the cash ratio down to 25 per cent.—a low figure for this period—and gold rose in price from £3. 10s. 0d. an ounce in January to £4. 10s. 6d. in August. So great was the demand for cash in the summer and autumn that—in spite of the Usury Laws—speculators were paying 3, 4, and even as much as 10 per cent. a month for short-term loans.[26] Perhaps the most telling evidence of the intensity of the demand for cash, however, was that of a London brazier who said that he had sold more iron chests during September and October than in all his trade before.[27]

The South Sea Bubble was part of a movement that affected France, Holland, and, to some extent, Denmark, Spain, and Portugal. Large numbers of foreigners invested in the South Sea Company and Englishmen had much to do with the stock-market boom in Paris and Amsterdam. Funds moved suddenly from centre to centre, with violent effects on rates of exchange.

In April 1720, when the South Sea Company had made an offer of £2 million of stock, demand for sterling by foreigners who wished to participate in the venture raised the exchange on Amsterdam, from 35–4 on 1 March to 36–1 a month later.[28] Early in July, however, a downward trend set in and by 1 September the rate was as low as 33–11: evidently the foreign speculator had lost his taste for English securities. At the height of the panic, however, the reaction ran true to form. By 4 October, when the demand for cash was at its

---

[26] See R. A. C. Parker, *The Financial and Economic Affairs of the Cokes of Holkham, Norfolk, 1707–1842* (thesis submitted for the Degree of D.Phil. in the University of Oxford, 1956), pp. 73–74.

[27] Most of the details in this and the preceding paragraph are drawn from Scott, op. cit. iii. 295–328. The statement of the brazier is from a letter of Craggs to Stanhope cited by Eric Wagstaff, *The Political Aspect of the South Sea Bubble* (thesis submitted for the Degree of M.A. in the University of London, 1934), p. 152.

[28] Scott, op. cit. iii. 308. The first instalment of the loan was payable in cash, India bonds, or the bonds of the Sword Blade Company.

peak, the rate had risen to 35–2—only to sink again, as crisis gave way to depression, to 33 on 1 November.

In February 1721 it is reported of London that 'no money is stirring' and that it is 'as difficult to borrow fifty pounds now as it was five thousand six months ago'.[29] That the effects of the collapse were not confined to Change Alley but were felt in areas remote from the metropolis is attested by William Stout of Lancaster. 'The great distraction the stock buyers and sellers made last year, and the prosecution of them made this year', he wrote in his Diary in 1721, 'have almost wholly discouraged trade, and put a stop to the circulation of money.'[30] In the iron industry, in particular, production suffered from lack of orders and falling prices.[31] From 1718 the annual figures of bankruptcies had been rising, but in 1721 they touched a point above any previously recorded, and in the following annual period were still abnormally high.[32] It was only slowly that confidence was restored and that money trickled out of the iron chests of the merchants and the stockings of the smaller tradesmen.

In the summer of 1720 an Act had been passed prohibiting, under extremely heavy penalties, the formation of joint-stock companies without charter from the Crown. This Bubble Act, together with the memories of the losses of 1720, prevented the recurrence of any major stock boom in the eighteenth century. It did not, however, put an end to sudden expansions and contractions of credit: all that happened was that henceforth these manifested themselves less in the creation of new corporate enterprises than in speculation in the stock of existing companies and in commodities.

The depression of 1721 was followed by four years of improving trade and rising investment. Perhaps activity in building and construction tended to outrun current savings or in other ways to create tensions. A sharp rise in the note circulation and an equally sharp decline in the Bank's holding of bullion brought the cash ratio down to less than 21 per cent. in August 1725. It was not, however, until early in the following year that the demand for cash expressed itself in rising rates of exchange, and not until the autumn that the approach of war with Spain brought clear signs of crisis. Between

[29] J. H. Plumb, *Sir Robert Walpole*, p. 339 n.
[30] Stout, op. cit., pp. 89–90.   [31] Ashton, op. cit., p. 130.
[32] Chalmers's totals for yearly periods ending in June are: 1718, 90; 1719, 125; 1720, 220; 1721, 288; 1722, 240. But, as Chalmers remarked, 'it was public, rather than private, credit, which was chiefly affected, during this unhappy year of projects' (loc. cit., p. 292).

1 October and 1 November 1726, Bank stock fell from 127¼ to 120¼ and East India stock from 147¼ to 133; and the decline continued in December. At the beginning of the year the rate of exchange on Hamburg had been 33–10; by August it had reached 34–9. In October it rose to 35–2 and in December to 35–3.[33] There were many complaints of the shortage of money in the Wiltshire clothing area —and no doubt elsewhere—at this time.[34] The effects are to be seen in a marked increase of bankruptcies in 1727 and the continuance of a high level in 1728.[35]

Seven years later there was again monetary stringency. As was observed by Sir John Clapham, the passing of Sir John Barnard's Act against stock-jobbing 'reflects some rather unwholesome financial activities of the early thirties'. The failure, for nearly half a million, of the Charitable Corporation 'for lending money to the industrious, but necessitous, poor at a moderate interest' led to widespread distress.[36] At the same time the agitation against Walpole's Excise scheme may have led to loss of confidence. It was, however, the outbreak of the War of the Polish Succession that aroused most anxiety, for it seemed possible that Britain might again be involved in a major struggle with both France and Spain. Between October and December Bank stock fell from 143 to 131, East India stock from 150 to 137, and South Sea stock from 102 to 92. India bonds, which had been at a premium of £2 in September, were at a discount of 8s. in October and of 2s. in November. The exchange on Amsterdam rose from 35–4 in September to 35–8 in December, and there was a sharp increase of discounting at the Bank in 1734. It is unlikely, however, that these financial movements were of much consequence: there was a rise, not a fall, in the reserve of the Bank and in its cash ratio; and there seems to have been no significant increase of bankruptcies in 1734 and 1735.[37]

---

[33] B.P.P. (1810–11), x. 197.

[34] I am indebted to Miss Julia de L. Mann for information about this.

[35] The number of bankruptcies for annual periods ending in June were 1726, 313; 1727, 454; 1728, 417.

[36] It was one of the many projects of 1708 which had been greatly extended in the booms of 1719 and 1725, and had recently suffered from frauds committed by its servants 'such as loans on fictitious pawns, embezzlements, etc.' (Macpherson, op. cit. iii. 5).

[37] In the summer of 1735 there was a fall in the prices of the leading stocks 'occasioned 'twas thought from the apprehension that there was no hope of securing the balance of Europe without Great Britain's taking part in the war' (Gentleman's Magazine (1735), p. 330).

Nor did the outbreak of hostilities in 1739 bring a crisis. It is true that there was some fall of stock prices in the second half of the year; but the 'Merchants' War' had come gradually and was not unpopular; the exchanges remained steady; and the increase of bankruptcies was small. There was shortage of bread but no shortage of money, it would seem, in 1740, and even when war with France broke out in 1743, there was little sign of financial disturbance.

When, however, in September 1745, the Young Pretender unfurled his banner in Scotland, the reaction was swift. There was a run on the Bank and notes fell to a discount. Lending was brought to a halt. 'Those who have great riches in the Public Funds . . . are as poor as those that have none, for they cannot raise money upon any of them', wrote a partner in the firm of Lascelles & Maxwell on 22 September.[38] Four days later a meeting was held at which 1,600 merchants pledged themselves to support the Bank notes,[39] but confidence in securities continued to decline. The subsequent story of the crisis is told in the following figures:

	3% annuities	Bank stock	East India stock	India bonds 5%		Exchange on Amsterdam
				£	s.	
1745						
Nov.	86	139	173	—1	2	35–7½
Dec.	86	133	170	—3	8	36–6
1746						
Jan.	76	125	162	—2	12	36–10
Feb.	75	122	155	—1	17	37–6
Mar.	75	119	155	—	11	37–2
				4%		
Apr.	82	117	157	—1	1	36–11
May	82	124	166	+	18	36–2

Not all these quotations are for the same day, but all are for an early point of time in the month. The Pretender reached Derby in January and this event is registered in the low stock quotations and high exchange rate for February. The upturn is already visible in April, but it was not until after Culloden (which was fought that month) that recovery was pronounced.

No marked financial disturbance attended the later years of the

[38] Cited by A. H. John, 'Insurance Investment and the London Money Market of the Eighteenth Century', *Economica* (N.S.), xx. 139.

[39] Macleod, *History of Banking*, i. 302.

War of the Austrian Succession; and the early years of the peace were marked by plentiful supplies of loanable funds and low rates of interest. In 1750 a turnpike trust was able to borrow at $3\frac{1}{2}$ per cent.,[40] and after Pelham's conversion of the national debt capitalists were only too ready to place loans at 3 per cent.[41] It is true that 1753 appears in Sir John Clapham's list of years that were 'marked by some culmination, usually amounting to a danger point or crisis, in English or European economic affairs'.[42] But the only evidence offered is an external drain resulting from the repatriation by the Dutch of sums they had invested in British Funds during the war, with a slight consequential fall of gold coin and bullion at the Bank of England.[43] There is no indication of any internal drain, no marked fall in security prices, and no sudden rise in rates of exchange: in other words, no crisis.

In 1754 there was panic in Ireland: several Dublin banks failed and the two that survived retired their notes; but there is no sign that England was affected, other than by a rise in the Dublin rate on London.[44] In this year, however, the first forebodings were felt of the approach of another war with France, and in February 1755 news was received that fighting had broken out between British and French settlers in America. Whether or not the year 1755 saw a crisis depends on the definition of that word. Rates of exchange moved upward, especially between July and October; there was a fall in the 3 per cent. stock and in the premium on India bonds in August and September; but the Bank ratio moved upward; and there was no appreciable increase of bankruptcies. The situation seems to have been one of nervousness rather than of panic. The declaration of war itself made no impress on any of the statistical series; and once the shortage of food resulting from the harvest failures of 1756–7 had passed, output and investment were brisk.

From the early months of 1760 rates of exchange began to move against Britain, and in the spring of 1761 were low enough to make it profitable to export bullion. When, however, in August Spain

---

[40] The New Cross Turnpike Trust. See *J.H.C.* xxix (1763), 661. I am indebted to Dr. P. L. Payne for this reference.

[41] 'My Bro. tells me no one knows at present how to make 3 per cent of money, the stocks are so much above Par', wrote a northern merchant this year. Edward Hughes, op. cit., p. 80.   [42] Clapham, op. cit. i. 224.

[43] Ibid., pp. 235–6. Rates of exchange moved against Britain immediately the war was over in April 1748. They were especially low from the autumn of 1752 to the spring of 1754. The ratio declined only from 40 in 1752 to 37 in 1753.   [44] F. W. Fetter, *The Irish Pound*, p. 11.

again joined in the Family Compact with France, there occurred a sudden fall in the price of securities. Between June and December the 3 per cent. consolidated stock fell from 86 to 66, Bank stock from 114 to 95, East India stock from 143 to 112, and 5 per cent. India bonds from a premium of £2. 14s. to a discount of 5s.[45] At the same time the exchange on Amsterdam rose from 33–10 to 34–10, and the upward movement continued after the proclamation of war against Spain in January 1762. In August 1761 the Bank's ratio was down to 28·6. It is true that the figures of bankruptcies were hardly affected,[46] but at least one important merchant—Samuel Touchet—was among the casualties.[47]

After the signing of preliminaries of peace in November 1762 there was a vast expansion of credit in Amsterdam and Hamburg, and this, together with deflation and recoinage in Prussia, led to an efflux of silver from these centres.

It was unusual for one crisis to follow hard on another, for some time had to pass before the undertow was reversed and a new wave of credit swelled to breaking-point. But hardly had the British economy recovered from the panic of 1761 than it was involved in a larger one. The sequence of events seems to have been this. During the war the neutral Dutch had made large advances to the belligerents on both sides. After the signing of preliminaries of peace in November 1762, Frederick the Great was withdrawing the base money that had circulated during the war and was seeking bullion for the new coinage. For this purpose further loans were required from abroad, and these were obtained on the security of the indemnity he had laid on Silesia. Heavy drawings on Amsterdam, Hamburg, London, and Paris put strain on the exchanges and led to an efflux of bullion. The chief financial house concerned with these transactions was De Neuvilles of Amsterdam, and the rashness with which this house extended credit brought retribution in July 1763. In spite of assistance from the Hopes, Cliffords, and other international bankers, De Neuvilles went down and another

---

[45] The fall was especially marked in October, when Pitt resigned from the Ministry.

[46] According to the *Gentleman's Magazine* there were 184 bankruptcies between July 1761 and June 1762, as compared with 171 in the previous annual period. Both figures are unusually low, and may be suspect.

[47] Wadsworth and Mann, op. cit., p. 246. The withdrawal of funds from Scotland in the late months of 1761 led to serious deflation and industrial depression. Henry Hamilton, 'Scotland's Balance of Payments Problem in 1762', *Ec. Hist. Rev.*, vol. v, no. 3 (1953), pp. 344–57.

great concern, Grills, followed suit. There was an intense demand for ready money in both Amsterdam and Hamburg and trade in both cities was brought to a halt. The crisis extended to most of the great cities of northern Europe: many bankruptcies occurred in Bremen, Berlin, Leipzig, and Stockholm.[48] As the Dutch threw their holdings of British securities on the market the prices of these went down, rates of exchange moved against London, and bullion flowed out. It was not only the Jewish bullion merchants who were involved: ordinary traders found it profitable to pick out the heavier guinea pieces and ship them to their clients abroad. On 20 June Henry Hindley of Mere in Wiltshire wrote a foreign correspondent, T. M. Liebenroode, to say he had been selling heavy gold coin in London at £4. 1s. 0d. an ounce, but that since the price had fallen to £4, he had ordered a friend to ship a parcel direct to Liebenroode.[49] It was this external drain, rather than the demand for coin to hold, that brought the Bank's Treasure down to a mere £367,000 in August. The cash ratio, of 5·3 per cent., was by far the lowest on record.[50]

Throughout the century two separate rates were quoted on Amsterdam, one 'at sight', the other at usance. Normally the first was a little below the second: for if a man were willing to wait for his guilders he received slightly more than if he demanded payment immediately. At times of crisis in Amsterdam the difference between the two rates tended to widen, because of the greater urgency for cash—the higher rate of interest—there than in London. The following figures suggest that the continental crisis was at its height in August and September:

Rates on Amsterdam

	Sight	'Money'
1 July	34–7	34–10
2 Aug.	34–7	35–1
2 Sept.	33–11	34–11
4 Oct.	35–5	35–9

[48] C. H. Wilson, op. cit., p. 168. For further details see L. S. Sutherland, 'Sir G. Colebrooke's Corner in Alum, 1771–3', *Economic History*, vol. iii, no. 11 (1936), p. 237. [49] Hindley MSS.

[50] The Bank had given substantial aid to houses in Amsterdam. It had also made a substantial loan to the East India Company, which was in difficulties. See L. S. Sutherland, *The East India Company in 18th Century Politics*, p. 111.

The rise of the rate and the fall of the differential in October indicates either an easing of pressure or a shifting of the storm-centre to London. Between the beginning of June and the beginning of October the 3 per cent. Consols had fallen from 92 to 83, Bank stock from 122 to 111, East India stock from 172 to 154, and India bonds from a premium of £5. 3s. to one of only 5s.

The crisis of 1763, then, was continental in origin. The fall in the prices of securities in London was less than in 1761; and it may be that it was the recollection of the losses of that year that preserved England from undue creation of credit and speculation, and enabled her to come to the aid of Amsterdam. As it was, there was some slackening of trade, a fall in the prices of commodities, and a moderate increase in the number of bankruptcies.[51]

During the following decade the disturbances in Change Alley and Throgmorton Street were no more than ripples. In 1769 there was much speculative activity in East India stock. 'I expect it [the good town of London] will set itself on fire at last, and light the match with India bonds and bills', wrote Horace Walpole on 19 July.[52] But when news came of fighting in the Carnatic and famine in Bengal, East India securities slumped.[53] In 1770 some excitement was displayed in the City when word was received that France had joined Spain in a raid on the Falkland Islands; but though Bank stock fell from 153 in August to 137 in October, there was no drain of coin, no upward movement of rates of exchange, and no marked increase of bankruptcies.

Two years later, however, Britain suffered from one of the fiercest financial storms of the century. Heavy investment in houses, turnpikes, canals, and other public works had been in process for several years, at a rate that probably tended to outrun current savings. This investment had been both cause and effect of the creation of many private banks. There had been an expansion of

---

[51] The fall in prices was not confined to Europe. In Jan. 1764 the *Maryland Gazette* declared that 'The bankruptcies in Europe has made such a scarcity of money, and had such an effect on credit, that all our American commodities fall greatly' (Quoted by Paul H. Giddens, 'Trade and Industry in Colonial Maryland 1753–1769', *Journal of Economic and Business History*, vol. iv, no. 3, p. 518). In the year ending June 1763 the number of bankruptcies was 208, in the following year 310. According to Clapham (op. cit., p. 239) 'no firms of outstanding importance collapsed'; but it was in this crisis that Samuel Touchet finally went down. His position as a Member of Parliament prevented his being declared bankrupt.

[52] *Letters*, vii. 299.   [53] Sutherland, op. cit., p. 191.

note issues, and excessive drawing of accommodation bills; and a reduction of interest on a large part of the public debt had made men look (as they had looked between 1717 and 1720) for outlets that would give higher returns. Optimism in Amsterdam and Hamburg helped to force up the prices of British securities, and, in particular, of East India stock, at a time when the Company itself was feeling the full weight of its commitments.[54]

Industrial output seems to have reached a peak in 1771, for in the spring of 1772 prices were beginning to move downward: as so often, the financial crisis appeared at an early stage in the downswing. It was in Scotland, where the pace of economic growth had been especially high, that speculative tendencies were most marked and the strain on resources greatest. In June 1772 Alexander Fordyce, a partner in the London house of Neale, James, Fordyce & Down, who had been speculating in East India stock, absconded to France. The firm, which had intimate relations with Scotland, was forced to close its doors, and within a fortnight ten other banks also failed. A panic demand for coin developed in Edinburgh, and on 25 June the Ayr Bank (the notes of which were said to represent two-thirds of the currency of Scotland) suspended payments. Money was so hard to come by that building was brought to a standstill, and great concerns like the Forth and Clyde Canal and the Carron Company found themselves seriously embarrassed.[55]

The crisis spread rapidly to England. There were runs on the banks, and among others Henry Thrale, the brewer, who held funds deposited by clubs and other customers, was unable to meet his obligations.[56] Money was so scarce that the more important part of the East India Company's sale had to be postponed from September to November. This time (in contrast to 1763) the crisis seems to have appeared first in Britain and to have spread to Holland.[57] When, in October, the great firm of Clifford & Sons of Amsterdam went down, panic spread through most of the centres of northern Europe. That things were not worse in England was due largely to the courage of the Bank, which, when the crisis was at its height,

[54] Wilson, op. cit., p. 170.
[55] Henry Hamilton, 'The Failure of the Ayr Bank, 1772', *Ec. Hist. Rev.*, vol. viii, no. 3 (1956), pp. 405–17.
[56] Peter Mathias, 'The Industrial Revolution in Brewing', *Explorations in Entrepreneurial History*, vol. v.
[57] Partly because of the action of the Bank in refusing, or limiting discounts to Jews with Amsterdam connexions.

discounted liberally (in spite of a sharp fall of the reserve of bullion), and also to the merchants of London and the provinces who (as in previous times of stress) joined to support the credit of both the Bank and the private bankers.[58] How well confidence in the Bank of England was maintained is indicated by the relative slightness of the fall of its stock—from 151 in June to 143 in January 1773. Over the same period East India stock fell from 224 to 160, though this was largely because of military reverses in India. In June the exchange on Amsterdam was 34–8; by the following January it had reached the extraordinary figure of 36–5. The intensity of the crisis is most clearly revealed, however, in the figures of bankruptcies which rose from 398 in 1772 to 623 in 1773.

Complaints of a shortage of money were numerous in 1773. The difficulties of traders were intensified by measures taken for the reform of the gold coinage. It had always been profitable for dealers to pick out the heavier coins for export, and during the sixties the temptation to clip or send abroad the full-weight guineas, as they came from the Mint, had been especially great. In 1773 orders were given to the receivers of taxes to deface all coin of less than a minimum weight that came into their hands, and the Bank of England was also buying the deficient pieces by weight.[59] The effects of the announcement that the old money was to be withdrawn are indicated in a letter written by Thomas Bland from Kendal to John Gurney jr. of Norwich, dated 7th mo. 1773:

People here in these parts where we have been are all in Confusion about the Act . . . to put a stop to the circulating of light Gold, as little is to be seen in the North but what has been clipped; nobody will take a Guinea scarcely without weighing it, [so] that all payments may be said to be totally at a stand. . . . Its reported that the Act is to take place next 7th Day . . . if so no doubt you will take Care not to be catched . . . every one to whom light Money (Gold) is tender'd, is to have a power of breaking it & selling it to the Goldsmiths at the current price for Acco^t. of the person who may offer it in pay^t.—So much trouble will now be attendant on Cash Transactions, that I think the fewer we have the better.[60]

In the following year official tellers and receivers were appointed

---

[58] Clapham, op. cit. i. 247; L. S. Sutherland, op. cit., p. 224; Wadsworth and Mann, op. cit., pp. 251, 401. The income of the Bank from discounts rose from £95,303 in 1772 to £124,293 in 1773.

[59] A. E. Feavearyear, The Pound Sterling, p. 156.

[60] I thank Dr. L. S. Pressnell for sending me a copy of this letter.

to buy up the old pieces, and about £16½ million was recoined. These operations must have helped to prolong the depression that followed the crisis.

With a return of confidence, and the rehabilitation of the gold currency, industry and trade revived. Business was affected by a worsening of relations with the American colonists, but this was a gradual process, and the declaration of open hostilities in 1775 brought little or no financial disturbance. In June of the following year it was reported of Scotland that there was 'great plenty of money now in the circle', and that over half a million sterling had been lent out at Edinburgh at 3 per cent.[61] It is probable that something of the nature of a boom appeared in the following year, and that credit was once more inflated; and when, at the beginning of 1778, the French entered the war all the familiar signs of crisis appeared. Three per cent. Consols dropped from 72 in January to 61 in April, Bank stock from 120 to 107, and East India stock from 164 to 137. India bonds, which had been at a premium of £3. 3s. in December, were at a discount of 9s. in January. The rate on Amsterdam moved up from 34–2 at the beginning of the year to 35–10 in April and 36–6 in August. There was a rush to the Bank for both notes and coin, and a consequent fall of the cash ratio. Sir William Forbes declared that 'trade of every kind seems to be at a perfect stand owing to an uncommon great and general scarcity of money'.[62] The number of bankruptcies rose from 471 in 1777 to 623 in 1778 and 634 in 1779.

During the later stages of the war heavy remittances to the forces abroad led to a severe fall in the exchanges and a serious drain of metal overseas.[63] The value of the pound sterling remained low until long after the signing of preliminaries of peace;[64] for, according to Clapham, there were heavy sales of British securities by the Dutch in the early months of 1783. The outflow of treasure led the Bank to curtail its discounts, but by August the reserves were down to the perilously low level of £590,000.[65] The return of peace had

---

[61] M. L. Robertson, 'Scottish Commerce and the American War of Independence', Ec. Hist. Rev., vol. ix, no. 1 (1956), p. 126.

[62] Sir William Forbes, Memoirs of a Banking House, p. 55.

[63] A good deal seems to have gone to America. 'The enormous expense of the armies, sent out to subdue them [the American colonists], in reality enriched them with a profusion of hard money, infinitely beyond what was ever seen in the country before' (Macpherson, op. cit. iii. 719).

[64] With the United States on 30 Nov. 1782, and with France, Spain, and Holland on 20 Jan. 1783.   [65] Clapham, op. cit. i. 254–6.

led to large speculative shipments overseas, especially to the United States. Writing in June 1783 to a business connexion in London, an American merchant referred to the 'amazing influx of goods from almost every part of the world' that had come in 'under an idea of the country's being in great want of goods, when in fact, the country was full at the conclusion of the war'. And another merchant, who wrote in the same month and to the same effect, predicted that in a year's time trade would become 'regular' again. 'Till then', he added, 'mushrooms will wither.'[66] In the autumn of 1783 an internal drain on a large scale reinforced the external drain of coin and bullion. Between September and January the 3 per cent. Consolidated stock fell from 66 to 57; Bank stock from 127 to 113; and East India stock from 141 to 118. At the same time there was the usual upward movement of the Amsterdam exchange—from 34–5 in September to 35–10 in January.[67] Marked as these movements were, however, Clapham's verdict was almost certainly correct: 'There had been a real crisis of peace but no panic.'[68] Nevertheless, as late as the end of 1784 merchants complained of the shortage of money.

For some years after 1783 the course of finance was steady, while manufacture and trade moved forward at accelerating pace. The cotton industry was reaping the rewards of technical invention, and the increase of output that followed the cancelling of Arkwright's patents was matched by an expansion of credit which, in some cases, overstepped the bounds of honest dealing. In particular, the great calico-printing firm, Livesey, Hargreaves & Co., issued not only ordinary accommodation bills, but bills drawn on, and payable to, fictitious persons, which they were nevertheless able to discount.[69] In Lancashire the mood of optimism was heightened by the Anglo-French treaty of trade of 1786, and the boom in output was associated with speculation in both raw materials and finished wares. In October or November 1786, S. & W. Salte referred to calicoes 'laid up snug in Warehouses to come into the market by and by', but asserted that 'they will never suit the French trade nor

---

[66] Anne Bezanson, *Prices and Inflation during the American Revolution, Pennsylvania, 1770–1790* (University of Pennsylvania, Research Studies, xxxv), p. 300.

[67] The fact that the rise in rates continued and reached the extraordinary point of 37–11 in April 1785 suggests something more than the normal reaction in a period of crisis.

[68] Clapham, op. cit. i. 256.

[69] For details see L. S. Pressnell, op. cit., pp. 91–92, 454–5.

any other Trade at the Price, and must come down, & many *Persons down with them*.[70] In another letter of 25 April the same correspondent refers to 'sad times' and goods selling for an old song.[71] But it was not, apparently, until the spring of 1788 that the crisis reached its height. After the failure of some of the largest London houses in the Manchester trade, came the collapse in May of Livesey Hargreaves themselves, as well as of the Manchester bank of Byrom & Co., with which the calico printers had very close connexions.[72] In the summer of 1788 there was deep depression. 'We do assure you', wrote S. Salte to Oldknow on 25 June, 'it is necessary for every man to curtail his trade, almost to stand still, look about him and collect in his debts.' And in the following month he wrote of his own difficulties: 'Very few persons that owe us money pay it. . . . We really hardly know who to trust.'[73] The crisis of 1788 was largely, though not exclusively, a matter of the cotton industry; it had little or no repercussions on the stock market, and Dr. Pressnell speaks of it as 'the crisis of accommodation bills'.[74] It is remarkable in that it came a full year after the trade depression in the cotton industry had set in, and that there was no general hoarding of cash and no widespread panic.[75] Bankruptcies, however, increased from 471 in 1787 to 599 in 1788 and 666 in 1789.[76]

Two years later, in 1790, fears of a rupture with Spain about Vancouver Island led to some excitement in the City. Consols fell from 80 in April to 73 in May, Bank stock from 186 to 170, and East India stock from 173 to 155. In the following month the premium on India bonds fell from £5. 18s. to £2. 10s. Rates of exchange, however, were hardly affected and within a few weeks the nervousness had passed.

It was far otherwise in 1792–3. For some years trade and invest-

---

[70] Unwin, op. cit., p. 88.

[71] Ibid., p. 89.

[72] Wadsworth and Mann, op. cit., pp. 307–8; Leo H. Grindon, *Manchester Banks and Bankers*, pp. 45–46.

[73] Unwin, op. cit., p. 102.

[74] Pressnell, op. cit., p. 92.

[75] In Aug. 1788 the premium on India bonds fell from £3. 4s. to £1. 15s. and the Hamburg exchange rose from 37–9 to 38–2. But both movements were reversed in September.

[76] Writing in Dec. 1788, an American observed, 'Cotton in Europe is very low owing to many bankruptcies in that branch.' Anne Bezanson, op. cit., pp. 279–80. Silberling's figures taken from the *London Gazette* are as follows: 1787, 607; 1788, 754; 1789, 586. There is a concentration of bankruptcies in the second and third quarters of 1788.

ment had been growing rapidly; there had taken place a phenomenal increase in the number of country banks and the creation of
notes and finance bills. Prices of raw materials, including wool,
leather, tin, and sugar, were rising, and from the beginning of 1792
there are indications that prosperity had created conditions of
boom. Political events on the Continent led to foreign sales of
British Funds and to a fall in the exchange value of sterling; and
this was accentuated when, after a wet summer and a poor harvest,
it was necessary to make relatively large purchases of grain abroad.
Trade and manufacture had already taken a downward turn. It
needed only some political or economic misfortune for the external
drain to be followed by an internal run on the banks for coin. The
course of events in Europe made it increasingly evident that Britain
could not remain long at peace with revolutionary France, and in
November 1792 a sudden fall in the prices of stocks and a rise in
rates of exchange heralded a crisis of the first magnitude. It was not
until early in February 1793 that France actually declared war on
this country; but that, as on other occasions, the war crisis preceded the war can be seen in the following figures:

	3% Consols	Bank stock	East India stock	East India bonds		Exchange on Amsterdam
1792				£	*s.*	
2 Nov.	90	200	210	5	11	37–4
4 Dec.	76	179	180	1	5	38–3
1793						
Jan.	78	175	184		11	38
2 Feb.	75	171	180			38–9
1 Mar.	72	164	195		10	39–2
5 Apr.	77	168	207		1	40–3

In March 1793 there were heavy runs on the country banks and
drains on the Bank of England. Bank failures and the hoarding of
coin made it impossible for many manufacturers not only to meet
commercial debts, but even to pay wages. The situation was
relieved, however, by emergency issues of £5 notes by the Bank,[77]
and of Exchequer bills which were lent by the government to
traders (on the deposit of goods with the Customs officers) and

[77] Before this time the Bank of England had been prohibited from issuing
notes of less than £10 denomination.

could pass from hand to hand or be discounted for cash at the Bank. By April the extreme demand for money had abated, and by the summer the crisis was over. There was, however, much wreckage in all parts of the country. The number of bankruptcies (which included many country bankers) had risen from 612 in 1792 to 1,037 in 1793 and was still at the high figure of 948 in 1794.

After nearly four years of free circulation (though not of unbroken prosperity),[78] panic once again brought constriction. Already in 1795 there was severe pressure on the exchanges, for, in addition to the payments to the forces overseas, remittances on account of the Austrian loan, granted this year, pressed down the value of sterling. Furthermore, after a long period of wild inflation, the French were taking steps to return to specie payments, and balances that had been held for safety in London were now being repatriated by way of Hamburg. In February 1795 the rate on Hamburg had been as high as 36; in June it was down to 33–6, and in August to 32–4. The specie points varied with the nature of the metal—gold or silver, bullion or coin—and, with rates of freight and insurance. But at 32–4 it must certainly have paid to remit gold rather than bills to Hamburg. In the following year heavy payments had to be made for imports of corn, and the other causes of an adverse balance of payments continued. Government expenditure at home was also rising. Exchequer bills and other instruments paid to contractors were presented to the Bank and exchanged for notes. As prices and incomes rose there was a growing need for guineas and small change. Hence an internal drain was added to the drain overseas.

There are signs of an increasing pressure for money in the later months of 1796;[79] again, it needed only some political mishap to precipitate panic; and when in February 1797 a few French troops were landed near Fishguard there was a run on the banks. The story of the Restriction crisis has been told too often to need repetition here. Suffice it to say that, as the following figures indicate, it was especially intense in April and May, when the rate on Ham-

---

[78] According to Francis Baring: 'The tranquillity, confidence, and general prosperity which succeeded the first six months of the year 1793, and continued for those of 1794, 1795, and part of 1796 was wonderful. . . .' Cited by Gayer, Rostow, and Schwartz, i. 44.

[79] 'What a Mercy it is, that Trade has been in such a flourishing state during the whole of the present War, and during the late uncommon dearness and scarcity of Corn' (*The Diary of Thomas Butler*, under date 8 Oct. 1796). 'Money is particularly scarce just now. We can hardly collect as much Money as will pay our Workmen's Wages' (ibid., p. 80).

burg (which as late as September 1796 had registered only 33–7)
rose above 36.

1797	3% Consols	Bank stock	East India stock	5% India bonds	Hamburg rate
				£ s.	
Jan.	54	140	167	..	35–6
Feb.	53	139	160	9	35–2
Mar.	50	136	152	—1 3	34–9
Apr.	..	124	150	4	36–8
May	48	119	149	1 10	36
June	50	123	..	1 10	36–4

In February the Bank's Treasure was down to £1 million and the
ratio to 9 per cent. Conditions of crisis are further attested by a rise
in the figures of bankruptcies: from 697 in 1796 to 875 in 1797. It
would be easy to give many illustrations of the difficulty of obtaining cash in the early months of 1797. But one or two will suffice. 'I
have found Money and Orders particularly scarce', wrote Thomas
Butler of Kirkstall Forge on 10 March. 'Trade in General is very
bad, and I fear there is no prospect at the present of an amendment.'
Six days later his *Diary* records: 'I have had very bad success to day
in collecting money; instead of receiving 1000 £ as I ought to do
I came home pennyless.' And on 1 April Butler wrote: 'I have had
a very unsuccessful Journey in regard to Money—Orders are not
amiss.'[80]

During this phase of the war the commercial and financial centre
of Europe had moved from Amsterdam to Hamburg. In the summer
of 1799 there was crisis in Hamburg,[81] where there had been excessive speculation in West Indian produce,[82] and between August and
November eighty-two houses failed for about £2½ million. The
panic was so great as to force up the discount rate in Hamburg to
15 per cent., and funds were attracted from London. Already, a
calamitous harvest had led to imports of grain on a large scale, and
for this reason also the exchanges were against Britain. Perhaps

---

[80] *The Diary of Thomas Butler*, pp. 121, 122, 125.

[81] The crisis seems to have been acute in April and May, for sterling fell in
value as follows: April, 37–4; May, 35–6; June, 34–6. By October the rate was
31–6. It looks as though the Hamburgers had an intense demand for liquidity
and were selling their sterling assets. See H. D. Macleod, *Theory and Practice
of Banking* (6th ed.), i. 538.

[82] Gayer, Rostow, and Schwartz, op. cit. i. 29.

because of the failure of the expedition to Holland, or for some other reason connected with the war, there was a fall of confidence at home and a disposition to hoarding. There is evidence of weakness among country banks and an unwillingness of the public to take payment in their notes. On 24 September Thomas Butler recorded that when he went to Leeds to get cash to pay wages he did not receive a shilling. The local bank, Sykes & Co., was under suspicion, and in the following month Butler was able to buy three of their guinea notes for £3. (He managed, however, to pay them away immediately.) Difficulties of obtaining money led to a loan by the state of £500,000 in Exchequer bills to the West India merchants in Liverpool.[83] But the suspension of cash payments two years before had made it possible for the Bank to meet most reasonable demands and there was no general panic. The fall in the prices of securities was mild and the increase of bankruptcies relatively small. Such distress as there was in England in 1799–1800 was due more to the shortage of food than to a shortage of money.

III

In the nineteenth century the course of industry and trade was marked by clearly defined cycles. Prosperity, boom, crisis, slump, and recovery succeeded one another with a regularity that suggested inevitability: it was natural to think of the crisis as arising out of the boom—just as, in turn, the depression arose out of the crisis. In the eighteenth century there is less evidence of periodic cycles: there were expansions and contractions of activity, and crisis might appear at any point of these. Events connected with war or domestic conflict are sufficient explanation of the panics of 1701, 1715, 1745, 1778, and, perhaps, 1797. To those who suffered from them these crises appeared not as something in the order of nature, which a man of experience might have foretold, but as bolts from the blue. They were (or at least seemed to be) causes rather than consequences of economic disorder.

Nevertheless, this chapter is not just a chapter of accidents. There was another kind of crisis in which politics seem to have played only a small part, and economic or financial pressures a large one. Such were the crises of 1720, 1763, 1772–3, 1788, all of which occurred in periods of peace, and all of which were international.

---

[83] Gayer, Rostow, and Schwartz, op. cit. i. 34; Macpherson, op. cit. iv. 485.

It is obvious that fears arising from war, or the prospect of war, are not a sufficient condition: otherwise there would have been far more crises in this century than in fact there were. 'That such things take place independent of war is therefore proved by experience, and the manner in which they are brought about is simply by a longer or shorter chain of distrust, aided by a very rigorous usury law.' So wrote William Playfair in 1793. If it had been possible for the banks to ration credit by raising discount rates, undue expansions might have been checked and the consequences of crisis mitigated.[84]

Each crisis manifested itself in sharp movements of stock prices. When the existing political order was threatened, as in 1710, 1715, and 1745–6, government stock fell as sharply as the stock of the chartered companies. In some of the later crises, as in 1772–3, when there was no fear for the régime, the decline in the price of 3 per cent. Consols was small: some investors may even have come to treat these as a haven and have sold other securities in order to take them up—as they did in the crises of the nineteenth century.

Each crisis meant an intense demand for cash, or, in other words, an obstruction to circulation. The depression that followed was usually proportioned to the height to which speculation and the creation of credit had previously gone; but in the last decade of the century, when all was set for expansion, even the severe panics of 1793 and 1797 did little more than halt for a few months the upward rush of industry and trade. The process of creating credit was closely bound up with investment, in the sense of the purchase of paper titles to wealth and also in that of the creation of capital goods; and after each crisis there was a lull in the process. But this is a topic on which sufficient has already been said in Chapter 4.

[84] William Playfair, *Better Prospects to the Merchants and Manufacturers of Great Britain* (1793), p. 8.

6

CONCLUSIONS

I

THE fluctuation in the diverse parts of the economy did not always coincide. It was not only the smugglers and highwaymen whose numbers increased as employment languished elsewhere: the same was true of those in several, well-respected occupations. Most women knew how to spin (ignorance of the art was almost a social disgrace), and when times were hard many who were normally maintained by their menfolk joined the ranks of the wage-earners —with disastrous effects on the earnings of the regular spinners. The fishing industry, like hand-loom weaving in the nineteenth century, was one of the last resorts of the poor: only under pressure of want would men face the hardships of life at sea in small boats. Hence it was (as Mrs. Schumpeter pointed out) that English exports of fish rose in times of distress and declined in times of prosperity.[1] When trade was bad the number of itinerant salesmen increased: one of the compensations for the slump in the cotton industry in the late eighties was that 'it called into employment a vast number of hawkers of muslins, &c., who, by dint of low prices, diffused a taste for these goods in the remotest villages of the country'.[2]

More important than any of these were the movements in the constructional industries. For here, as with all durable goods, the annual output was small compared with the stock already in existence. An increased demand of 5 per cent. for houses or ships might mean a 50 per cent. increase in the demand for new ones; and hence the fluctuations in output were much wider than in those for immediately consumable goods. Construction sometimes varied inversely with exports (if only because when the export industries were slack more productive resources were available to builders and contractors). And this 'anti-cyclical' behaviour had the effect of making the economy less unstable than its parts—just as, to borrow a simile

[1] Elizabeth B. Schumpeter, *Trade Statistics and Cycles in England, 1697–1825* (thesis), p. 231.   [2] Macpherson, op. cit. iv. 134.

from the bimetallists of the nineteenth century, two tipsy men link-ing arms are likely to keep a steadier course than if each walks alone.

Some sections of the economy were slower than others in their response to stimulus or pressure. Re-exports were always quick off the mark: the movement of English exports came some months later. An increased demand for textile goods showed itself first in spinning, then in weaving, and lastly in fulling, bleaching, and dyeing. The annual figures of output of linen in Scotland (and, for the short periods for which they are available, in England) show rises and falls in advance of those of printed goods. But again it was in the constructional industries that the lag was most pronounced. Some time must have elapsed before a growth of prosperity gave rise to new demands for houses, ships, docks, roads, and canals; entrepreneurs would need to be assured that the improvement was more than a flash in the pan before they embarked on schemes involving heavy expenditure;[3] and some plans requiring Parliamen-tary sanction might be held up for months, or even years, at West-minster. In any case, the period between inception and completion of a project was necessarily a long one; and hence if employment was slow to expand it was also slow to contract. The existence of lags tended to make short-period changes in the economy less jerky and more cyclical than in individual industries.

Unfortunately there is no satisfactory index, such as a sensitive quarterly price series, to which one might appeal to substantiate this last statement. The upward and downward swings in overseas trade show irregularities introduced by political incidents. There are no figures representative of the internal trade of the country—but those in Table 22, of sales of goods and property by auction, show a high degree of continuity of movement. All that can be said is that the less specific the nature of the data—the closer a series comes to representing activity in the country as a whole—the fewer the departures from the wave-like movement. Differences in the accounting periods make it impossible to demonstrate the existence of general tendencies by presenting the various series in the form of graphs on the same diagram. If we wish to measure the fluctuations

---

[3] The lag in decision-making is stressed by Dr. Ralph Davis, op. cit., p. 337. Dr. Davis makes the further point that 'when the proportion of investment goods has itself become a very high proportion of total business activity, then the time-lag of investment indices behind an index of general activity may disappear or become negligible'.

and determine the points at which depression gave way to rising
activity, prosperity to boom, and crisis to slump, we must do so
by fumbling with material already considered and making judge-
ments of the extent to which the various influences reinforced or
offset one another. The following narrative will offer new illustrations relating to work and wages, about which little has so far been
said. But some repetition is unavoidable. In accordance with common practice, a fluctuation is taken to be the movement between
one depression and the next, not between peak and peak.

II

The seventeenth century had ended in gloom. Trade with Flanders
had been cut off, and unemployment, falling wages, and rising poor-
rates were reported from several industrial centres. In these circumstances Parliament had taken steps to remove one grievance of the
woollen manufacturers by prohibiting the wearing of Oriental silks
and printed calicoes, and another by abolishing the export duties
on woollen fabrics. These reliefs, together with an abundant
harvest, may explain why, in spite of a financial crisis in January,
the first year of the new century should have been marked by the
high activity reflected in the figures of exports, the consumption of
beer and spirits, and imports of coal into London. With the outbreak of war in the following year, however, there was a sharp
downward turn. In the textile areas of the west employers were
complaining of the embezzlement of materials, and workers of
payment of wages in truck. Such evils were endemic in eighteenth-
century industry, but they tended to increase in hard times; and the
fact that the government passed measures against both implies that
conditions were especially bad in 1702. The first fluctuation to be
distinguished was thus an extremely short one.[4]

The next two years saw a revival of exports, imports of timber,
and shipments of coal. Good harvests led to high outputs of malt,
beer, and spirits; and enlistment in the forces must have tended to
keep unemployment low. But military reverses on the Continent
and a financial crisis in the autumn of 1704 brought a set-back
which is reflected in a fall of exports and a high level of bankruptcies; and, since at this time the costs of the war were met almost
wholly by taxation, little or no alleviation was afforded by deficit
expenditure. The year 1705 saw a return of general depression.

⁴ Wadsworth and Mann, op. cit., pp. 89, 132.

Improvement began in 1706. The yields of both arable and grass-land farming were high; the Union with Scotland in 1707 widened the area of domestic trade; and growing government expenditure, financed by loans, also tended to increase the demand for goods and labour. High prices of wool and expanding exports of fabrics point to prosperity in the leading industry.[5] Rates of interest were low and building and construction active. Heavy imports of raw cotton and other materials, together with a brisk market for securities, suggest that a boom was well under way in 1707–8. The relatively poor harvest of 1708 and the almost complete failure of that of 1709 brought depression to industries dependent on grain, and reduced the volume of exports;[6] but they did not prevent continued speculation in stocks, and the appearance of a boom in the promotion of joint-stock companies, in the early months of 1710. Large shipments on government account brought exports (and the employment of merchant seamen) to a peak in this year; but, partly because of the previous bad harvests, and partly because of rising expenditure on the war in Europe, the balance of payments must have moved against Britain. Large outward shipments of bullion, reinforced by an internal drain of currency, put a strain on the Bank; and political tension in the summer and autumn turned financial stringency to panic.

The two years from the summer of 1710 to that of 1712 must have been among the worst of the century. The scarcity of bread continued, and the output of beer (though not of spirits) fell to low figures. A sharp decline of imports of timber in 1710 and 1711 suggests depression in building. It was probably shortage of work that led to a strike of the London stocking-makers against the employment of workhouse children in 1710; there was severe depression in the cutlery trade of Sheffield in 1711; and the sailors on the collier vessels were reduced to such straits that, it was said, they could not so much as feed their families on bread and water.[7] Evidence of the poor state of the woollen industry is afforded by the

[5] It is suggested also by the building of cloth halls in the West Riding: at Halifax in 1708 and at Wakefield in 1710. The cloth hall at Leeds was not opened till 1711, when depression had set in, but it was probably begun earlier.
[6] The number of seamen's sixpences collected also indicates a recession of overseas trade in 1708–9.
[7] Paul Mantoux, *The Industrial Revolution in the Eighteenth Century*, p. 82; R. B. Leader, *History of the Sheffield Cutlery Company*, i. 68; Edward Hughes, op. cit., p. 161.

fall of exports of woollens and worsteds in 1711 and by the low price of wool at the August sales in the following year: it was partly, no doubt, for reasons of revenue, but partly also to relieve distress in the woollen areas, that an excise duty was laid on printed linens and calicoes and a customs duty on foreign striped linen. In *1711* high deficit expenditure may have done something to mitigate depression; but in the following year, when, so far as Britain was concerned, the war was virtually over, the excess of expenditure over ordinary revenue was small.[8] The decline of exports of woollens in 1712 was probably connected with reduced shipments to the forces; as early as June some 400 men were dismissed from the government establishments at Deptford and Woolwich,[9] and demobilization—100,000 men were involved—had probably begun. Between 1706 and 1712 economic life had run through the successive phases of recovery, prosperity, boom, crisis, and depression. How far the fluctuation was 'autonomous' and how far the result of operations of the state it is impossible to say.

The Treaty of Utrecht was signed in March 1713, but the failure of the attempt to negotiate a treaty of commerce with France, and a continuance of war in Spain, impeded recovery. It is true that there was an increase of exports and that the number of seamen in English merchant vessels rose sharply. But it was not until 1714 that the post-war peak in overseas trade was reached. Several series speak of rising activity this year. But the political uncertainties that followed the death of Queen Anne in August, the disturbances that led to the Riot Act, and the outbreak of the rebellion, in 1715, were all unfavourable to enterprise. A doubling of the excise duty may explain the fall in the output of printed goods in *1715*, and the hard frost of the following winter, which lasted for three months, may have had something to do with a decline in the output of paper; but it was the financial crisis of 1715 that was responsible for the general depression which extended into the early months of 1716. Politics had determined that the fluctuation should be short.

With a clearing of the political situation and a restoration of credit, industry and commerce again expanded. Overseas trade mounted in 1717; there was an upward turn in the price of wool, the output of printed goods and paper, and shipments of coal; and in spite of the fact that the harvest had been only moderately good,

---

[8] The decline was from £10 million in *1711* to £2·1 million in *1712*.

[9] *Supra*, p. 72.

the consumption of beer and spirits rose sharply. As both cause and effect of the conversion of the public debt, market rates of interest were low; and that the building industry responded is shown by the rising imports of timber. The prosperity continued during the first half of 1718: in the summer the price of wool rose from the already high figure of 23s. to 27s.

The outbreak of war with Spain in August 1718 struck a blow at the export trades, and the textile industries entered on a period of decline. The Spitalfield weavers were said to be 'in a starving condition' and there was severe distress among the woollen workers at Norwich.[10] On the other hand, the trades dependent on agriculture continued to prosper; the war gave a stimulus to the production of iron; money remained cheap; imports of timber increased, and building progressed. Encouraged by rising prices of securities, a speculative movement developed, and schemes were launched for the improvement of rivers and the construction of docks, as well as for many astonishingly foolish purposes. All this makes it impossible to think of the years 1718–20 as a time of general depression. When, however, in the summer of 1720 the South Sea boom collapsed the demand for liquidity brought a sharp contraction of industry and trade of all kinds. Employment in the merchant service declined and remained low in the following year; and conditions in the woollen industry went from bad to worse. Once again the woollen and silk workers attributed their miseries to the competition of printed fabrics, and engaged in rioting and 'calico-chasing';[11] and in 1721 the government took drastic action and, by what came to be known as the Calico Act, prohibited the manufacture or wear of the obnoxious fabrics.[12]

The period from the spring of 1716 to the end of 1721 had thus seen an upward swing of general activity; then depression in one section of the economy, offset by prosperity in others; a mania of speculation; a crisis; and finally universal stagnation and distress.

Peace and abundant harvests brought a return of prosperity in 1722. Exports of English manufactures moved upward and (after a recession in 1723) mounted rapidly. The production of printed goods doubled in 1723. Imports of timber expanded, and there is abundant evidence of great activity in building in 1724–5. If the prices of wool remained low the reason is probably to be found in

[10] M. D. George, op. cit., p. 193.
[11] Wadsworth and Mann, op. cit., p. 134.   [12] 7 Geo. I, c. 7.

conditions of supply rather than of demand; for exports of woollen goods reached an exceptionally high level in 1725. Employment in the merchant service was well maintained, and here again a peak was reached in 1725. The prosperity of the workers in the neighbourhood of Lancaster is attested by William Stout, who notes in his autobiography that in 1723 corn was cheap and 'our linen manufactory and spinning [being] at good prices, the poor subsisted well', and that in 1725 the demand for linens and cottons and the wages paid for spinning were high. The same observer supports the belief that in this year the growing activity culminated in a boom; for he remarks on the rise in the price of materials—including raw cotton, iron ore, charcoal, and bar-iron—used in the chief local industries.[13] If the movement was general it may have been the principal cause of an external drain of gold and silver which, coinciding, as it did, with a rising demand for cash to meet the needs of the home trade, brought the Bank's ratio down from 36·6 in 1724 to 20·7 in 1725.

Most of the excise series show increases of output in *1726*, but, on the other hand, exports decreased in the calendar year that overlaps this, and there was also a decline of imports of timber. It seems probable, therefore, that the prosperity came to an end in the second half of 1726, and that the crisis arising from the outbreak of war with Spain was the turning-point. Employment in the mercantile marine ebbed, and there are signs of a low demand for labour elsewhere. There were strikes or lock-outs in Gloucestershire in 1727, and the passing of an Act prescribing the death penalty for the destruction of machinery implies that these had been marked by violence. Deficient harvests added to the distress. According to Stout, in 1728 the linen industry about Lancaster was 'very low' and the wages of the spinners were reduced by a third. The wave that had reared itself from the trough of 1721 was spent.

The year 1728 saw some improvement. With the restoration of peace in March there was a partial recovery of overseas trade and shipping; and, as a result of the conversion of debt (in 1727), and perhaps of the low demand for capital in some parts of the economy, money was cheap. It is not surprising, therefore, to read of 'a great advance in purchase of lands', as well as of a rising demand of landlords and farmers for servants, so that the wages of these were raised by as much as 20s. a year.[14] There was some opening up of

---

[13] Stout, op. cit., pp. 102, 107.　　　　　　　[14] Ibid., p. 110.

new mines; and a sharp rise of imports of timber implies a recovery of enterprise in building. The revival, however, was not sustained; and whether because of the poor harvest, the renewal of tension with Spain, or some other malign influence, 1729 seems to have seen a return of depression. There was a downward movement of output in trades dependent on agriculture, as well as of exports and employment of sailors. In Lancaster the poor-rate was doubled, and a workhouse was opened so that the poor could be maintained 'without going a begging'.[15] It looks as though the improvement of 1728 had been due to passing circumstances and not to any fundamental economic change.

During the next four years the upward movement was unbroken. In 1730 the volume of goods sent abroad increased sharply, and a high price of wool at the August sales also implies activity in the most important export industry.[16] Stout observes that the manufactures of linen, wool, and iron were doing well, and that the wages of spinners were raised by a quarter. His reports on the next three years are to the same effect: in 1731 spinning is 'at its highest'; in 1732 'the labouring people lived well'; and in 1733, 'though the low price of grain went hard with poor farmers and broke many and lessened the rent of lands', all the local industries were thriving and 'great wages were paid to spinners and other labouring people'.[17] The output of nearly everything subject to the eye of the excise officers was rising; exports increased; and relatively high imports of timber indicate at least moderate activity in building. There are scraps of evidence that prosperity again bred speculation; and the expansion of credit was sufficiently great for news of the outbreak of the War of the Polish Succession to bring about at least a minor financial crisis. In 1734 some of the indices—exports, the price of wool, imports, employment in ships and so on—point to recession. The undulation was contained within a period of four to five years.

Between 1734 and 1738 harvests were abundant, and both imports of timber and exports of English manufactures high. There were, it is true, temporary set-backs. A slight fall in the sales of beer in 1735–6 may be explained by a transfer of demand to spirits, the production of which soared at this time. A decline in the figures for

---

[15] Ibid., p. 116.
[16] Widespread foot-rot in the flocks may also have helped to raise the price of wool at this time.
[17] Stout, op. cit., pp. 120, 121, 123.

printed goods in *1736* was due to a reopening of the fustian contro-
versy: once it was determined by the Manchester Act that fustians
were not covered by the prohibitory clauses of the Calico Act of
1721, output resumed its upward trend. There were riots in Spitalfields against undercutting by Irish weavers in 1736, and others in
the south-west against exports of grain in the following year.[18]
Some slackness appeared in the woollen industry of Wiltshire in
1737, owing to French competition in the markets of the Levant;[19]
and an epidemic of colds and fever—probably influenza—may
have reduced industrial activity in the country generally. But all
these were minor affairs. If farmers and landlords continued to
grumble at continued low prices they found some compensation
in large, subsidized, exports of grain; and the prosperity of the
workers is attested by an increase in the output of beer and by high
sales of cattle and sheep at Smithfield.

In November 1737 reports came in of fighting between British
and Spanish merchantmen in the West Indies;[20] and an outbreak
of rioting against a proposed reduction of weavers' wages in the
south-west was a symptom of lowered sales of cloth overseas in
1738.[21] In November of the following year there was a renewal of
disorders at Spitalfields and a 'mutiny' of the workmen at Woolwich.[22] The declaration of war in December, coinciding as it did
with the beginning of the great frost, marked the end of the prosperity of the thirties.

The years 1740 and 1741 saw widespread distress. To the dearth
of grain resulting from the failure of the harvest was added a shortage of cattle products, including candles and soap. Exports and
employment in shipping declined. There was a slump in textiles of
all kinds, and a London warehouseman told those who normally
supplied him that they had better wear their cloths themselves.[23]
According to Stout, the wages of spinners fell from 7*d.* to 5*d.*—at
a time when the cost of living had soared. In February 1741 it was
reported that 'at Spittle-fields, and in divers parts of the Isle the

[18] *Cal. Treasury Papers* (1735–8), p. 341; Rowe, op. cit., pp. 33–34; George,
op. cit., p. 180.
[19] I am indebted to Miss Mann for information about this.
[20] Macpherson, op. cit. iii. 215.
[21] Wadsworth and Mann, op. cit., p. 357; *Gentleman's Magazine* (1739),
pp. 123–5, 205.
[22] Ibid., p. 602.
[23] Ibid. (Dec. 1741).

manufacturers are starving by thousands for want of work'.[24] Bankruptcies increased and gold and silver piled up in the Bank. The only outlet for unemployed men was in the forces. The only sign of energy was that of the rioters who burnt down mills and attacked corn dealers and bakers. And, apart from workhouses, almost the only new constructive enterprise of which mention is made in the annals is, significantly, a burial club, set up by the sail-makers of London.[25] The wave that had begun its upward course in 1734, and had reached its crest in 1738, was in full reflux.

Most of the series point to recovery in 1741 and 1742. It is true that, in consequence of the heavy losses of sheep in the great frost, the production of soap and candles remained low. But the harvests were abundant, and the production of beer, spirits, and other products of grain recovered. The figures of cloth milled in the West Riding were well above those of the prosperous years of the late thirties, and exports were at a reasonably high level. Everything points to general prosperity in 1743. A rise in exports to a figure higher than any previously recorded was due partly to government shipments, partly to purchases by the French of woollens for their armies, and partly to the building up of stocks by foreign merchants in anticipation of an extension of the war.[26] There was a similar increase in the volume of re-exports, as well as in the number of seamen in English ships. High industrial activity is reflected in a sharp rise in the price of raw wool and a leap in the figures of broad cloth. The demand for munitions led to a great bustle at the arsenals; and among the bits of evidence that conditions were favourable to labour is the report of the *Gentleman's Magazine* of 28 February 1744 that 'A mob of nailers consisting of several thousands . . . got together in Staffordshire in order to raise their wages'.

With the formal beginning of war in 1744, however, the prosperity came to an end. There was a drop of more than £2 million in total exports, and employment in shipping was lower than in any year since 1726. 'A terrible summer' for the coal trade was followed by a lowering of prices or an advance of measure: it was, said Mathew Ridley, 'the worst year I ever saw'.[27] The 'forty-five and

[24] Ibid. (Feb. 1741).
[25] Sidney Pollard, *The Economic History of British Shipbuilding, 1870–1914* (thesis submitted for the Degree of Ph.D. in the University of London, 1951), p. 146.   [26] Smith, *Chronicum Rusticum*, ii. 769.
[27] Hughes, op. cit., pp. 85, 247.

the crisis that accompanied it brought a decline of the circulation, a fall of prices, and a drop in the output of most commodities, including leather, paper, and printed calicoes.[28] With the restoration of confidence, in 1746, there was a sharp increase of English exports and employment in shipping; but perhaps because hopes of an early peace were frustrated (and perhaps because of a serious outbreak of smallpox)[29] the following year was one of low activity. Overseas trade declined; there was a drastic fall in the receipts of seamen's sixpences; and if the circumstances of the builders improved, the cattle disease (which had broken out in 1745) brought losses to many farmers and others. The period from 1744 to 1748 is to be thought of as one of depression engendered by war, broken only by a single brief spurt of activity in 1746.

Between 1748 and 1751 a strong upward movement developed. The reopening of markets abroad brought prosperity to the staple export industries; and since, in the first two of those years, government expenditure by deficit finance was actually above the wartime level, there arose a brisk demand for consumers' goods at home. Following a reduction of duties on the import of raw silk, several new mills were set up in Cheshire; and low rates of interest stimulated investment in sugar refineries in London and the outports.[30] There are signs of speculation in commodities in 1750–1; but the boom—if boom it was—seems to have died down rather than to have been cut short by crisis. English exports fell off in 1751–2 and at the same time there was a halt in the production of most consumers' goods, including (though this was a result of legislation) gin. A drastic fall in the price of wool was recorded at Sturbridge Fair in 1752, 'trade being so bad in the clothing counties';[31] the woolcombers at Norwich, threatened by a reduction of wages, left the town 'and betook themselves to a kind of Aventine at Rockheath'.[32] The fall in the demand for woollens and for consumers' goods in general was accentuated by the ending of deficit financing[33] and by the poverty of the harvest of 1753, which led to

[28] The price of wool fell from 21s. to 16s. 6d. in 1745. In the same year that of sugar declined by 10s. or 12s. a cwt. Pares, loc. cit., pp. 264–5.

[29] It was 'one of the worst years of the century for deaths from this cause' in London and Leeds. See *Thoresby Miscellany*, vol. xli, pt. 2, p. 161.

[30] George, op. cit., p. 185 n.

[31] *Gentleman's Magazine* (30 Sept. 1752), p. 430.

[32] Mantoux, op. cit., p. 80 n.; *Gentleman's Magazine* (1752), p. 476.

[33] There was a surplus of income over expenditure of £1·4 million in 1753.

widespread riots. In 1754 most of the indices tell of continued depression.

By this time figures of the output of glass are available. If we may take these, together with the returns of imports of timber, as a guide, building and construction had not shared fully in the expansion of investment of the early years of the peace. But cheap money, associated with Pelham's conversion of the public debt, led to important developments from 1751 onward. The turnpike principle was applied to old roads, and new highways were constructed. Imports of timber soared in 1752–3, and the production of glass increased by a third between 1752 and 1754.[34] The growth of employment in building at this time must have done much to offset the effects of the fall of overseas trade and the replacement of a deficit by a large surplus in government finance.

The overall movement from 1748 to 1754 is thus one of increasing liveliness for four years, culminating in high prosperity, if not in boom, and followed by a depression, though this was less deep than some of its predecessors by reason of continued investment in building and public works.

Already in 1754 news had been received of fighting between British and French settlers in America, and this may have had, at first, a dampening influence. But, paradoxical as it may appear, as prospects of a new war with France became stronger conditions began to improve. It may be simply that the depression had lasted long enough for there to be a need for merchants to replenish stocks, but it may also be that government demands for stores aided the revival. There was a remarkable increase in the number of men and boys in English ships in 1755; and in spite of a failure of the harvest and many food riots, the improvement of output continued. Exports increased in 1756. 'Trade is very brisk here', wrote Jedediah Strutt of Nottingham early in the following year;[35] and that the prosperity was not confined to the hosiery industry is shown by a rise in the price of wool, an increased output of glass and printed goods, and a further slight growth of exports. With better harvests the pace of advance steepened. Between 1758 and 1761 exports rose to an entirely new level. Employment in shipping was good; and figures

[34] The output of stained paper, which had been rising from 1747, reached a peak in 1753.
[35] I thank Dr. R. S. Fitton for this extract from a letter of April 1757, written from Alfreton to Mrs. Strutt in London.

of the production of glass, greater than any previously recorded, point to an advance of building. As has been seen, large public works were initiated at this time; and, perhaps because the success of British arms went to men's heads, grandiose schemes were concerted for the exploitation of far parts of the earth. Rising prices of commodities and securities, and high imports of cotton and other materials, suggest conditions of boom in 1761. There are many indications that the prosperity extended to the wage-earners. In 1759 it was reported that the check-weavers of Manchester 'were never in better humour in their lives'; their pieces were shortened, their wages raised . . . provisions are plenty, and work enough to be had'. At Liverpool, the wages of the cabinet-makers were raised by 2s.[36] In 1760 Matthew Boulton complained that the iron-chape-makers of Birmingham had entered into combinations and declared they would raise the price of their work by 3s. in the £.[37] In 1761 the London cabinet-makers were indicted for having combined to raise wages and shorten their hours of work, and there were similar reports of this 'growing evil' among the shoe-makers, tailors, and peruke-makers.[38] Even the Irish harvesters, at Kings Langley and in the Isle of Ely, were at odds with the farmers about wages.[39] Among other statistical evidences of prosperity was a marked rise in the number of christenings in London.[40]

Heavy government expenditure overseas and the rise of prices and wages at home put pressure on the exchanges, and there may have been some restriction of credit. The textile areas seem to have been the first to suffer: at the end of April the manufacture of woollen stuffs at Tiverton suddenly ceased.[41] In May the celebrated merchant, financier, and adventurer, Samuel Touchet, stopped payment. It looks as though economic forces alone had brought the boom to an end. But it was the alarming news of the Family Compact between France and Spain that precipitated the general crisis in August. The result can be seen not only in the statistics of finance —the upward movement of exchange rates, the fall in the prices of securities, and the drop in the Bank's ratio—but also in the fall of the price of wool, and a general decline of production. In *1761* the output of printed goods was 6·88 million yards: in *1762* it fell to

[36] Wadsworth and Mann, op. cit., pp. 369, 377.
[37] *J.H.C.* xxviii. 882.   [38] George, op. cit., p. 368 n.
[39] *Annual Register*, 8 Aug. 1761.
[40] From 14,951 in 1760 to 16,000 in 1761.
[41] Dunsford, op. cit., p. 244.

5·62 million yards. Similar, if less steep, decreases occurred in the manufacture of paper and glass—and presumably in the volume of building. In 1762 English exports declined by £1·4 million, and there was a marked fall of employment at sea.

The distresses were intensified by adverse weather. The 'unparalleled drought' of the summer of 1762, with a consequent shortage of hay, led to a scarcity of meat, butter, and cheese. The fields of oats had been scorched, so that the price of meal, the staple of Lancashire diet, rose steeply; and in July the colliers of Oldham and Saddleworth marched into Manchester to vent their rage on the millers.[42] Later in the year, in December, an intense frost which lasted five weeks put a stop to operations in agriculture, manufacture, and inland navigation over wide areas.[43] The depression was at its lowest point in the last months of 1762 and the first months of 1763.

Preliminaries of peace were signed at Fontainebleau on 3 November 1762, and the definitive treaty was concluded at Paris on 10 February 1763. As after the War of the Spanish Succession, the first year of the peace was, at best, one of moderate prosperity. It is true that re-exports were extraordinarily high, and the number of men in the shipping industry registered a peak. But the war had given rise to inflation, and, though the crisis of 1761 had done something to reduce the volume of credit, there was a marked premium on gold: in May 'the Jews' (i.e. the bullion merchants) were paying as much as four guineas an ounce for coin the par value of which was £3. 18s. 6d.[44] The reserves of the Bank were being drained. As has been seen, the crisis of July 1763 was not so much of British as of continental origin,[45] but it was followed by deflation and depression here. Industries that had supplied the needs of the forces—those concerned with linen and iron especially—were seriously depressed; and the ending of war-time protection to the silk trade resulted, in October, in riots and destruction of machinery at

[42] *Gentleman's Magazine* (July 1762), p. 340; *S.P. Dom. Geo. II* (1757), p. 178.

[43] *Annual Register*, 26 Dec. 1762.

[44] *Gentleman's Magazine* (30 May 1763), p. 256.

[45] According to George Chalmers (op. cit., p. 141), however, speculation in American land was an important factor. 'Every man, who had credit with the ministers at home, or influence over the governors in the colonies, ran for the prize of American territory . . . millions of productive capital were withdrawn from the agriculture and manufacture and trade of Great Britain to cultivate the ceded islands, in the other hemisphere.'

Spitalfields.[46] The government sought to ease the lot of the disbanded sailors and soldiers by an Act permitting them to set up in every corporation in the kingdom; but large numbers must have remained unemployed. We may set the terminal date of the fluctuation that began in 1755 at the autumn of 1763.

The year 1764 saw general prosperity. The previous harvest had been good, and though the prices of meat and dairy produce were high, the poorer classes had a margin for expenditure on other things. The figures of production of beer, starch, candles, soap, and printed calicoes give evidence of rising consumption; those of glass point to a high level of investment in building. A rise of over £2 million in shipments of English goods implies activity in the export industries; and the high prices of stocks, and the large number of patents taken out, reflect confidence and enterprise. But, as with most post-war booms, there was a speedy reaction; the following year saw the beginning of a depression that dragged on for the rest of the decade. Some industries that had expanded during the war, and had managed to keep going during the boom, now found themselves with redundant labour and equipment. A war-time shortage of workers on the coalfields had led to high wages and binding fees; and the attempt made by the coal owners to alter the conditions of hiring, now that pitmen were easier to come by, brought extensive disorders in Northumberland and Durham.[47] Between August and October 1765 the trade of the northern ports was paralysed, and thousands of keelmen, sailors, and distributors of coal were put 'out of bread'. The pitched battles that came a little later between the sailors and coal-heavers of the Thames were part of a struggle for employment between rival groups, and the same was true of the quarrel between the 'engine-weavers' and the 'single-handed loom weavers', as well as between men and women workers, in Spitalfields.[48] The iron industry was short of orders: it was in order to keep its men in work that, in 1767, the Coalbrookdale Company turned to the making of rails for its own wagon-ways.[49] It is difficult to make an assessment of the state of the woollen industry. A rise in the price of wool in 1766–7 may have been due to heavy losses of sheep rather than to any rise in the demand for cloth. The figures of the output of milled cloth in the West Riding

[46] *Annual Register*, 3 Oct. 1763.   [47] Ashton and Sykes, op. cit., p. 90.
[48] *Annual Register*, 10 Jan. 1765, 30 Nov. 1767; George, op. cit., pp. 181–2.
[49] Ashton, *Iron and Steel in the Industrial Revolution*, p. 134.

jumped to an entirely new level in 1766; but this was due to the reformed system of supervision and measurement, and it would be unwise to place much reliance on the figures for the next two or three years. Something may be gathered from the statistics of the drawbacks of duty on soap used in the woollen industry of England and Wales: they show a decline from 1764 to 1767 and after that some recovery. There are indications, however, of low prices of cloth in Gloucestershire in 1768–9, and of falling wages elsewhere.[50]

Among the reasons for continued depression was the high price of food. In the earlier years the chief complaint was of a shortage of meat and dairy produce. At Michaelmas 1765 the price of milk in London was raised from 1½d. to 2d. a quart, and in the following year cheese at Sturbridge market was 'dearer than ever known'.[51] Bad weather played a part. In February 1766 large numbers of sheep were drowned, and floods prevented the wagons laden with pork, veal, and other provisions from reaching the market at Newgate. The drought of the following summer had serious effects on the herds; between 1766 and 1768 the number of cattle and sheep brought to Smithfield was exceptionally low; and the shortage of hides led to a rise in the price of leather, from 9s. 6d. in the first of these years to 14s. 6d. in the second.[52] It was, however, the increase in the price of grain that was of most concern to the industrial classes. The harvest of 1764 was the first of a series that gave poor yields of wheat and oats. In 1766 and 1767 the deficiency was such that the government prohibited the use of grain by distillers, laid an embargo on the export of corn, and allowed foreign wheat to come in free of duty. Food riots were widespread in both these years and continued into 1768: it was not until 1769 that the price of bread came down to normal. As usual, dear bread was associated with a low demand for labour. In June 1768 a Painswick clothier announced that he must part with his spinners, adding 'What they will do I cannot tell, I fear they will not find employ elsewhere.'[53]

At the same time there was a depression in overseas trade, and especially in that with America, where, in reprisal for the attempts of the British government to raise revenue and assert its authority in other ways, the colonists instituted boycotts of British goods. The

---

[50] E. A. L. Moir, 'The Gentleman Clothiers' in H. P. R. Finberg, *Gloucestershire Studies*, pp. 225–66.

[51] *Annual Register*, Sept. 1765.

[52] *Supra*, p. 39.

[53] Moir, loc. cit., p. 248.

following figures of shipments to New England, New York, Pennsylvania, Maryland, Virginia, the Carolinas, and Georgia reflect the effects of the economic war:

1764	1765	1766	1767	1768	1769
		(in £ million)			
2·49	1·94	1·80	1·90	2·16	1·34

The decline in 1765 was part of a reaction—common to all overseas markets—from the post-war boom; but it was intensified and prolonged by the organized opposition to the Stamp Act and other measures. With the adoption of a more conciliatory attitude by Britain and the calling off of the boycott, things improved in 1768; but retaliation against the Townshend duties brought the American trade to a very low point in 1769. The consequences for employment in England were serious. In 1765, according to Samuel Garbett, some thousands of artificers in Birmingham and the surrounding district were suffering from want of remittances from America.[54] In February of the following year another merchant said that, owing to the countermanding of orders, 300 of his workers were unemployed; and in the same month the cutlers of Sheffield complained of the decay of their trade with North America.[55] Similar instances of depression arising from the same cause could be offered for the succeeding years. It may be suggested, however, that some historians, their eyes on later events, have tended to overstress the influence of the colonial struggle on English exports in the sixties. Even more serious was the downward trend of shipments to Germany (from £2·4 million in 1764 to £1·3 million in 1769) and, at the end of the decade, to Spain and Portugal. But for the expansion of trade across the Irish Channel, the slump in several English industries must have been severe indeed.

The chief support for employment in these years came from building and public works. A reduced demand for capital by the export industries may have been one reason for the low rates of

---

[54] Ashton, *Iron and Steel in the Industrial Revolution*, p. 132. On 24 Feb. 1766 the *Annual Register* reported that upwards of 3,000 letters had been sent from the General Post Office in Lombard Street on the previous Saturday night by merchants anxious that their correspondents should know that a Bill to repeal the Stamp Act had been brought in. The bells in most of the churches rang from morning till night.

[55] *J.H.C.*, vol. xxx, 27 Feb. 1766. 'Nor can I get out of my head the present stop to all sorts of trade in these parts', wrote Richard Whitworth, the engineer, in November. J. Phillips, *Inland Navigation*, p. 128.

interest that were a condition of expansion here; and the release of able-bodied men from the army may have provided a large part of the labour force. However that may be, from the first year of the peace there was a marked upward movement of import of timber and output of glass and stained paper; and the verbal, no less than the statistical, evidence is eloquent of the energy given to 'improvement'. Never before, and rarely since, can so high a proportion of English workers have been engaged in constructing roads, cutting canals, making docks, and extending and rebuilding the towns. The rising demand of those engaged in the production of capital goods must have provided at least partial compensation for the declining demand of workers in the export trades. And hence, except in the dearth of 1766–7, employment in the consumers' goods industries seems to have been maintained. Nevertheless, the evidence of social unrest and distress is sufficient to justify our regarding the period from 1765 to 1769 as one of depression.

From 1769 to 1774 the story is different. In the first of these years the volume of English exports was the lowest recorded for more than a decade. But the output of consumers' goods as a whole was high; there had been a remarkable expansion of production of printed goods and starch in the excise year 1769; and there is verbal evidence of rising demand elsewhere. Writing to Bentley on 30 September, Josiah Wedgwood refers to the shortage of labour for his pottery works at Burslem and Etruria: 'Hire more you say. Aye, but trade is as good with others as ourselves, allmost everybody wants hands.'[56] Largely because of the ending of non-importation in America, overseas trade recovered in 1770, rose outstandingly in the following year, and, it would seem, remained at a high level for at least the first half of 1772. From the end of the sixties it is possible to place reliance on the statistics of the fulling mills in the West Riding. The production of broad cloth (four-fifths of which was sold abroad) increased from 2·7 million yards in 1769 to 3·6 million yards in 1772. Other series also tell of great activity in this year: printed goods show a rise from 8·74 million yards in 1771 to 9·17 in 1772. At the same time the output of copper in Cornwall touched a point not to be reached again until the late eighties. The decline in the production of glass, which had continued for three years, was reversed: a sharp rise in 1722 implies a revival of building. The development of public works, many instances of which can

[56] Wedgwood, *Letters*, i. 295.

be found in England, was especially marked over the border, in Scotland, where large schemes, including the building of New Edinburgh and the digging of two great canals, put a strain on resources of capital and labour. In 1770 the proprietors of the Forth and Clyde Canal complained that the Monkland Company was enticing away its skilled workers; and on the Monkland itself the contractors of different sections were similarly poaching on each other's labour.[57]

The upswing of trade and investment stimulated, and was stimulated by, a creation of many private banks in the provinces and an expansion of the issues of notes and bills. There was a sharp rise in the circulation of the Bank of England in 1771—and an equally sharp fall in the bullion reserve in the following year. A stock-exchange boom in Amsterdam and Hamburg encouraged dealings in securities in London; and that speculation extended to commodity markets is suggested by the excessive prices of raw cotton, wool, and other materials.[58]

Sooner or later the drain of specie—external and internal—must have enforced a restriction of credit and brought the boom to an end. But, in fact, a whole series of untoward events conspired to this end. Early in 1771 the price of food, especially oatmeal, moved upward: at Derby the framework-knitters were given higher wages to meet the rising cost of living.[59] The harvest of the following year was seriously deficient, and the ravaging of Poland by the neighbouring powers cut off supplies of corn and cattle from western Europe. There was war between Russia and Turkey. A crisis had developed in the affairs of the East India Company, which was heavily indebted to the Bank.[60] Above all, the situation in America was deteriorating.

In the spring of 1772, when the turmoil in Europe raised doubts about the financial stability of Amsterdam, the Bank of England discontinued its discounts to firms with Dutch connexions. At this

[57] Hamilton, op. cit., p. 415.
[58] The price of wool was, it was said, the highest recorded between 1741 and 1790. *Penny Encyclopaedia* (1843), p. 549. I thank Dr. Max Hartwell for this reference. The rise in the price of cotton was attributed to the manipulations of a group of dealers in Manchester. Wadsworth and Mann, op. cit., p. 234.
[59] *Derby Mercury*, 12 July 1771. I am indebted to Dr. R. S. Fitton for this reference.
[60] L. S. Sutherland, *The East India Company in 18th Century Politics*, p. 223.

time Scotland was the most vulnerable part of the British economy. The prohibition of the issue of small notes by the Scottish banks in 1766 was, no doubt, desirable in itself, but it had resulted in a great increase of commercial paper, including accommodation bills. When the Bank applied to houses associated with Scotland the same policy as to those connected with Holland, credit collapsed; and the panic spread rapidly to England. The shortage of currency was such that many concerns, in Lancashire and Yorkshire in particular, were obliged to pay wages in notes they themselves created. Manufacturers of repute, like Matthew Boulton, John Roebuck, and Henry Thrale, were in difficulties.[61] According to Boulton, the trade of Birmingham was 'so dead . . . that the London waggons have to make up their loading with coals for want of merchandise'.[62] In December Josiah Wedgwood wrote to his partner to say, 'We are laying by for Christmas at our works. The men murmur at the thought of play these hard times.' In the following April the pottery manufacturers made an agreement to reduce their prices by 20 per cent.; and even Wedgwood, who was more favourably situated than most, had to turn off some of his workers.[63] The distress was intensified by the high cost of food. A silk manufacturer, William Wilmott of Sherborne, said that his workpeople were starving, and that he was having to distribute bread to keep them alive.[64]

Perhaps naturally, the depression was most acute in industries that had expanded rapidly before the crisis, and among these was the manufacture of linens. No figures of output are available for England and Wales, but between 1769 and 1771 exports (exclusive of linens produced in Scotland and Ireland) had increased by more than a third. In February 1773 Henry Hindley of Mere wrote of 'a miserable trade all over the Kingdom, and especially in these Western Parts'.[65] At this time the government was seeking for means to relieve distress, industry by industry, rather than by general measures: it sought to aid one branch of textiles by repealing the

---

[61] Thrale's debts amounted to £130,000, and it was only by the energy of Mrs. Thrale in collecting money from their friends that he was saved. Peter Mathias, 'The Industrial Revolution in Brewing', *Explorations in Entrepreneurial History*, vol. v, no. 4. For Roebuck's difficulties see T. S. Ashton, *Iron and Steel in the Industrial Revolution*, p. 135.

[62] *Hist. MSS. Comm. Rept.* xv, pt. 1, p. 198.

[63] Wedgwood, op. cit. ii. 14, 31, 63.

[64] Frank Warner, op. cit., p. 334.   [65] Hindley MSS.

Calico Act of 1721, and another by passing the Spitalfields Act. Its proposals for the linen manufacture—important for England, and vital to Scotland and Ireland—was to levy higher duties on foreign-produced yarn and cloth. These were strongly opposed not only by the merchants engaged in trade with Russia and Hamburg, but also by the manufacturers of woollens, cottons, printed goods, and hardware, who feared that any raising of the tariff would lead to retaliation and loss of markets in Europe. The industrial politics of 1773 would repay special investigation: the organization of the opposition foreshadows the movement of the eighties which led to the General Chamber of Manufacturers. Its interest for the present purpose, however, is that a committee of clothiers and stuff-makers of the West Riding, associated with industrialists elsewhere, prepared for Parliament a detailed report on the state of their affairs, which gives information about the effects of the crisis on wages and employment in this area.[66]

Stress was laid on the importance of the American market. James Thompson of Ramsden, a Trustee of the Mixed Cloth Hall at Leeds, gave evidence that 'before the demand from America was stopped', in 1769, he had paid 2s. 6d. for spinning 6 lb. of warp and 1s. 4d. for spinning the same quantity of weft. When the Americans ceased to buy, the wages of both fell by about a penny in the shilling; but in 1771 and the first half of 1772, 3s. was paid for spinning warp and 1s. 8d. for weft. In 1774 the corresponding rates were 2s. 2d. and 1s. 3d. Before the boom it had been usual to employ two weavers at each loom at a rate of 10d. for 3 yards of cloth. During the period of brisk demand the price rose to 1s. 1d. or 1s. 2d. 'About this time', [1771–2] he remarks, 'was introduced the practice of weaving Broad Cloth by one man only at the Loom.' This, it may be conjectured, was because of the difficulty in obtaining sufficient labour during the boom. In 1774 the rate paid to the weavers by his neighbours had sunk to 9d.: his own weaving was now done by the members of his family.

Another producer of white, broad cloth gives similar figures:

[66] The report was drawn up by Thomas Wolrich of Leeds. Fears lest useful information should be given to foreign competitors led the committee to refuse permission to publish it. But Wolrich deposited the document with his bankers, Abel Smith & Co. of Nottingham, and it has, fortunately, been preserved by this bank and its successor. I am much indebted to Dr. L. S. Pressnell for letting me make use of it.

	Spinning warp	Spinning weft	Weaving per string	Wool cleaning per stone
	s. d.	s. d.	s. d.	s. d.
1769 . . .	2 10	1 4	10	9
1770 . . .	2 9	1 3	9	8
1771 . . .	3 1	1 6	1 1	10
1772 . . .	3 4	1 8	1 4	1 1
Since 1772 to 1774 .	2 6	1 2	8	6

Those engaged in producing stuffs or worsteds underwent much the same vicissitudes. Catherine Ibbertson of Harewood, who had 'put out worsted to spin for several gentlemen in Leeds for near forty years', said that in 1771 and 1772 she had paid 7*d*. for spinning a pound of wool into thirteen hanks: now she paid only 4½*d*. And John Sutcliffe, stuff manufacturer of Houldsworth, lodged the following statement of the prices he paid to outworkers for spinning worsted yarn:

	At or near Halifax		In Lancashire and at a distance	
	Warp	Weft	Warp	Weft
	d.	s. d.	d.	s. d.
21 Aug. 1771 .	11	1 2	10	1 1
26 Oct. 1772 .	10	1 1	9	1 0
1 Mar. 1773 .	9	1 0	8	11
7 Mar. 1774 .	8	11	6	9

According to the same witness, the decline in wages was 12½ per cent. for the relatively well-paid wool-comber, 16½ per cent. for the weavers, 20–27 per cent. for the spinners near Halifax, and 30–40 per cent. for those at a distance—often twenty to forty miles away from Halifax. In normal times, it appears, the weaver might earn about 6*s*. and the spinner about 2*s*. 6*d*. a week. Cuts in pay of the order mentioned above must have meant destitution: it is little wonder that the poor-rates rose sharply in many towns of the West Riding and east Lancashire, as elsewhere. The slump led to widespread emigration from Scotland and Ireland, and according to the *Leeds Mercury* of 17 May 1774, the same thing was happening here: 'scarce a week passes without some setting off from this part of Yorkshire for the Plantations'.[67]

---

[67] According to the returns of the Custom House 7,756 people migrated from England and 1,253 from Scotland in 1774. For 1775 the figures were

In 1774 employment in the shipping industry was at a low point and there were many reports of distress and of outbreaks of violence in different parts of the country. The 'pitched battles' between English and Irish haymakers on the outskirts of London in July may have been due to competition for work.[68] Many able-bodied men took to crime. 'Our roads are so infested by highwaymen, that it is dangerous stirring out almost by day', wrote Walpole on 6 October 1774. 'All the freebooters, that are not in India have taken to the highway. The Ladies of the Bedchamber dare not go to the Queen at Kew in an evening.'[69] The consequences of the slump were felt in high places.

By the middle of 1774, however, the undertow of the wave was exhausted, and a new upward movement had begun. The American trade was open and English exports were rising. An increase in the price of wool at the August sales signified recovery in what was still the leading industry, and high imports of cotton suggest activity in the one that was beginning to rival, and was before long to outstrip it. In the slump of 1773 producers concerned with the home market had suffered less than those dependent on overseas demand: the fall in the production of narrow cloth was much smaller than that of broad cloth, and in 1774 the output of the first of these reached a figure higher than any previously recorded. The decline in the output of glass—and presumably of buildings—had also been slight, and in 1775 there was recovery here also. Other series that show development in this year include those for beer, spirits, and candles: the run of bad weather and poor harvests was drawing to an end.

In the early months of 1775 Britain drifted once more into war. The first shot was fired at Lexington in April and the first real battle at Bunker's Hill came in July. That these events should have brought no serious economic or financial disturbance was due to a variety of circumstances. There had been insufficient time for credit to build up very much since the collapse of 1772–3: the deterioration of the political situation had been gradual, and merchants and investors had made their dispositions in advance.[70] The

---

5,113 and 1,180. I. Ferenzi and W. F. Willcox, *International Migrations*, i. 626. For emigration from Yorkshire see *Thoresby Miscellany*, vol. xli, pt. 2, p. 175; and for that from Ireland and Scotland see *Annual Register* (1773), p. 118.   [68] George, op. cit., p. 357.   [69] *Letters*, ix. 63.

[70] On 19 Oct. 1774 the government had taken a precautionary step by prohibiting the export of firearms and powder. Macpherson, op. cit. iii. 580 n.

ending of direct trade with the rebel colonies brought disarrangements of shipping: in August the wages of seamen at Liverpool were reduced from 30s. to 20s. a month; and by November some 600 vessels formerly engaged in the American trade were lying idle in the Thames.[71] But the decline of total exports in 1775 was small, for there was a notable recovery of trade with the East Indies, as well as with Spain; and shipments to places from which goods could be smuggled to the Americans—Quebec, Nova Scotia, Newfoundland, Florida, and the West Indies—increased substantially. The outbreak of the war slowed down, but did not reverse, the recovery from the great slump.

In spite of a further decline in overseas trade, the next two years saw at least moderate prosperity. The yield of the fields was good, and the output of almost all the trades dependent on agriculture was rising. Government expenditure must have helped to sustain the demand for iron, linen, and wool. The output of cloth in the West Riding continued its upward course. There was prosperity in the silk industry: in 1776 William Wilmott raised the wages of his workers at Sherborne, and bid up for the labour of workhouse children;[72] and in the following year the weavers of London felt strong enough to form a union to enforce the provisions of the Spitalfields Act. In the Potteries also employment was good and the workers were demanding higher wages.[73] Activity in building and construction was well sustained, and in 1777 there was a remarkable increase in the output of glass. Scotland, which had suffered even more than England in the slump, had made full recovery: her merchants had found compensation for the loss of American markets in increased trade with Europe; and work had been resumed on the large projects of internal development. When in August 1777 Lord Gower made two expeditions into Lancashire (from Buxton where presumably he had been taking the waters), he found prosperity on all sides.[74] If he had crossed the Pennines he would have observed the same activity, for the output of broad cloth increased spectacularly that year. As has already been said, large-scale investment was taking place in building and construction —houses were being run up in London almost, it seemed, overnight

---

[71] C. N. Parkinson, *Rise of the Port of Liverpool*, pp. 124–5.
[72] Warner, op. cit., p. 251.
[73] Wedgwood, *Letters*, ii. 177, 187.
[74] Ibid. 266.

—and sharply rising prices of wool and sugar, together with large imports of raw cotton, speak of conditions of boom.

Towards the end of the year, however, there were signs that the activity was drawing to an end. In November came reports from Scotland of 'an uncommon stagnation in the sale of every species of linen'.[75] In this same month the number of bankruptcies in the United Kingdom was sixty-three, and, though there was a seasonal decline in December, high figures were again recorded in the following January and February: not since 1773 had there been anything approaching this. On 21 February 1778 Josiah Wedgwood wrote of the financial plight of a friend, Mr. Dobson, 'through some failures in London', and added, 'I have not recovered the shock this alarming account has given me. If such men as these fail where is safety to be found? And yet I am afraid these failures are only slight forerunners—mere warnings of what we are to expect.'[76] Since his letter was written within a few days of the declaration of war by France, the failures can scarcely have been due to this. Premonitions of an extension of the war may, it is true, have played a part in the recession that had set in in the later months of 1777; but it is reasonable to believe that the boom, like its predecessor of 1771–2, had carried within it the seed of decay, and that economic forces were mainly responsible for the slump.

However that may be, the financial crisis brought about by the war with France was followed by a further increase of bankruptcies and depression in trade, manufacture, and building alike that persisted for nearly three years. In June 1779 the Spaniards joined in the war: Gibraltar was besieged and the Mediterranean closed to British ships—with serious consequences for several industries, including the Cornish fisheries.[77] The Irish non-importation agreement cut off another important outlet of trade. Employment in shipping, which had been at a peak in 1778, dropped suddenly. And though an increase of shipments to the East Indies brought some relief in 1780, and increased greatly the number of merchant seamen, the accession of Holland to the list of Britain's enemies brought the figures down again in the following year.

Fortunately for England the harvests were good and the industries

---

[75] Robertson, op. cit., p. 126.   [76] Wedgwood, op. cit. ii. 293.
[77] Rowe, op. cit., p. 636. Building was at a low ebb. In 1780 the Oxford Canal passed its dividend, and in October it was recorded in the Minutes that 'the trade upon this Canal has decreased very much for these three months passed'. Information provided by Dr. L. S. Pressnell.

dependent on agriculture flourished. The demand for munitions, the cessation of imports of iron from America, and fears that the Armed Neutrality might put an end to those from the Baltic, led to the setting up of new furnaces and forges in South Wales, Shropshire, Staffordshire, Yorkshire, and Derbyshire.[78] The small-arms trade also was busy: it was said that at Birmingham 300 new houses were required annually during the war.[79] The demand for naval vessels and privateers was such that the established shipyards were unable to cope with it, and new yards were opened even in remote parts of Scotland and Wales. But notwithstanding these compensations, there was widespread distress and tumult. In June 1779 riots broke out at Nottingham as a result of a refusal of Parliament to regulate wages and frame-rents. In Lancashire, disorders, which included the burning down of Arkwright's factory at Birkacre in October, were attributed to unemployment resulting from the loss of the Irish market. In the following year anti-machinery riots occurred at Leeds;[80] and in the summer came the Gordon riots in London. According to Wedgwood, the colliers and potters in the neighbourhood of Etruria were conspiring to follow the example of the London mobs, but the danger was averted.[81] In both London and Staffordshire sectarian prejudice was at the root of the trouble, but it is possible that anti-Irish, as well as anti-Catholic, sentiment played a part: it was always latent and tended to flare up in times of economic stress.

The depression continued throughout the year 1781. 'What, too, is the condition of the great body of the poor, employed in the several branches of this manufacture?' asked a pamphleteer on the woollen industry in the following year. His answer was: 'Deplorable beyond expression. Some quite destitute of employment, others half-employed, and almost all obliged to fly (where else can they fly?) to the landed interest for at least partial support. . . . It is a fact (I speak it from knowledge) that many parishes, at this instant, pay the carriage of wool, to and from the spinning houses, at the distance of twenty, thirty, and even forty miles, for the sake of obtaining some employment for their poor.'[82]

[78] T. S. Ashton, *Iron and Steel in the Industrial Revolution*, pp. 136–7.
[79] In 1781 the number of houses subject to window tax in the town was 2,291. Macpherson, op. cit. iii. 704.   [80] Paul Mantoux, op. cit., p. 270.
[81] Wedgwood, op. cit. ii. 420.
[82] *An Answer to Sir John Dalrymple's Pamphlet upon the Exportation of Wool*, Anon. (1782), pp. 29–30.

Between 1774 and 1781 economic activity had followed a course very similar to that of the years 1769–74. In each case two years of recovery had been followed by a boom, and this, in turn, by crisis and depression. The only difference was that in the later period the boom appeared more abruptly, and, since war pressed heavily on both exports and building, the depression was prolonged.

As the war drew to an end signs of improvement appeared. As early as 1781 there was an expansion in the output of printed goods, and shortly afterwards in that of broad cloth. A sharp rise of imports in 1781 and of employment in shipping in 1782 suggests that merchants and manufacturers were replenishing stocks (purchases of raw cotton and timber were especially high). The growth of English exports in the same year was not due to any increase of shipments to America or Europe, for it was not until late in the year that the first of the peace treaties—that with the United States—was concluded: it consisted largely of goods sent to the East Indies. The upward movement continued in 1783, but several factors prevented the development of an authentic post-war boom. The harvests of 1782 were deplorably low, not only in England but throughout western Europe, and those of the following year were even worse. Grain was being sought from as far afield as Pennsylvania,[83] and in February 1783 the Lord Mayor of London declared that the price of wheat was so excessive, and that of barley so exorbitant, that it almost amounted to the prohibition of the use of it.[84] There was a sharp decline in the output of beer, spirits, starch, candles, and soap in 1783; and it is probable that the reduction of the disposable income of the workers, after they had paid for essentials, was partly responsible for a lowered demand for some classes of textiles.[85] The figures of seamen's sixpences indicate unemployment in shipping. Building remained depressed: it was not until 1785 that the output of glass began to rise. The crisis of the autumn of 1783 seems to have been due partly to an external drain and partly to losses sustained by merchants who had overestimated the strength of overseas demand for British goods. There was no serious panic but the result was to slow down the circulation of money and

[83] Anne Bezanson, *Prices and Inflation during the American Revolution*, p. 96.
[84] *Gentleman's Magazine*, Feb. 1783.
[85] The fall in the output of beer was probably connected with the refusal by the government of the request of the brewers for an increased price of beer. Peter Mathias, op. cit., p. 97.

to hamper the process of recovery from the war-time depression. Manufacture was sluggish at a time when technological improvements ought to have allowed of considerable expansion.

Until 1785 the existence of a large mass of unfunded debt, a legacy of the war, had kept rates of interest high and made private borrowing difficult.[86] But from this year it was possible for industrialists, including builders, to obtain the money they required for expansion at, or below, the legal rate of 5 per cent. Innovation was in the air. Henry Cort's process of puddling and rolling was effecting a revolution in the production of iron. James Watt's rotative engine was bringing a new source of power to a variety of processes, including, with spectacular results, the spinning of cotton. The cancellation of Arkwright's patents opened the way to a boom in the construction of factories: a count of the number in Great Britain in 1787 gave a figure of 143 (119 in England, of which 80 were in the three counties of Derby, Lancaster, and Nottingham). The cotton area—Lancashire, in particular—had its own special currency of small bills, and hence the expansion, and subsequent contraction, are hardly registered (as those of earlier booms and slumps are) in the returns of the Bank of England. A brief sketch has already been given of the events of 1786–9; but a few figures may be added to indicate the amplitude of the fluctuation:[87]

	Raw cotton imported (million lb.)	Price per lb. (pence)	Exports of manufactured cottons £000
1785	18·4	14–28	864
1786	19·5	22–42	915
1787	23·3	19–34	1,101
1788	20·4	14–33	1,252

There are no figures of the production of cotton yarns and cloth; but the output of the printers (most of whom had by this time left

---

[86] 'But, every war leaves many unliquidated claims which are the more distressful to individuals and the state, as these unfunded debts float in the stock market at great discount; as they depreciate the value of all public securities; and as, from these circumstances, they obstruct the financial operations of government, and prevent private persons from borrowing for the most useful purposes of productive industry. Of such unfunded debt there floated in the market, in October 1783, no less than £18,856,542.' Chalmers, op. cit., p. 174. As late as 1785 the yield on the 3 per cent. stock was higher than in any of the preceding years of war.

[87] Richard Burn, *Statistics of the Cotton Trade* (1847), pp. 20, 26.

London for Lancashire and were concentrating on calicoes) reached a peak in 1787. The woollen industry of Yorkshire, less affected by technical change, was also expanding rapidly; and although the crest of the wave for broad cloth had been reached earlier, in 1786, a sharp rise in the price of wool in 1787–8 suggests market conditions not unlike those across the Pennines.

Unlike many of its predecessors, the crisis of 1788 was not precipitated by political events: it was largely a result of undue optimism and over-expansion of credit in a single part of the economy. The decline of output that followed was not, however, confined to the cotton industry, for a fall of demand in the North was bound to have general repercussions.[88] But the reduction in the output of bricks in 1789 was probably due directly to a slowing down of the building of factories and houses in the cotton areas.

The two fluctuations of the eighties—those of 1781–4 and 1786–9 —were short and of limited amplitude. In both cases the crisis was relatively mild, and the increase of bankruptcies relatively small. In several series the following recessions appear as a retardation of the secular upward trend rather than as a declivity.

The course of economic activity from 1790 has been treated in detail by Gayer, Rostow, and Schwartz. The account that follows owes much to their work, though most of the illustrations have been drawn from other sources.

There is evidence that in 1789 the depression was lifting. Though a poor harvest led to distress and lack of employment in some parts of the country—notably in Cornwall—the figures of exports, and most of those of output, bear witness to rising activity. Better crops and rising incomes in the following three years allowed of increased production of beer, spirits, starch, candles, and soap. Exports of British merchandise—largely to the United States and the West Indies—expanded by 44 per cent. There was a rapid growth of the output of broad and narrow cloth in Yorkshire; and between 1789 and 1792 the production of printed goods increased by a half. The large imports of raw material suggest growing activity in the cotton industry, but since Lancashire and Scotland were increasingly producing the finer types of fabric, the figures give an inadequate

---

[88] The crisis was certainly not localized. 'The general consternation which seized the mercantile part of the City of London at the beginning of the present month has gradually affected the whole kingdom . . .' (*Gentleman's Magazine* (May 1788), p. 460).

impression of what was taking place. In January 1792, when Lord Auckland was seeking estimates of industrial output, Josiah Wedgwood, referring to the cotton manufacture, replied: 'One must here shoot flying, for this darts forward at such an amazing rate, as to leave all the others far behind.'[89] Perhaps even more important however, was the expansion in building and construction. Rates of interest were falling and all sorts of plans were launched for canals, turnpikes, and other public works. Between *1789* and *1792* the production of bricks increased by 54 per cent. (Since the growth of imports of timber and output of glass was much less, it seems probable that most of the bricks were used by the canal contractors.)

There are many indications that prosperity had created conditions of boom in 1792. Writing to Benjamin Gott on 24 November, John Dennis of Penzance remarked that 'the demand for tin has been astonishingly great of late. . . . This country promises to be very flourishing, every mine is going back to work and we are all Mining Mad.'[90] Between January 1790 and January 1792 the price of tin had risen by about 13 per cent. But even greater increases had taken place in the prices of other commodities: notably in those of wool, leather, and sugar.[91] Nowhere, however, were manifestations of the boom clearer than in the market for securities. In December 1792 a share in the Birmingham Canal of an original value of £140 could be sold for £1,250; one in the Wolverhampton Canal of a nominal value of £130 fetched £1,100; and a share in the Grand Trunk, which had been bought for £200, was now worth between £600 and £700.

There are signs of pressure on existing supplies of labour. In Staffordshire the potters were demanding higher rates and were 'punishing some of their comrades who attempted to work at their usual prices'.[92] The trustees for a new harbour at Swansea found it difficult to get masons to carry out the work, and were looking for recruits in Cornwall. Early in 1793 farmers in various parts of the country were complaining of a shortage of hands and sending petitions to Parliament for a measure to prohibit labourers from being employed in cutting canals during the months of harvest.[93]

---

[89] Wedgwood, op. cit., p. 206.   [90] Crump, op. cit., p. 200.
[91] In March 1792 a resolution of the Court of the East India Company referred to 'the present enormous price of sugar' and attributed this to the fact that annual imports were unequal to the demand for consumption at home and for exportation. *Gentleman's Magazine* (15 Mar. 1792), p. 275.
[92] Wedgwood, op. cit., p. 206.   [93] *Sheffield Register*, 8 Feb. 1793.

The high activity was associated, both as cause and effect, with an expansion of currency. Between 1789 and 1791 refugee money had been pouring into the Bank of England from France; and the increase of Treasure had led to an expansion of both the note circulation and the drawing accounts. There had been a rapid growth in the number of note-issuing private banks and an increase of the bill circulation. All the abuses of this most volatile type of credit were in evidence, as they had been in 1763, 1772, and 1788. In the later months of 1791 an external drain set in. The poverty of the harvest of 1792, and the necessity of paying for large imports of wheat, intensified the outward flow of bullion, at a time when the rise of wages and a state of high employment called for larger supplies of guineas and half-guineas for domestic circulation. It seems probable, therefore, that even if there had been no limit to the resources of labour and capital, the boom must have been brought to an end by a shortage of hard money.

Once more, however, the transition from boom to slump was accelerated by political forces. From April 1792 threats of a new war in Europe were forcing down the price of the Funds and raising the rate of interest on loans. In November pressure culminated in crisis; and when, on 24 January 1793, the French ambassador was ordered to leave the country, there was universal panic. Until the late summer of this year the situation was one of an acute shortage of cash. Coin was at a premium and employers had to resort to all sorts of shifts for the payment of wages.[94] 'Every day and every hour', wrote William Rowbottom in April, 'furnishes us with fresh evidences of the times. Money is not to be obtained on any account whatsoever, so that the poor are in the most wretched situation imaginable.' In May it was said that upwards of 7,000 people were 'destitute of employment' in Manchester.[95] The issue of the 'commercial Exchequer bills' by the government, and of £5 notes by the Bank brought some relief to merchants; and a rapid minting of gold coin helped to relieve the harassed employers and manufacturers. But the crisis left a legacy of ruined firms and unemployed labour.

---

[94] 'Edward Bourne has failed and as he has taken every means in his power of tempting persons to furnish him with cash by a high premium he has injured a great number of little shopkeepers.' Josiah Wedgwood, jun., to his father, on 22 Apr. (Wedgwood, op. cit., pp. 213–14.) For the paper money issued by Oldknow see Unwin, op. cit., pp. 176–93.

[95] Clapham, op. cit., p. 263.

It is not possible to disentangle the effects of the crisis from those arising from the state of war itself. The volume of English merchandise exported fell from £17·5 million in 1792 to £13·1 million in 1793. The output of industries dependent on overseas trade declined sharply: there were substantial falls in the production of printed goods and of Yorkshire broad and narrow cloths. Falling output meant reductions of wages. Even before the crisis had reached its height, in February 1793, a wholesale ironmonger, Abraham Chamberlain, wrote to Peter Stubs of Warrington: 'As there seems to be a general reduction of wages about to take place in most parts of the kingdom, your file cutters we should suppose will be among the rest.[96] Among those who suffered most severely were the textile workers of Lancashire. 'The relentless cruelty exercised by the fustian masters upon the poor weavers is such that it is unexampled in the annals of cruelty, tyranny and oppression', wrote Rowbottom on 11 August, 'for it is nearly an impossibility to earn the necessaries of life so that a great deal of families are in the most wretched and pitiable situation.' In December Rowbottom reported that 'the hatters have dropt one half of their wages' and that further cuts in the prices paid for weaving had 'caused a great deal of heads of familys to enlist'.

It would be wrong, however, to think of the distress as universal. Fortunately the harvests were moderately good: there was little or no decline in the output of beer in 1793–4 and the production of leather, candles, and soap increased. Building and construction— always late to react—continued at a high level. In 1793 the output of bricks was at the highest point since the series of figures began, and that of glass continued its upward course in both this and the following year. It was not until 1795 that rising rates of interest and, no doubt, a shortage of timber, as well as of labour, brought depression to this group of industries.

A restoration of the normal circulation of money, and of access to overseas markets, as well as rising government expenditure at home and abroad, led to a revival of activity in the spring of 1794. There was a substantial increase in exports of cotton yarn and manufactured goods, and a rising demand for labour was reflected in an upward movement of wages. On 24 May Rowbottom observes 'with the greatest satisfaction that the price of labour in this country is considerably advancing'; on 3 August he notes that the manufacturers

[96] Stubs MSS. The University of Manchester.

of calicoes, nankeens, and other light goods are rapidly increasing the prices paid to their weavers and that 'hats are increasing prodigiously; and in September he remarks that 'the astonishing demand for all kinds of light goods surpasses belief', and that wages are still advancing.

The harvest of 1794, however, was defective; in the following winter food was dear, and at Christmas it was 'impossible for people with large families to get what nature requires'. There is evidence of distress in the early months of 1795: in February a distribution of bread and coal was made to 'the most necessitous poor in Oldham'. In London the price of the peck loaf increased from 35*d*. in January to 52*d*. in August. Whether because of the effect of this on the ability of the poorer classes to buy clothing or for some other reason, there was a fall in the demand for cotton goods. In March the wages for weaving nankeens and dimities were reduced; and in May, according to Rowbottom, though the trade in hats and the higher qualities of cotton goods was brisk, fustian weaving (which produced cloth for the working classes) was at its lowest pitch. At the same time depression set in in building: the output of bricks and glass was sharply curtailed in the year ended July 1795.

From this point, however, the upward movement was resumed. Prospects of a better harvest and rising government expenditure led to increased employment, not only in industries that ministered to the needs of war, but generally. In 1796 employment in shipping rose to a figure higher than any previously recorded. The silk weavers of Spitalfields obtained an advance of wages, and the rise of rates in the cotton industry was remarkable. Whereas at the beginning of the year the price paid for weaving a piece of nankeen had been 16*s*., in June it had risen to 26*s*., and even the earnings of the fustian weavers were increasing.[97] The Austrian Loan and subsides to other allies, amounting in all to £5·7 million (a good deal of which was spent in this country), must have played some part in the rising activity of both 1795 and 1796: in the second of these years no fewer than eighteen Bills came before Parliament relating to canals and harbours, and the output of bricks and glass, as well as the import of timber, suggests some revival of building.

By the autumn, however, there were signs of financial pressure. 'Money is particularly scarce just now, we can hardly collect as much Money as will pay our Workmen's Wages' (wrote Thomas

[97] Rowbottom, op. cit.

Butler on 8 October 1796), 'tho' our Orders are plentiful enough
and we are now doing business—well—to advantage'.[98] A few days
later Thomas Atkinson of the Salford Twist Company wrote as
follows to Boulton & Watt of Birmingham: 'From the great scarcity
of money in Scotland we have been disappointed in getting bills
discounted as usual and even prolonging the credit to six months,
which lays us under the unpleasing necessity of remitting you a bill
at that period. . . . We assure you that nothing but the great scarcity
of money in the commercial world would have induced us to ask
for a longer credit. . . .'[99] From the beginning of the year the Bank
of England had been rationing its discounts; the prices of long-term
securities were falling and in July the rate on India bonds had been
raised to 5 per cent. It was the beginning of the crisis—due largely
to an external drain arising from the Imperial Loan and the restoration of a gold standard in France—that was to lead to the restriction
of cash payments in 1797.

The effects of the crisis can be seen in the decline of the figures
of exports, imports of cotton, output of Yorkshire woollens and
other commodities in 1797, as well as in the production of printed
goods in 1797 and 1798. Employment in shipping fell sharply. There
was acute distress among the weavers of Spitalfields, as well as of
those in the cotton industry. 'This year concludes with the most
distressing times ever experienced by the oldest person living, in
respect of weaving and hatting being down', wrote Rowbottom
on 26 December 1797. Even in the iron trade, which had been
generally prosperous throughout the war, there are reports of a
decline in wages. 'How changeable are all earthly things', said
Thomas Butler, on 5 January 1798. '4 or 5 years ago they [the
workers] were all Masters, they behaved very insolently. . . . We
were obliged to agree to their terms—they had then the whip hand
—Now we have it. But we do not use it so insolently as they did.'[1]
The upward movement that had begun in the summer of 1795 had
been brought to an end not, it would seem, by forces inherent in
the productive system, but by those of politics and war. In its
abruptness and brevity the fluctuation is similar to that of 1716–18.

The year 1798 saw recovery, with mounting exports and rising
outputs of nearly every commodity for which we have records. The

---

[98] Butler, op. cit., p. 80.
[99] Boulton & Watt Letters. Birmingham Central Library.
[1] Butler, op. cit., pp. 190–1.

harvests of the past two seasons had been good. Lavish government expenditure financed by loans kept up general demand; and, since the Bank was no longer forced to ration discounts in accordance with the state of the Treasure, credit was easy. But once again hostile influences beyond the control of industrialists or statesmen brought the prosperity to an end in the autumn of the following year. The commercial and financial crisis in Hamburg, which had superseded Amsterdam as the leading centre of European trade and finance, had serious repercussions in England. Large-scale hoarding reduced the circulation of money and brought a sharp upward movement of rates of interest. The summer had been one of the wettest on record and the harvest was an almost complete failure. The necessity of purchasing large amounts of grain overseas put a strain on the exchanges and tended to a further restriction of credit. The following harvest was even worse; and the records are full of accounts of distress and riots. Not all industries suffered: those concerned with munitions continued to thrive; employment in shipping rose steadily. After a brief set-back, the upward surge of enterprise in Lancashire was resumed; and there was a strong upward movement of building and public works.[2] It was not, however, until after the Peace of Amiens had been signed in 1802 that the cycle that began in 1800 culminated in boom.

It may be convenient to set down the findings of this study in summary form:

Depression	Turning-point	Peak	Crisis
	1700	1701	Feb.–Mar. 1701
1702	1702	1704	Oct.–Dec. 1704
1705	1706	1708	Aug.–Dec. 1710
1711–12	1712	1714	July–Dec. 1715
1715–16	1716	1717–18	Mar. 1719; Aug.–Dec. 1720
1718–21	1722	1724–5	Oct.–Dec. 1726
1726–7	1727	1728	..
1729	1730	1733	Oct.–Dec. 1733
1734	1734	1738	..
1739–41	1742	1743	..
1744–5	1746	1746	Sept. 1745–Apr. 1746
1747	1748	1751	..
1752–5	1755	1761	June–Dec. 1761

[2] The output of bricks rose from 421 million in *1799* to 543 million in *1800* and 842 million in *1803*. For developments in construction see Macpherson, op. cit. iv. 503.

Depression	Turning-point	Peak	Crisis
1762	1763	1764	July–Oct. 1763
1765–9	1769	1771–2	June 1772–Jan. 1773
1773–4	1775	1777	Jan.–Apr. 1778
1778–81	1781	1783	Sept. 1783–Jan. 1784
1784	1784	1787	May–June 1788
1788–9	1789	1792	Nov. 1792–Apr. 1793
1793	1794	1796	Feb.–June 1797
1797	1798	1799	Aug.–Nov. 1799
1800	1800	1802	..

It should be borne in mind that the movements varied greatly in amplitude. The inclusion of a year among the peaks does not necessarily mean that things were good, but only that they were better than they had been or were to be. Crises might appear at any point of the fluctuation, but generally they came just after a peak: they were precursors of depression.

III

The short-term movements of economic activity were far from uniform. Occasionally in a graph of output, trade, or finance, some one year stands out like a steeple in an otherwise featureless landscape; but generally the line traced is that of a series of arches, varying in height and span, and sometimes broken, but essentially of the same order. In the nineteenth century the undulations were more regular: in the early part, at least, booms, each culminating in a crisis, followed one another at intervals of ten or eleven years. Reasons for the greater frequency, shorter duration, and abrupt ending of the fluctuations of the eighteenth century are implicit in the account given above, but it may be useful to summarize them here.

In the simpler economic life of the earlier period a leading role was played by agriculture. Sometimes good harvests appeared in series, but the runs were never long, and the coming of dearth was sufficient in itself to halt, or reverse, an upward movement of activity. In the nineteenth century agriculture was still the most important of English industries, but its dominance was weakened by the growth of imports; and dearths were fewer and less acute.

Until 1800 or thereabouts, the mobility of factors of production was imperfect, and, in particular, the supply of industrial labour was, over short periods, inelastic. For though there were in rural England large numbers of under-employed men, most of them were unskilled and unaccustomed to discipline; and only when special inducements (including the provision of houses) were offered, or when want was acute, could there be any quick transfer from the countryside. It was partly because of this difficulty of recruitment that employment in building and construction tended to vary inversely with that in manufacture. At times when activity in both was high, as in 1764, 1772, and 1792, there were complaints of a shortage of labour, and it is possible that the ending of the booms was due to this influence quite as much as to growing pressure on supplies of capital or money.

In recent studies short fluctuations are associated with international trade and longer ones with the creation of investment goods in fixed form. In the eighteenth century the proportion of the energies of Englishmen that went to the production of exports was extraordinarily high. Merchants had no immediate contact with the ultimate purchases of their wares, and the possibilities of errors of judgement about demand in remote parts of the earth were great. 'The experience of merchants demonstrates that when abundance has glutted foreign markets in one year, repletion is cured in the next by sending a scanty supply', remarked a writer on the wool trade in 1782.[3] No doubt slower sailings and poorer means of obtaining information meant that the oscillations were a little longer than those of nineteenth-century trade; but compared with those arising from investment in durable capital-goods they were short. That the building of houses and ships and the construction of roads and canals had multiple effects is plain; but the proportion of the nation's resources employed in these must generally have been smaller than that employed in overseas trade: there was nothing in our period quite like the boom in the erection of factories in the early eighteen-twenties or the mania for railways in the following decades.

Equally important differences are to be seen in the sphere of money and finance. In the earlier period banking was still at an experimental stage. The Bank of England, it is true, seems to have taken a serious view of its responsibilities to the public; but the

---

[3] *The Propriety of Allowing a Qualified Exportation of Wool*, Anon. (1782), p. 50. Further reasons for the existence of short-term or 'inventory' cycles in international trade are given by W. W. Rostow, *British Economy of the Nineteenth Century*, pp. 39–40.

country bankers were often careless about reserves and apt to forget the maxim about the importance of distinguishing between a bill and a mortgage. The supply of currency created by merchants was highly elastic, and, at times when confidence was high, undue use was made of accommodation bills. An upward movement of prices and incomes might go far before an automatic check was administered. For though an adverse movement of the exchanges might lead to an export of bullion and foreign coin, it was forbidden to ship British coin overseas; and, in any case, most of what was euphemistically called 'hard money' consisted of pieces which, as the result of sweating and clipping, had a low bullion value and were unacceptable to exporters except at a high discount. After 1821 an expansive movement might be slowed down or ended by a legal export of the new, full-weight golden sovereigns.[4]

More important than this, however, was the relative ineffectiveness of the rate of interest as a brake to the creation of credit. Modern economists have pointed to the consequences of a minimum, below which rates of interest cannot, in practice, fall—a 'floor' which, it is argued, may make full employment impossible. They have paid less attention to the results of a ceiling, such as existed in the eighteenth century. There is a good deal of evidence that the Usury Laws were respected;[5] in so far as they were effective in keeping down the rate of interest, they may have enabled investment to go farther, over short runs of time, than would otherwise have been possible. As Henry Thornton put it:[6]

At some seasons an interest, perhaps, of six per cent per annum, at others, of five, or even four per cent, may afford that degree of advantage to borrowers which shall be about sufficient to limit, in due measure, the demand upon the bank for discounts. . . . In times of peace, the bank has found it easy to confine its paper by demanding five per cent for interest; whereas in war, and especially in the progress and towards the conclusion of it, as well as for some time afterwards, the directors have been subject, as I apprehend, to very earnest solicitations for

---

[4] That the existence of a coinage with low bullion value meant that credit expansion could go farther in the eighteenth than in the nineteenth century was pointed out to me by Jacob Viner.

[5] The penalty imposed for a breach of the law was a fine of three times the capital of the transaction. For examples see the *Annual Register*, Dec. 1762 and July 1765. In the second of these a man who had charged 16s. for discounting a note of hand for £30, which had six weeks to run, had to forfeit £90.

[6] Thornton, op. cit., p. 254.

discount, their notes, nevertheless, not being particularly diminished. . . .
The borrowers, in consequence of that artificial state of things which is
produced by the law against usury, obtain their loans too cheap. That
which they obtain too cheap they demand in too great quantity.

When the limits to loans at 5 per cent. had been reached—when the
reserves of the banks had fallen to a dangerously low fraction of
their liabilities—the Usury Laws prevented a full use of the brake:
all the banks could do was to ration credit, and this, in practice,
meant refusing some necessitous would-be borrowers, and so
precipitating the panic everybody was anxious to avoid. The un-
fortunate results of the laws were manifested most clearly in the
experience of industries concerned with investment goods, but
manufacturers of consumers' goods and traders also suffered.
Whether or not the laws tended to lengthen the cycles they must
certainly have increased their amplitude. In the nineteenth century
they were increasingly disregarded, though it was not until 1854
that they were finally repealed.

By far the greatest difference between the two periods lay in
the field of politics. In the eighteenth century the intervention of the
state in the money market and the stock market (as well as in the
markets for labour and commodities) was on a grand scale; and
generally the influence was destabilizing. Some of the speculative
booms, like those of 1708–10 and 1720, arose directly out of operations on the national debt by the government and the chartered
companies associated with it. And the almost complete prohibition
of new joint-stock companies by the Bubble Act, which concentrated stock-exchange dealings on a narrow range of—mainly
government—securities, may have tended to increase the violence
of speculative movements. It was, however, the recurrent needs of
the state to finance wars that was the chief disruptive influence:
over a large part of the century fluctuations arising from 'investment in war' blurred those originating in the decisions of entrepreneurs and individual investors.

Nor was it only the wars in which Britain was involved that
affected the course of English industry and trade. For the greater
part of the century the chief centre of European finance was
Amsterdam, and it was through Amsterdam that tremors in any
part of Europe were transmitted to this country. In the nineteenth
century the leadership in international finance passed to London;

and London was less vulnerable to political shocks than any continental city. It was less because of this, however, than because the settlement of 1815 put an end to the disturbances themselves that the fluctuations generated by industry and commerce were able to run a more regular, periodic course—until the seismic movements of our own age brought a new distortion of economic processes.

Historians, their eyes on the long-term movements that transformed economic and social life at this period, have paid insufficient attention to short-term fluctuations. They have observed that, over the century, there was a growth of income and capital, but they have also observed much that indicated extreme poverty and distress; and they have sought to explain the conjunction by all sorts of misty theories. The paradox disappears, or at least loses its sharpness, when it is realized that the upward slope was not continuous but was broken throughout by declivities, and that it was at these points that most of the instances of misery were concentrated.

It may be added that a more extended study than has been possible here would throw light on aspects of social life which are not, in the narrow sense, economic: on diet and dress, crime and punishment, and the attitude of both individuals and the state to the problems of poverty. It might seem, at first sight, that the social classes that are the subject of Jane Austen's satires would hardly be touched by the rude influences with which we have been concerned. But that economic forces found their way through the doors of London clubs and the assembly rooms at Bath and Tunbridge Wells can be seen by a glance at a set of figures provided by the Office of Excise.[7] As a means of raising revenue to meet the costs of the War of the Spanish Succession, in 1711 a duty of 6d. a pack was imposed on playing-cards and another of 5s. a pair on dice. (For these taxes the revenue period ended on 31 March: most of the receipts must have come in during the previous calendar year.) Running one's eye down the column showing the amounts derived from the tax on these toys, one cannot fail to notice the rise at the time of the Bubble in 1720, and of the boom of 1725–6, or the fall in the dearth of 1741, and the much greater drop, following the outbreak of war with France, in 1745. There was a less easily explained rise in 1755, and a sharp fall in the following year. According to Horace

[7] See Table 23.

Walpole, the disaster at Lisbon in November 1755 had a sobering effect on the man about town of his set. 'The earthquake has made us so good', he wrote, 'that the Ministry might have burned the latter [cards and dice] in Smithfield if they had pleased.'[8] High yields of revenue were obtained in *1758–9, 1762–5, 1771–3*, and *1787–90*; and, though in the last decade of the century the trend was steeply downward, there are signs of revival in *1800–1*. The correlation with our indices of activity is by no means perfect.[9] But generally, men and women seem to have enjoyed themselves when economic conditions were good, and to have become unsociable, or less disposed to take unnecessary risks, when they were bad. Observers of our own century have asserted that men tend to drink more in times of hope or excitement, and to smoke more in times of adversity:[10] drinking, like gaming, is essentially a social activity.

It is tempting to go farther and suggest that the pulsations of economic life were felt in courts and chancelleries, and that they played at least a minor part in the rise and fall of ministries and the shaping of policies. This is dangerous ground for an economic historian to tread. But perhaps some other kind of historian may think it worth while to survey the century once more with this possibility in mind. A chronological study of the public revenues, in detail, might serve as the starting-point.

[8] *Letters*, iii. 403. The letter was dated 4 Mar. 1756.

[9] Partly because of increases of duties in *1756, 1776*, and *1789*. The rise of revenue in each year immediately preceding these may have been due to purchases made by dealers to avoid payments at the higher rates.

[10] D. H. Robertson, *A Study of Industrial Fluctuation* (1915), p. 197 n.

APPENDIX
STATISTICAL TABLES

1. *Prices of wheat per bushel at Windsor and of the quartern loaf in London*

	Wheat		*Bread*		*Wheat*		*Bread*		*Wheat*		*Bread*
	s.	*d.*	*d.*		*s.*	*d.*	*d.*		*s.*	*d.*	*d.*
1700	4	9		1734	5	3		1768	6	11¾	6½
1701	4	2		1735	5	9	5½	1769	5	6¾	6
1702	3	7		1736	5	3	5¼	1770	6	10½	6½
1703	5	3		1737	4	7½	5¼	1771	7	3	7¾
1704	4	4		1738	4	3	5	1772	8	6	8
1705	3	6		1739	4	11	6	1773	8	3	7½
1706	3	3		1740	7	10½	7¼	1774	8	0	8
1707	3	10		1741	4	6	5½	1775	6	1½	6½
1708	6	6		1742	3	9	4¾	1776	6	0	6½
1709	11	6		1743	2	11	4¼	1777	7	3	7¼
1710	8	0		1744	3	1	4¼	1778	5	4½	6
1711	7	3		1745	3	8	4¾	1779	5	0	5¾
1712	4	9		1746	4	6	5½	1780	6	9	7¼
1713	8	0		1747	4	1	5	1781	6	9	7
1714	4	10		1748	4	9	6	1782	8	1½	8¼
1715	6	3		1749	4	9	5¼	1783	7	0	7¼
1716	6	0		1750	4	3	5¼	1784	7	1½	7½
1717	5	9		1751	5	6	6	1785	6	6	6¼
1718	4	6		1752	5	3	5½	1786	6	0	6½
1719	4	8		1753	5	6	6½	1787	7	0	6½
1720	4	9		1754	4	0	5	1788	6	9	6¾
1721	4	4¼		1755	4	6	5	1789	8	0	7¼
1722	4	6		1756	6	9	7½	1790	7	6¾	7½
1723	4	6		1757	6	6	7¼	1791	6	3	6½
1724	4	9		1758	5	6	6	1792	7	6	7¼
1725	6	10½		1759	4	8	5	1793	6	4	7½
1726	5	0		1760	4	9	5½	1794	7	0	7½
1727	5	10½		1761	3	9¾	4½	1795	11	6	12¼
1728	6	8		1762	4	9	5½	1796	8	0¾	8½
1729	5	6		1763	5	6	6	1797	6	9	9½
1730	4	6		1764	6	3	6½	1798	6	9	8
1731	4	0		1765	6	6	7	1799	11	7	13
1732	3	3		1766	6	6	8	1800	16	0	17½
1733	3	6		1767	8	3	8¼	1801	10	0	10

J. Marshall, *Digest of All the Accounts* (Statistical display of finances, &c.), pp. 88–89. Prices of wheat at Michaelmas, of bread at beginning of each mayoralty on 9 November.

2. *Prices of malt per bushel and numbers of victuallers*

	Malt		Victuallers		Malt		Victuallers		Malt		Victuallers
	s.	d.			s.	d.			s.	d.	
1700	3	6	39,469	1734	2	10	45,849	1768	4	3	
1701	3	0	41,841	1735	2	10	46,822	1769	3	7	
1702	3	6	43,434	1736	3	0	46,409	1770	3	3	
1703	3	0	44,654	1737	3	6	45,559	1771	4	3	
1704	3	6	49,838	1738	3	6	46,070	1772	4	7	
1705	3	4	48,015	1739	3	4	46,122	1773	5	0	
1706	3	4	48,754	1740	4	0	46,140	1774	5	0	
1707	3	8	47,433	1741	4	0	45,140	1775	4	11	
1708	4	0	47,265	1742	3	10	45,219	1776	4	7	
1709	4	8	46,860	1743	3	4	46,055	1777	3	11	
1710	5	0	40,559	1744	3	2	47,620	1778	3	11	
1711	5	0	38,671	1745	2	10	48,933	1779	3	11	
1712	4	2	32,294	1746	2	9	48,239	1780	3	9	
1713	4	0	41,043	1747	2	10	48,197	1781	3	9	
1714	4	0	42,418	1748	3	0	48,758	1782	4	3	
1715	4	8	42,201	1749	3	2	48,370	1783	5	5	
1716	4	0	41,818	1750	3	2	48,421	1784	5	5	
1717	3	8	41,384	1751	3	4	47,999	1785	5	3	
1718	3	8	41,354	1752	3	4	47,940	1786	5	1	
1719	3	8	43,443	1753	3	6	47,405	1787	4	9	
1720	3	10	43,872	1754	3	6	46,422	1788	4	9	
1721	3	6	43,463	1755	3	2	43,432	1789	4	9	
1722	2	8	43,490	1756	3	4	45,048	1790	4	6	
1723	3	2	44,333	1757	4	6	40,101	1791	4	9	
1724	3	8	46,227	1758	4	6	39,252	1792	5	3½	
1725	3	6	45,440	1759	4	4	39,723	1793	5	2	
1726	3	6	44,629	1760	3	3	40,166	1794	5	3	
1727	3	6	45,030	1761	3	1	40,180	1795	5	5	
1728	4	0	42,383	1762	3	9	39,064	1796	5	1	
1729	4	4	40,971	1763	4	9		1797	4	9	
1730	3	3	44,077	1764	4	3		1798	4	9	
1731	3	3	46,702	1765	4	3		1799	5	5	
1732	3	2	46,751	1766	4	3		1800	9	2	
1733	2	10	46,611	1767	4	3		1801	9	8	

Marshall, op. cit. (Statistical display of finances, &c.), pp. 88–89; Harrowby MSS., State of the Revenue of Excise, vol. 285, p. 27.

3. *Net exports of wheat (including flour):* *Net imports (−)*

	'000 quarters		'000 quarters		'000 quarters		'000 quarters
1700	49	1726	142	1752	429	1778	35
1701	98	1727	30	1753	300	1779	217
1702	90	1728	−71	1754	356	1780	220
1703	107	1729	−21	1755	237	1781	−57
1704	90	1730	94	1756	103	1782	64
1705	96	1731	130	1757	−130	1783	−532
1706	188	1732	202	1758	−11	1784	−128
1707	74	1733	427	1759	227	1785	22
1708	83	1734	498	1760	394	1786	154
1709	170	1735	153	1761	442	1787	62
1710	14	1736	118	1762	296	1788	−66
1711	77	1737	462	1763	400	1789	27
1712	145	1738	581	1764	397	1790	−192
1713	176	1739	280	1765	62	1791	398
1714	175	1740	54	1766	154	1792	278
1715	166	1741	45	1767	−493	1793	−313
1716	75	1742	293	1768	−342	1794	−173
1717	23	1743	371	1769	46	1795	−295
1718	72	1744	232	1770	75	1796	−854
1719	128	1745	325	1771	7	1797	−407
1720	83	1746	131	1772	−18	1798	−337
1721	82	1747	267	1773	−49	1799	−424
1722	179	1748	543	1774	−273	1800	−1,243
1723	158	1749	629	1775	−470	1801	−1,397
1724	246	1750	948	1776	190		
1725	204	1751	661	1777	−145		

Marshall, op. cit. (Statistical display of finances, &c.), pp. 88–89. The figures relate to Great Britain.

4. *Imports into England and Wales*

(in £ million)

1700	6·0	1726	6·7	1752	7·9	1778	10·3
1701	5·9	1727	6·8	1753	8·6	1779	10·7
1702	4·2	1728	7·6	1754	8·1	1780	10·8
1703	4·5	1729	7·5	1755	8·8	1781	11·9
1704	5·4	1730	7·8	1756	8·0	1782	9·5
1705	4·0	1731	7·0	1757	9·3	1783	12·1
1706	4·1	1732	7·1	1758	8·4	1784	14·1
1707	4·3	1733	8·0	1759	8·9	1785	14·9
1708	4·7	1734	7·1	1760	9·8	1786	14·6
1709	4·5	1735	8·2	1761	9·5	1787	16·3
1710	4·0	1736	7·3	1762	8·9	1788	16·6
1711	4·7	1737	7·1	1763	11·2	1789	16·4
1712	4·5	1738	7·4	1764	10·4	1790	17·4
1713	5·8	1739	7·8	1765	11·0	1791	17·7
1714	5·9	1740	6·7	1766	11·5	1792	17·9
1715	5·6	1741	7·9	1767	12·1	1793	17·8
1716	5·8	1742	6·9	1768	11·9	1794	20·8
1717	6·3	1743	7·8	1769	11·9	1795	21·5
1718	6·7	1744	6·4	1770	12·2	1796	21·5
1719	5·4	1745	7·8	1771	12·8	1797	19·5
1720	6·1	1746	6·2	1772	13·3	1798	26·0
1721	5·9	1747	7·1	1773	11·4	1799	24·5
1722	6·4	1748	8·1	1774	13·3	1800	28·4
1723	6·5	1749	7·9	1775	13·5		
1724	7·4	1750	7·8	1776	11·7		
1725	7·1	1751	7·9	1777	11·8		

From tables compiled by Elizabeth Schumpeter.

5. Exports from England and Wales
(*in £ million*)

	English products	Re-exports	Total		English products	Re-exports	Total
1700	4·3	2·1	6·5	1751	8·8	3·6	12·4
1701	4·6	2·2	6·9	1752	8·2	3·5	11·7
1702	3·6	1·2	4·8	1753	8·7	3·5	12·2
1703	4·6	1·6	6·2	1754	8·3	3·5	11·8
1704	4·3	1·9	6·2	1755	7·9	3·2	11·0
1705	..	..	5·3	1756	8·6	3·1	11·7
1706	4·7	1·5	6·2	1757	8·6	3·8	12·3
1707	4·8	1·6	6·4	1758	8·8	3·9	12·6
1708	5·1	1·5	6·6	1759	10·1	3·9	13·9
1709	4·4	1·5	5·9	1760	11·0	3·7	14·7
1710	4·7	1·6	6·3	1761	10·8	4·1	14·8
1711	4·1	1·9	6·0	1762	9·4	4·4	13·8
1712	..	..	6·9	1763	9·5	5·1	14·7
1713	4·8	2·1	6·9	1764	11·5	4·7	16·3
1714	5·6	2·4	8·0	1765	10·1	4·5	14·6
1715	5·0	1·9	6·9	1766	9·9	4·2	14·1
1716	4·8	2·2	7·0	1767	9·5	4·4	13·9
1717	5·4	2·6	8·0	1768	9·7	5·4	15·1
1718	4·4	2·0	6·4	1769	9·0	4·5	13·4
1719	4·5	2·3	6·8	1770	9·5	4·8	14·3
1720	4·6	2·3	6·9	1771	11·2	5·9	17·1
1721	4·5	2·7	7·2	1772	10·5	5·7	16·2
1722	5·3	3·0	8·3	1773	8·9	5·9	14·8
1723	4·7	2·7	7·4	1774	10·0	5·9	15·9
1724	5·1	2·5	7·6	1775	9·7	5·5	15·2
1725	5·7	2·8	8·5	1776	9·3	4·5	13·7
1726	5·0	2·7	7·7	1777	8·8	3·9	12·7
1727	4·6	2·7	7·3	1778	7·8	3·8	11·6
1728	4·9	3·8	8·7	1779	7·0	5·6	12·6
1729	4·9	3·3	8·2	1780	8·0	4·3	12·3
1730	5·3	3·2	8·5	1781	7·0	3·5	10·6
1731	5·1	2·8	7·9	1782	8·6	3·8	12·4
1732	5·7	3·2	8·9	1783	10·1	3·8	13·9
1733	5·8	3·0	8·8	1784	10·5	3·7	14·2
1734	5·4	2·9	8·3	1785	10·3	4·8	15·1
1735	5·9	3·4	9·3	1786	11·2	4·2	15·4
1736	6·1	3·6	9·7	1787	11·3	4·4	15·8
1737	6·7	3·4	10·1	1788	11·9	4·3	16·3
1738	7·0	3·2	10·2	1789	13·0	5·2	18·2
1739	5·6	3·3	8·8	1790	14·1	4·8	18·9
1740	5·1	3·2	8·2	1791	15·9	5·5	21·4
1741	6·0	3·6	9·6	1792	17·5	6·2	23·7
1742	6·1	3·5	9·6	1793	13·1	6·2	19·4
1743	6·9	4·4	11·3	1794	15·9	9·8	25·7
1744	5·4	3·8	9·2	1795	15·7	10·7	26·3
1745	5·7	3·3	9·1	1796	18·0	11·2	29·2
1746	7·2	3·6	10·8	1797	15·8	11·8	27·7
1747	6·7	3·0	9·8	1798	18·3	13·6	31·9
1748	7·3	3·8	11·1	1799	22·5	11·6	34·1
1749	9·1	3·6	12·7	1800	22·5	18·4	40·8
1750	9·5	3·2	12·7				

From tables compiled by Elizabeth Schumpeter. The figures of re-exports from 1700 to 1714 are provided by Dr. A. H. John.

6. Tonnage of ships cleared outward from ports of England and Wales

(in thousand tons)

	British	Foreign	Total		British	Foreign	Total
1760	471	103	574	1781	548	163	711
1761	508	118	626	1782	553	209	761
1762	480	120	601	1783	796	158	954
1763	562	87	649	1784	846	113	959
1764	584	75	659	1785	952	103	1,055
1765	651	68	719	1786	982	117	1,099
1766	684	62	746	1787	1,105	132	1,237
1767	646	63	709	1788	1,243	122	1,365
1768	669	73	742	1789	1,344	100	1,444
1769	710	63	773	1790	1,261	144	1,405
1770	703	57	761	1791	1,333	178	1,511
1771	773	64	837	1792	1,396	169	1,565
1772	818	73	891	1793	1,101	180	1,281
1773	771	55	826	1794	1,247	210	1,457
1774	798	65	864	1795	1,030	370	1,400
1775	783	65	848	1796	1,108	455	1,563
1776	779	72	851	1797	972	380	1,351
1777	736	83	820	1798	1,164	345	1,509
1778	657	98	755	1799	1,145	391	1,536
1779	591	139	730	1800	1,269	656	1,924
1780	619	135	754				

George Chalmers, *An Estimate of the Comparative Strength of Great Britain* (1802), p. 234.

7. *Public income and expenditure of Great Britain:*
Surplus income, or excess of expenditure (–)

(in £ thousand)

1700	1,143	1734	−913	1768	984
1701	327	1735	−200	1769	1,560
1702	−141	1736	−32	1770	848
1703	248	1737	948	1771	881
1704	−133	1738	991	1772	308
1705	−581	1739	610	1773	510
1706	−1,408	1740	−415	1774	1,047
1707	−3,276	1741	−1,144	1775	747
1708	−2,534	1742	−2,118	1776	−3,469
1709	−3,954	1743	−2,412	1777	−4,154
1710	−4,524	1744	−2,822	1778	−6,504
1711	−9,966	1745	−2,468	1779	−7,861
1712	−2,116	1746	−3,554	1780	−10,082
1713	−582	1747	−4,492	1781	−12,630
1714	−824	1748	−4,744	1782	−15,469
1715	−681	1749	−5,049	1783	−10,832
1716	−1,494	1750	283	1784	−11,031
1717	629	1751	672	1785	−10,305
1718	−264	1752	−45	1786	−1,732
1719	−126	1753	1,386	1787	969
1720	321	1754	797	1788	442
1721	81	1755	−182	1789	651
1722	−828	1756	−2,583	1790	215
1723	321	1757	−3,224	1791	510
1724	334	1758	−5,253	1792	1,654
1725	445	1759	−7,227	1793	−491
1726	−25	1760	−8,786	1794	−9,974
1727	243	1761	−11,518	1795	−19,942
1728	237	1762	−10,581	1796	−22,981
1729	584	1763	−7,930	1797	−36,269
1730	691	1764	−466	1798	−20,476
1731	733	1765	−1,089	1799	−15,636
1732	829	1766	−27	1800	..
1733	927	1767	229		

B.P.P. Accounts and Papers (1868–9), vol. xxxv, no. 2, App. 6, pp. 280–5. The figures are for years ending at Michaelmas.

8. Number of men in the armed forces
(in thousands)

1700	20	1726	41	1752	39	1778	155
1701	46	1727	53	1753	37	1779	204
1702	86	1728	43	1754	39	1780	221
1703	104	1729	44	1755	65	1781	228
1704	111	1730	39	1756	100	1782	237
1705	114	1731	35	1757	132	1783	190
1706	123	1732	32	1758	159	1784	60
1707	139	1733	33	1759	176	1785	52
1708	136	1734	49	1760	186	1786	51
1709	150	1735	63	1761	186	1787	55
1710	160	1736	43	1762	205	1788	52
1711	186	1737	36	1763	159	1789	59
1712	153	1738	45	1764	52	1790	78
1713	46	1739	50	1765	51	1791	95
1714	29	1740	78	1766	49	1792	74
1715	32	1741	101	1767	47	1793	216
1716	14*	1742	95	1768	47	1794	296
1717	13*	1743	102	1769	48	1795	437
1718	32	1744	107	1770	51	1796	264
1719	37	1745	107	1771	75	1797	380
1720	41	1746	136	1772	57	1798	389
1721	37	1747	120	1773	52	1799	394
1722	30	1748	116	1774	51	1800	124*
1723	32	1749	47	1775	50	1801	474
1724	31	1750	41	1776	81	1802	482
1725	30	1751	39	1777	134	1803	278

* Seamen and mariners only.

B.P.P. (1863–9), vol. xxxv, no. 2, pp. 693 et seq. The figures are the totals of the numbers *borne in* the Navy and *voted for* the Army.

9. Approximate yield on 3 per cent. Funds

1731	3·1	1749	3·2	1767	3·4	1785	5·4
1732	3·1	1750	3·0	1768	3·3	1786	4·5
1733	3·0	1751	3·0	1769	3·4	1787	4·1
1734	3·2	1752	2·9	1770	3·4	1788	4·1
1735	3·2	1753	2·9	1771	3·6	1789	4·1
1736	3·1	1754	2·9	1772	3·4	1790	4·0
1737	2·8	1755	3·0	1773	3·4	1791	3·8
1738	2·9	1756	3·3	1774	3·5	1792	3·3
1739	3·0	1757	3·4	1775	3·4	1793	3·7
1740	3·0	1758	3·3	1776	3·4	1794	4·2
1741	3·0	1759	3·4	1777	3·7	1795	4·6
1742	3·0	1760	3·7	1778	4·2	1796	4·4
1743	3·0	1761	3·7	1779	4·9	1797	5·5
1744	3·1	1762	4·2	1780	5·0	1798	6·0
1745	3·3	1763	3·5	1781	5·0	1799	5·7
1746	3·7	1764	3·6	1782	5·3	1800	5·0
1747	3·5	1765	3·6	1783	4·8	1801	4·9
1748	3·6	1766	3·4	1784	5·0		

The figures are the reciprocals of the average annual (July–June) prices of the 3 per cent. stock calculated from the monthly quotations in Sir John Sinclair, *History of the Public Revenue of the British Empire*, App. II, pp. 28–46.

10. *Imports of deals and fir timber*

(*in £ thousand*)

1700	68	1726	70	1752	72	1778	120
1701	58	1727	61	1753	78	1779	86
1702	61	1728	86	1754	60	1780	86
1703	70	1729	62	1755	70	1781	79
1704	81	1730	65	1756	69	1782	85
1705	..	1731	63	1757	60	1783	125
1706	59	1732	68	1758	71	1784	144
1707	67	1733	63	1759	67	1785	115
1708	62	1734	72	1760	56	1786	172
1709	50	1735	69	1761	66	1787	169
1710	36	1736	73	1762	56	1788	175
1711	33	1737	69	1763	83	1789	157
1712	..	1738	67	1764	94	1790	190
1713	59	1739	54	1765	108	1791	190
1714	60	1740	59	1766	116	1792	307
1715	73	1741	59	1767	84	1793	232
1716	51	1742	56	1768	102	1794	199
1717	53	1743	59	1769	110	1795	179
1718	61	1744	43	1770	99	1796	235
1719	64	1745	56	1771	109	1797	158
1720	82	1746	54	1772	124	1798	187
1721	67	1747	57	1773	119	1799	..
1722	79	1748	51	1774	120	1800	..
1723	69	1749	56	1775	123		
1724	93	1750	60	1776	142		
1725	76	1751	59	1777	126		

Table compiled by Elizabeth Schumpeter.

11. *Stained paper charged with duty*

(*in thousand yards*)

1713	197	1732	230	1751	784	1770	2,119
1714	204	1733	237	1752	918	1771	2,275
1715	132	1734	245	1753	1,067	1772	2,190
1716	79	1735	240	1754	939	1773	2,053
1717	205	1736	273	1755	958	1774	2,279
1718	202	1737	294	1756	1,080	1775	2,109
1719	223	1738	292	1757	1,165	1776	2,284
1720	214	1739	324	1758	1,139	1777	2,441
1721	219	1740	320	1759	1,313	1778	2,401
1722	225	1741	396	1760	1,404	1779	1,893
1723	219	1742	419	1761	1,468	1780	1,828
1724	230	1743	378	1762	1,358	1781	2,256
1725	247	1744	399	1763	1,387	1782	1,886
1726	231	1745	380	1764	1,824	1783	1,703
1727	239	1746	343	1765	1,843	1784	2,096
1728	218	1747	442	1766	1,963	1785	2,101
1729	222	1748	516	1767	2,196	1786	1,885
1730	216	1749	653	1768	2,257	1787	2,028*
1731	230	1750	737	1769	2,301		

* To 10 May.
From Excise returns for years ended 24 June or 5 July.

12. *Glass charged with duty*

(*in thousand cwts.*)

1747	28	1762	100	1777	144	1792	169
1748	43	1763	99	1778	129	1793	161
1749	50	1764	108	1779	112	1794	182
1750	62	1765	118	1780	113	1795	132
1751	63	1766	118	1781	109	1796	149
1752	67	1767	129	1782	114	1797	157
1753	72	1768	138	1783	115	1798	139
1754	82	1769	132	1784	116	1799	146
1755	76	1770	128	1785	124	1800	165
1756	78	1771	125	1786	124	1801	171
1757	77	1772	139	1787	132	1802	180
1758	91	1773	134	1788	146	1803	195
1759	83	1774	133	1789	169	1804	173
1760	92	1775	134	1790	163		
1761	92	1776	134	1791	161		

Excise returns for year ended 24 June or 5 July. Common bottles, &c., excluded.

13. *Bank of England*

Column I: Notes in circulation *plus* balances in Drawing Accounts (*£ million*)
Column II: Percentage of bullion and coin to figures in column I

	I	II		I	II		I	II
1720	4·0	25	1747	6·1	32	1774	··	··
1721	3·0	34	1748	5·5	40	1775	11·2	63
1722	4·0	31	1749	6·1	34	1776	10·5	51
1723	4·1	43	1750	6·2	31	1777	10·6	37
1724	5·2	37	1751	7·1	42	1778	9·8	21
1725	5·7	21	1752	6·9	40	1779	11·3	33
1726	4·7	38	1753	6·1	37	1780	11·0	33
1727	6·6	45	1754	5·8	49	1781	10·0	33
1728	6·5	37	1755	7·4	51	1782	10·9	20
1729	6·1	38	1756	7·3	55	1783	9·6	14
1730	6·3	33	1757	8·2	45	1784	8·1	8
1731	7·1	38	1758	7·2	31	1785	8·4	33
1732	7·1	36	1759	6·4	34	1786	10·2	59
1733	6·6	51	1760	6·8	38	1787	10·9	52
1734	7·4	50	1761	7·1	29	1788	12·0	48
1735	7·7	49	1762	8·0	44	1789	12·5	58
1736	7·7	51	1763	6·9	5	1790	12·9	62
1737	7·0	47	1764	7·7	24	1791	14·9	53
1738	7·2	41	1765	··	··	1792	14·2	46
1739	6·7	61	1766	7·3	25	1793	14·7	27
1740	7·3	66	1767	7·1	11	1794	13·6	51
1741	7·3	56	1768	7·6	21	1795	17·5	35
1742	7·7	44	1769	7·5	18	1796	13·5	19
1743	7·0	37	1770	7·1	41	1797	12·2	9
1744	7·1	24	1771	8·5	27	1798	19·2	30
1745	5·6	14	1772	7·5	21	1799	21·1	36
1746	5·8	40	1773	7·8	15	1800	23·9	26

Sir John Clapham, *The Bank of England*, vol. i, App. C. For 1798–1800 the figures are from Marshall, op. cit., pp. 170–1: since other liabilities (including the 'Rest') are merged with notes and Drawing Accounts the figures for these three years are not strictly comparable with those in the rest of the Table. Up to 1764 all statements are as at 31 August, thereafter as at 28 or 29 February.

14. *Prices of wool*

(*Lincolnshire long wool per tod of 28 lb.*)

	s. d.		s. d.		s. d.		s. d.
1706	17 6	1728	18 0	1747	17 3	1766	21 6
1707	16 6	1729	18 0	1748	18 6	1767	20 0
		1730	19 0	1749	19 0	1768	16 0
1712	15 0	1731	19 0	1750	18 6	1769	15 3
1713	..	1732	19 0	1751	18 6	1770	14 0
1714	18 0	1733	18 6	1752	20 0	1771	15 0
1715	..	1734	16 0	1753	15 0	1772	15 6
1716	..	1735	14 0	1754	14 6	1773	15 6
1717	23 0	1736	14 0	1755	14 0	1774	17 6
1718	27 0	1737	14 0	1756	15 6	1775	18 6
1719	21 0	1738	13 6	1757	18 0	1776	18 6
1720	21 6	1739	13 0	1758	20 0	1777	18 3
1721	20 0	1740	14 0	1759	20 0	1778	17 0
1722	20 0	1741	14 0	1760	18 6	1779	18 6
1723	17 6	1742	15 0	1761	18 0	1780	19 6
1724	16 0	1743	19 6	1762	17 0	1781	20 0
1725	16 0	1744	21 0	1763	20 0		
1726	15 9	1745	16 6	1764	20 0		
1727	16 0	1746	17 0	1765	21 0		

The Propriety of Allowing a Qualified Exportation of Wool, Anon. (1782), pp. 83–84. According to the anonymous author the figures to 1746 were taken from J. Smith, *Memoirs of Wool*, ii. 171–6; those for the later years were 'ascertained from the best manuscript documents that could be procured, comprising from five to ten different accounts'.

15. *Price of wool*

(*in pence per lb.*)

	Southdown	*Long Kent*		*Southdown*	*Long Kent*
	d.	d.		d.	d.
1759	8½	7½	1780	7½	6½
1760	8½	7½	1781	7½	5
1761	6½	6	1782	8	5½
1762	6½	6	1783	8	6½
1763	8	7	1784	8½	7
1764	8	8	1785	9	7
1765	7½	7	1786	9	7½
1766	8	8	1787	11	9½
1767	9	7½	1788	12	9
1768	7	6½	1789	12	8½
1769	7	6½	1790	12½	9½
1770	7½	7	1791	11½	9
1771	8	7½	1792	16	11½
1772	7	6½	1793	11½	9½
1773	7	7	1794	13	9½
1774	8	7	1795	15	10
1775	9	8	1796	16	9½
1776	8½	8	1797	15	9½
1777	8	7½	1798	15	9½
1778	6½	5½	1799	21	12
1779	6	6	1800	17	12½

Marshall, op. cit., p. 119. The prices are, apparently, those at the August sales in each year.

16. *Woollen cloths milled in the West Riding of Yorkshire*

(*in million yards*)

	Broad	Narrow		Broad	Narrow
1769	2·77	2·14	1785	4·84	3·41
1770	2·72	2·26	1786	4·93	3·54
1771	2·97	2·24	1787	4·85	4·06
1772	3·22	2·38	1788	4·24	4·21
1773	3·63	2·31	1789	4·72	4·41
1774	2·59	2·13	1790	5·15	4·58
1775	2·84	2·44	1791	5·82	4·80
1776	2·98	2·49	1792	6·76	5·53
1777	3·15	2·60	1793	6·05	4·78
1778	3·80	2·75	1794	6·07	4·63
1779	3·43	2·66	1795	7·76	5·17
1780	2·80	2·57	1796	7·83	5·25
1781	3·10	2·67	1797	7·24	5·50
1782	4·46	2·60	1798	7·13	5·18
1783	4·56	3·29	1799	8·81	6·38
1784	4·09	3·36	1800	9·26	6·01

Macpherson, op. cit. iv. 15, 525. The years to which the figures relate ended in March.

17. *Gilt wire charged with duty*

(*in thousand ounces*)

1713	72	1736	109	1759	102	1782	75
1714	95	1737	123	1760	121	1783	59
1715	89	1738	66	1761	125	1784	50
1716	84	1739	85	1762	163	1785	46
1717	95	1740	99	1763	152	1786	47
1718	89	1741	90	1764	165	1787	45
1719	76	1742	85	1765	134	1788	50
1720	70	1743	98	1766	116	1789	47
1721	56	1744	92	1767	140	1790	61
1722	71	1745	101	1768	146	1791	61
1723	75	1746	111	1769	152	1792	53
1724	78	1747	126	1770	129	1793	54
1725	86	1748	118	1771	113	1794	55
1726	77	1749	109	1772	78	1795	73
1727	56	1750	102	1773	75	1796	74
1728	65	1751	71	1774	66	1797	65
1729	57	1752	80	1775	74	1798	74
1730	68	1753	100	1776	75	1799	99
1731	90	1754	96	1777	63	1800	93
1732	78	1755	98	1778	65	1801	86
1733	89	1756	109	1779	73	1802	72
1734	99	1757	120	1780	69		
1735	87	1758	107	1781	75		

Excise returns for years ended in March.

18. *Common glass bottles charged with duty*

(in thousand cwts.)

1747	185	1762	214	1777	249	1792	258
1748	171	1763	231	1778	226	1793	272
1749	186	1764	265	1779	171	1794	243
1750	221	1765	258	1780	138	1795	237
1751	255	1766	262	1781	165	1796	236
1752	268	1767	244	1782	166	1797	229
1753	244	1768	241	1783	169	1798	166
1754	272	1769	237	1784	169	1799	199
1755	260	1770	221	1785	190	1800	226
1756	232	1771	225	1786	193	1801	247
1757	213	1772	240	1787	208	1802	262
1758	179	1773	233	1788	208	1803	281
1759	166	1774	230	1789	218	1804	261
1760	191	1775	226	1790	245		
1761	209	1776	236	1791	253		

Excise returns for years ended 24 June or 5 July.

19. *Tonnage of ships built in England and Wales*

1787	77,996	1795	56,946
1788	60,594	1796	75,270
1789	49,108	1797	69,425
1790	49,470	1798	67,955
1791	48,741	1799	72,713
1792	56,044	1800	101,776
1793	55,839	1801	92,000
1794	47,353		

P.R.O., Customs (17/12–30).

20. *Sums insured against fire in England and Wales*

(in £ million)

1783	173·3	1792	121·6
1784	154·9	1793	133·0
1785	136·6	1794	132·3
1786	132·8	1795	132·5
1787	136·9	1796	141·3
1788	101·3	1797	136·1
1789	104·9	1798	183·8
1790	108·7	1799	198·6
1791	113·2	1800	204·9

B.P.P. (1857), iii. 617–75. The years to 1799 ended 1 August. The figure for 1800 covers the period 2 Aug. 1799–5 Jan. 1801.

21. *Output of bricks*

	Million		Million
1785	358·8	1795	559·3
1786	495·6	1796	633·0
1787	635·8	1797	517·7
1788	668·2	1798	516·8
1789	590·3	1799	421·3
1790	711·2	1800	543·1
1791	749·9	1801	674·7
1792	808·0	1802	698·6
1793	908·9	1803	842·1
1794	787·7	1804	795·7

H. A. Shannon, 'Bricks: a Trade Index, 1785–1849', *Economica*, August 1934. The years ended 5 July.

22. *Auctions: amount of sales charged with duty*
(*in £ million*)

1778	1·16	1784	2·42	1790	2·47	1796	4·94
1779	1·69	1785	2·22	1791	3·19	1797	4·79
1780	1·83	1786	2·22	1792	3·87	1798	3·58
1781	1·87	1787	2·62	1793	4·14	1799	4·28
1782	2·13	1788	2·77	1794	3·53	1800	5·24
1783	2·01	1789	2·62	1795	4·13	1801	6·60

Excise returns for years ended 5 July.

23. *Revenue from the duties on cards and dice*
(*in £ thousand*)

1712	3·3	1735	10·2	1758	15·4	1781	27·5
1713	4·6	1736	9·8	1759	16·1	1782	26·7
1714	5·5	1737	10·3	1760	15·7	1783	25·9
1715	5·6	1738	9·9	1761	15·4	1784	26·1
1716	7·8	1739	9·6	1762	18·6	1785	27·1
1717	8·6	1740	9·9	1763	18·7	1786	27·7
1718	8·8	1741	8·5	1764	19·6	1787	28·3
1719	8·2	1742	9·4	1765	20·3	1788	29·9
1720	9·9	1743	9·0	1766	20·2	1789	31·2
1721	9·9	1744	9·9	1767	21·3	1790	35·6
1722	9·7	1745	7·9	1768	22·0	1791	34·9
1723	9·7	1746	9·7	1769	21·5	1792	31·8
1724	9·9	1747	10·3	1770	22·5	1793	29·5
1725	10·2	1748	10·5	1771	24·0	1794	25·4
1726	10·2	1749	10·7	1772	24·2	1795	24·8
1727	9·6	1750	10·8	1773	24·6	1796	21·7
1728	9·5	1751	10·7	1774	23·9	1797	20·5
1729	9·5	1752	10·8	1775	28·6	1798	22·5
1730	9·1	1753	10·1	1776	25·6	1799	7·8
1731	9·5	1754	10·1	1777	27·9	1800	23·8
1732	9·4	1755	14·6	1778	28·6	1801	30·9
1733	9·3	1756	13·3	1779	27·9		
1734	9·6	1757	14·8	1780	28·3		

First Report of the Commissioners of Inland Revenue. *B.P.P. 1857*, iv. 216–17. The years ended 31 March.

INDEX

Accommodation bills, 108, 128, 131, 132, 157.
Adam brothers, 99.
Allen, William, 41, 42.
Amsterdam, rates of exchange on, 126; as financial centre, 176.
Anderson, Adam, 94.
Annuities, 87.
Arkwright, Richard, 78, 131, 163, 165.
Armed Neutrality, 163.
Army and Navy, 51, 52; numbers of men, 187.
Arsenals, 72, 142, 146, 147.
Assize, of bread, 32, 36; of beer, 37.
Atkinson, Thomas, 171.
Auckland, Lord, 167.
Auction sales, duty on, 28; statistics, 193.
Austrian Loan of 1795, 134, 170.
Ayr Bank, 128.

Bakewell, Robert, 40.
Balance of payments, 46, 141.
Baltic trade, 10, 71, 72, 85.
Bank of England, loans and discounts, 65, 112–13; notes and deposits, 65, 66; cash ratio, 48, 113, 121, 124, 126, 135, 144, 150; rationing of discounts, 171; statistics of, 189.
Bankruptcies, 13, 33, 87, 99, 113, 114, 116 n., 121, 122 n., 125 n., 127 n., 162.
Banks, private, 66, 103, 107, 108, 127, 133, 136, 168.
Baptisms, 3, 21, 150.
Bargemen, 8, 9.
Baring, Francis, 134 n.
Barley, conditions of growth, 15; price, 24.
Barnard, Sir John, 122.
Barracks, 82.
Bath, 91, 93, 99, 104.
Beef, price of, 17, 18, 19, 21, 22, 25.
Beer and ale, seasonal variation of production, 6; price of, 37; retailers, 38, 182; elasticity of demand for, 65.

Billeting of troops, 82.
Bills of Exchange, inland, 66, 107 n., 108, 165; accommodation and fictitious, 108, 128, 131, 132, 157.
Bills of Mortality, 3, 17 n.
Bills, Navy, Exchequer, &c., 66, 106, 133, 134, 136, 168.
Birmingham, 97, 154, 157, 163.
Bleaching, 4.
Blight of wheat, 18, 23.
Bolton, 44.
Bonds, East India, 112, Ch. 5 *passim*.
Booms, stock market, 67; in Amsterdam and Hamburg, 156.
Bottles, glass, 80, 192.
Bouillé, Marquis de, 50.
Boulton, Matthew, 150, 157.
Boulton & Watt, 70, 171.
Bread, price of, 20, 21, 23, 24, 25, 32, 36, 153, 181.
Bricks, duty on, 28, 32, 103; output, 88, 89, 101, 103, 167, 193; regulation of size, 100.
Bridgewater, Duke of, 95, 97.
Bright, John, 9.
Bubble, South Sea, 92; Bubble Act, 89, 121, 176.
Building and construction, 4, 83, 138, 139, Ch. 4 *passim*; Acts, 91, 95, 99, 100; and exports, 94, 100, 138, 155; and war, 83, 104.
Bullion, *see* Gold.
Burials, 3, 17, 18, 20, 21, 147.
Burslem, 155.
Butler, Thomas, 6, 25, 134 n., 135, 136, 171.
Butter, price of, 17, 18, 20, 23.
Byrom & Co., 132.

Cabinet-makers, 150.
Calendar reform, 30, 31.
Calico Act, 143, 146, 158.
Calicoes, *see* Printed fabrics.
Canals, Oxford, 162 n., Forth and Clyde, 99, 100; Bills, 102, 103, 170; shares, 167; mania, 102, 167.
Candles, 6, 28, 39.
Cannon, 71.

PRINTED IN GREAT BRITAIN
AT THE UNIVERSITY PRESS, OXFORD
BY VIVIAN RIDLER
PRINTER TO THE UNIVERSITY